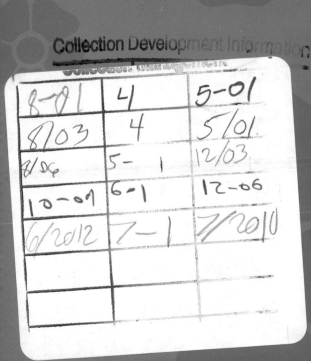

GODDARD PARENTING GUIDES

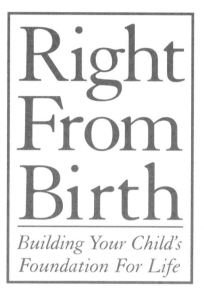

Right From Birth

Building Your Child's Foundation For Life

BIRTH TO 18 MONTHS

Craig T. Ramey, Ph.D. ❋ **Sharon L. Ramey,** Ph.D.

GODDARD PRESS

380 MADISON AVENUE

NEW YORK, NY 10017

Book design by Stan Adler Associates

Manufactured in the United States of America

PUBLISHER'S CATALOGING-IN-PUBLICATION DATA

Ramey, Craig T.

Right from birth: building your child's foundation for life — birth to 18 months

p.   cm. ill

Includes bibliographical references.   1. Parenting.   2. Child care.

ISBN 0-9666397-0-7

I. Ramey, Sharon L.   II. Title

HQ755.8 .R36 1999   98-96648

649'.1   dc–21   *649.1*   CIP

THE AUTHORS AND PUBLISHER GRATEFULLY ACKNOWLEDGE PERMISSION TO REPRINT
MATERIAL FROM THE FOLLOWING WORKS AND INDIVIDUALS:

Chap. 1. PET scans reprinted by permission of Harry T. Chugani, M.D., Children's Hospital of Michigan, Wayne State University. © Harry Chugani.

Chap. 2. Graph reprinted by permission of the publisher from "Regional Differences in Synaptogenesis in Human Cerebral Cortex," Peter R. Huttenlocher and Arun S. Dabholkar (University of Chicago), *The Journal of Comparative Neurology,* Vol. 387, 1997. © 1997 Wiley-Liss Inc. Adapted by permission of Wiley-Liss, Inc. a subsidiary of John Wiley & Sons, Inc.

Chap. 3. Photographs reprinted by permission, © Tony Young, 1998, all rights reserved.

Chap. 6. Graph reprinted from "Early Vocabulary Growth: Relation to Language Input and Gender," Janellen Huttenlocher, Wendy Haight, Anthony Bruk, Michael Seltzer, and Thomas Lyons (University of Chicago), *Developmental Psychology,* 1991, Vol. 27, No. 2. © 1991 by the American Psychological Association, Inc.

CHAPTER PHOTOGRAPHS: *Cover and Section I:* Telegraph Colour Library/FPG; *Chap. 1:* Donna Day/Tony Stone Images; *Chap. 2:* Jim Craigmyle/Masterfile; *Chap. 3:* Telegraph Colour Library/FPG; *Chap. 4:* Valerie Simmons/Masterfile; *Chap. 5:* Telegraph Colour Library/FPG; *Chap. 6:* Telegraph Colour Library/FPG; *Chap. 7:* Valerie Gates/Photonica; *Chap. 8:* Photex, Ltd-ZE/Masterfile; *Chap. 9:* Niyati Reeve/Tony Stone Images; *Chap. 10:* Telegraph Colour Library/FPG; *Section II:* Telegraph Colour Library/FPG; *Chap. 11:* David Muir/Masterfile; *Chap. 12:* Telegraph Colour Library/FPG; *Chap. 13:* Telegraph Colour Library/FPG; *Chap. 14:* Graham French MCMXC/Masterfile; *Chap. 15:* David Young-Wolff/Tony Stone Images; *Chap. 16:* Dale Sanders/Masterfile

We dedicate this book to our parents

Ellie and Gene Landesman
Belle and Jim Ramey

and to our children

Jane, Ann, Lee, and Sam

*with whom we have shared many wonderful years
of loving and learning.*

Acknowledgments

❈

CREATING THIS BOOK HAS BEEN A GREAT ADVENTURE. WE HAVE HAD THE JOY OF WORKING with many wonderful people. Diane Lansing, Editor in Chief, contributed immensely to *Right From Birth* with her tireless spirit and extraordinary enthusiasm. Special thanks to our publisher, Anthony Martino, who is also chairman of The Goddard Schools for Early Childhood Development. This book is a product of his vision and commitment to high quality care for children and to providing timely and important information to parents. Suzanne du Pont and Fran Ritter of the Goddard Schools provided invaluable insights and great help in defining the scope of this book to be as useful as possible to parents. Leslie Wells helped to polish our words, and shared personal insights as a mother of a very special two-year-old boy. Jay Poynor consistently provided sage advice about all aspects of book production, always with a twinkle in his eye.

Our friends, family, and colleagues who offered support, ideas, facts, and opinions are many. Our colleagues, whose decades of careful scientific inquiry form the true basis for this book, are acknowledged in a special section at the end. We owe them a debt of professional and personal gratitude, for they are the reason we look forward to going to work — to our offices and labs — every day. The fields of child development and developmental science are extraordinarily dynamic, and the findings are immensely exciting and applicable to the everyday lives of children and families.

Our friends who helped — often just through listening and being there — and who have shared their extensive parenting and grandparenting experience, as well as aunt and uncle experience, and godparent experience, include: Tika Benveniste, Alexis Collier, Janice Cotton, Ellen Dossett, Karen Echols, Tom Fulton, Robert Goldenberg, Jody Stein Kleinman, Robin Gaines Lanzi, Casey Morrow, Kathleen Nelson, Nancy Robinson, Holly Ransom, Jim Sackett, Felicia Sanders, Vicky and Mac Sauls, Anne Shealy, Donna Whisenhunt Thornell, and Wanda Washington. Our family also was fabulously supportive, and often quite patient. Sam, our six-year-old and youngest child, frequently announced, "I think you are finished now!" and "You really couldn't have written this book without me, right?" Ann, our twenty-eight-year-old and a world-class mother read drafts and offered her own scientific and practical perspectives about what parents really need to know. Georges-Guy, our great son-in-law, kept reminding us about writing for fathers, too. Our mothers, as always, were just a phone call away, with their ever-supportive words of wisdom. Even Aunt Gert Rose, upon learning the book was about the first eighteen months of life and how parents can stimulate positive development, exclaimed, "How fascinating! I didn't realize that you had to begin so early!"

We also thank our siblings, Kathy (Ramey) Forget, Benjamin Landesman, and David Landesman, for their valuable thoughts. David especially pitched in during the final week of editing with tremendous assistance.

Our personal assistants — currently, Zee Hildreth, Leslie Franklin, and Lori McClelland; previously, Marie Butts, Nancy Jenkins, L. Susanne Keller, Kitty Mabbatt, and Linda Maultsby — have been the best in the whole world. Their years of hard work and assistance on our many projects truly made it possible for us to write this book.

Very special thanks and recognition are extended to the many agencies and foundations that have supported our research over the past four decades. Most especially, we thank the Civitan International organization and the Civitan Foundation for the vision and $20 million grant that created the Civitan International Research Center at the University of Alabama at Birmingham, where we have had the honor and challenge to serve as founding directors; and the National Institute on Child Health and Human Development, which has supported our training and research continuously for more than thirty years. The Maternal and Child Health Bureau; the Administration on Developmental Disabilities; the Administration on Children, Youth, and Families; the Robert Wood Johnson Foundation; and the MacArthur Foundation also have supported our work in valuable ways.

Finally, we credit the media with awakening in us an awareness of how eager and capable both parents and the general public are to learn about scientific findings concerning brain development and early childhood experiences. Key among these have been Sharon Begley *(Newsweek)*, Walter Cronkite *(the Discovery Channel)*, Edwin Kiester, Jr. *(Reader's Digest)*, Betsy Butgereit *(Birmingham News)*, Peter Jennings *(ABC)*, Diane Sawyer *(ABC)*, Richard Whitmire *(Gannett News)*, Barbara Bolding *(Parenting Life)*, Madeleine Nash and Wendy Cole *(Time)*, and Sandra Blakeslee *(The New York Times)*. Thank you for your conscientious reporting and for your encouragement to us to share what we have learned in places beyond our scientific journals.

Above all, we are deeply grateful to the thousands of young children and families who have participated in our research projects over the past three decades. Thank you for sharing your lives with us and helping us to learn what really matters in young children's lives. ❀

— *Sharon and Craig Ramey, Birmingham, AL*

CONTENTS

Section I
What We Have Learned

❁

Section II
Your Baby's Development

❁

Introduction

✻

A NEW ERA IN PARENTING

Science and business are revolutionizing the way we parent. As a new or expectant parent, you face a staggering array of equipment, gadgets, toys, books, and expert advice.

Research on the brain and early learning has spawned a whole new industry that promises to enhance children's development. Infants well under two years old are being "taught" with flash cards, math games, and toy computers. Babies are having their "brains" stimulated with Mozart, natural sounds, and specialized baby massage.

Never before have parents had the wealth of resources and information available today. In many ways, this is wonderful. But it can also be overwhelming, intimidating, and confusing. It may appear that "expert advice" keeps changing, and that "experts" don't always agree.

What advice can you trust? What's the right way to give your baby the best foundation for life?

WHAT WORKS, WHAT COUNTS

In this book, we will tackle three issues at the core of all the current advice and trends on parenting. First, we will tell you what the newest research really says — and doesn't say. We will help you to separate proven facts from current fads. We will also show you which parenting practices really matter over the long term, and why.

Second, we will focus on your child's *total* development — how growth, learning, social interactions, emotional development, and communication all interact and depend on one another. In so doing, we hope to give you a fuller appreciation of your child's wonderful accomplishments during the first eighteen months, and a more balanced and enjoyable approach to parenting.

Third, we will help you put this knowledge to good use. We have organized the best scientific findings into "Seven Essentials" that children need in their everyday lives, and we show how to provide them as your baby grows. We also give specific ideas for these essentials at different stages of your baby's life. Our recommendations are all based on the best that research — and generations of successful parents — can offer. They are also practical, flexible, and appropriate in today's new world of childcare arrangements, diverse family lifestyles, and broad array of aspirations.

THE JOYS OF PARENTING

We believe that children are super. But this book is not about producing superaccelerated children. Rather, it provides an overview of what we know about the remarkable unfolding of human competence in the very early months of life. It also shows how parents can love and care for their infants, while also enjoying their own lives.

Being a parent is a great experience. Parenting affords untold joys and delights — moments to cherish, hours to reflect, weeks and months filled with love and amazement. Parenting is a life-transforming experience. Your child will contribute much to your own adult development and help to shape the rest of your life, just as you help to shape his or her future.

In writing this book, we think it's important to share our biases. These come from our experience as researchers connected to a dynamic community of scientists, and as parents with four children, ranging from six to thirty-one years old, and two grandchildren.

The biases we recognize are these: We believe that being a parent is one of the greatest things on earth; we think parenting, great though it is, should never be the one and only thing in life; and knowledge about parenting is good. We also believe balance is important: A combination of activities, values, and passions makes for happy and confident parents and children alike.

We have devoted our careers to improving children's development. We have spent years studying children in different programs and life circumstances to learn what provides the greatest and most lasting benefits. Our days are spent asking questions, gathering and analyzing data, writing, speaking, reading, thinking, and, we hope, contributing constructively to the growing and ever-changing body of knowledge that may help to improve the well-being of children everywhere.

The more you know about how infants and young children develop, the more you will understand why some parenting approaches are more effective than others in producing a good-natured, socially responsive, creative, and accomplished child. This book should encourage and reassure you. The approaches we suggest are enjoyable and practical.

The challenges and uncertainties of parenting won't go away. But the rewards can be greater the more you appreciate the amazing accomplishments of your baby's total development, the more you understand the lasting importance of the love and support you provide, and the more you delight in your child's uniqueness right from birth. We know of no better way to give your new baby the foundation to explore and develop to the fullest and to start a lifelong journey of loving, learning, enjoying, and contributing. ✿

Section I

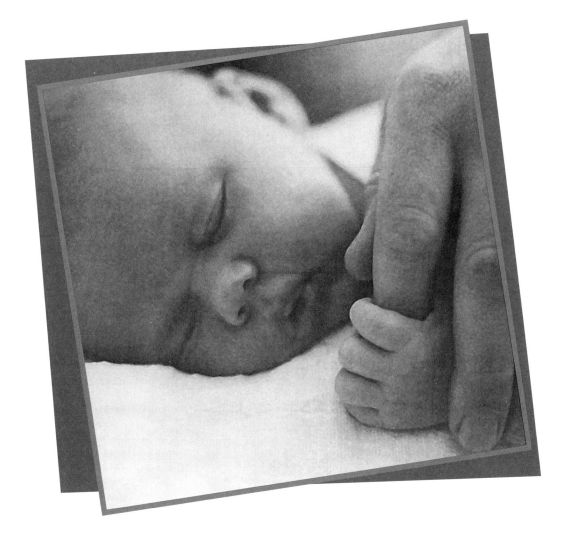

What We Have Learned

CHAPTER 1

What We Really Know

*How Science Is Changing
the Way We Parent*

THE MOST DYNAMIC AND DRAMATIC GROWTH IN YOUR CHILD'S ENTIRE LIFE — PHYSICAL, EMOTIONAL, SOCIAL, AND MENTAL — WILL OCCUR IN THE FIRST THREE YEARS. A WEALTH OF NEW RESEARCH SHOWS THAT MUCH MORE HAPPENS FROM BIRTH TO AGE THREE THAN WE PREVIOUSLY THOUGHT, AND SOME IMPORTANT DEVELOPMENTS HAPPEN EVEN IN THE FIRST FEW MONTHS.

Parents have always been fascinated by their infants' physical growth and motor development. But now, with the wealth of new discoveries, parents are increasingly aware of the progress their children are making in other areas. Many parents now know that, right from birth, their infants are responding to their environments more fully than we had understood in the past. Today's parents know that attachments begin to form right away between infant and parent, and a baby's emotional and social awareness progress rapidly.

However, these exciting new findings about infant development have also caused some confusion. Science news has become a hot topic. Recent discoveries have fueled an explosion in books, articles, and products to help parents give their children a competitive edge in the world. So parents regularly hear and read all about the latest research.

Unfortunately, many of the headlines have focused on early learning and intelligence, to the exclusion of findings in other areas where the impact of early experience is just as great. The lopsided coverage has given rise to a whole new industry bent on boosting early learning. The result is often a new source of concern for parents. How can my baby learn more and learn sooner? If I haven't done it perfectly so far, have I limited my child? Is it too late to help?

This chapter is designed to help you sort through what we really know — and don't know — from all the new research. We will also discuss how the media reports new findings. This should help you to assess such information and to know if it applies to you and your child. Then we will tell you what we now know about infant development, and how that development can be guided most effectively.

Keeping Up with Science

In recent decades, research has led to great progress on many fronts. New technology allows us to study what was once impossible — from subtle aspects of infant visual and auditory capabilities to the dynamics of a child's brain when solving problems. Breakthroughs in biomedical research and health care have dramatically improved maternal health and infant survival, even for the tiniest and most premature babies. Specially designed early interventions now address a host of problems previously not treated until school age, including learning and language delays, hearing and visual impairments, and developmental disabilities. Children with special needs, such as those with Down Syndrome and other genetic conditions, now have a world of learning open to them from infancy on, a wonderful change from the limited lives such children led not that long ago. Infants can be fitted with corrective lenses to see better, hearing impaired children and their parents can learn to use sign language in the first year of life, and many forms of "failure to thrive" can be prevented.

With such wonderful progress, parents want to keep up with the latest discoveries. They are understandably eager to know all they can about new ways to improve their children's chances in life, particularly given such well-publicized trends as falling test scores, poor performance compared to children in other countries, and a dramatic increase in learning disabilities and attention-deficit disorders. They want to know how to enhance their children's learning, while also encouraging their children to be well-rounded, athletic, and socially adept.

As parents wade through the mountains of new "expert" advice, they may find conflicting views or counsel that seems contrary to good sense.

Moreover, they repeatedly hear that anything they do can permanently help or hinder their child, and woe be to the parent who makes the wrong choice.

Early learning benchmarks have become the latest in the series of developmental milestones that parents now monitor. Most parents have these milestone "averages" down pat — when a "normal" child should sit, crawl, walk, and talk. Some parents even monitor sophisticated achievements such as understanding object permanence and early number concepts. They compare their child with these national norms, not to mention every other child they know.

Parents whose children are in a childcare center or preschool may be even more prone to such comparisons because they see their child among a sizable group of children of the same age — a virtual fishbowl of competition. The result can be more concern and less appreciation for the exquisite individuality of each child.

The effect of all these developments has been to add pressure to both parents and children, and to undermine the joy and spontaneity of family life. Such unhappy results are simply not justified. The late Dr. Benjamin Spock, the trusted pediatrician for generations of children and parents, had it right: Parents know a lot more than they think they do. Many parents will do a great job as parents without the advice contained in any book. With the best advice, parents can be assured that they are providing the right types of stimulation for their children, timed in ways that match their infants' development and adjusted to fit their own values and lifestyle.

New Research: What Does It Tell Us?

The most recent discoveries about infant development have captured public attention like nothing before. These are the findings on the infant brain. Among the most important are those that document the rapid growth and development of the brain in the first three years of life. Dr. Peter Huttenlocher, a neurologist at the University of Chicago, has used electron microscopy to document, for the first time ever, the density of neural synapses — the connections between cells —

in the infant's brain. He has found that there is an early, rapid, and large rise in the number of synapses, followed by a decrease — a selective pruning and refinement of the nervous system.

More recently, Dr. Harry Chugani, a pediatrician with the Children's Hospital of Michigan at Wayne State University, has used positron emission tomography (PET) to image the brains of young infants. In so doing, he has produced stunning visual evidence of the explosive growth of the brain during the early months of life. For the first time, we can see the "wiring" of the young brain take shape. We can also see how fast it happens and how important early experiences are in helping or hindering this growth.

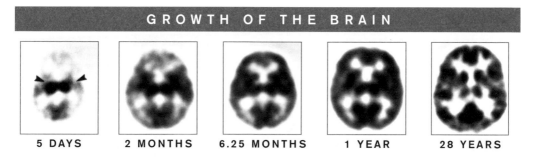

GROWTH OF THE BRAIN

| 5 DAYS | 2 MONTHS | 6.25 MONTHS | 1 YEAR | 28 YEARS |

Source: Harry T. Chugani, M.D., Children's Hospital of Michigan/Wayne State University

PET scans are not only breakthroughs in their own right, but they help to explain what other researchers have been finding. The scans show the neural activity that powers all the other early developmental activity that researchers have found in the past three decades. Because the pictures are so dramatic, they have helped to raise public awareness of how much development occurs in a child's earliest years. This, in turn, has helped focus public attention on the importance of high-quality care for children from birth to age three.

Unfortunately, this attention has focused on early cognitive learning devoid of its social context. In fact, rapid brain development is just as responsible for emotional expression and control and for social skills and responsiveness as for early cognitive learning.

But growth in each area affects other areas. The complexity of this interlinkage is profound. Your child's total "personhood" is being shaped on all fronts simultaneously. All facets of this personhood need to be nurtured and encouraged together. If they are, each is likely to be enhanced by the growth of the others. If they aren't, each may be hurt by the imbalance.

How to Understand Research

The discoveries of recent years are fascinating and should increase parents' appreciation of infants' abilities. The key is to understand these findings in the context of total human development — the process of growing throughout childhood and to mature adulthood — not just in the limited time frame of the first few years of life or in an isolated domain of development. It is also important to evaluate the merits of a single study in the broader context of the total body of research.

Because findings in early child development are so interesting, research now has a wide popular audience. The media now monitor each and every issue of the leading scientific journals in human development and neurobiology. The findings in these journals have been subjected to multiple peer reviews by other scientists. They often reflect the results of extensive research conducted over long periods of time.

But reporters typically encourage researchers to elaborate on their findings and to speculate on their implications for everyday life — something not usually encouraged in scientific journals. The flashier the implications, the more media attention. Reporters often dramatize the latest findings by emphasizing their newness or their provocative potential.

All too often, reporters reduce these findings to a few sound bites with only the briefest of explanations. At the other extreme, some reports provide highly detailed accounts with so many qualifiers that it's hard for parents to understand the practical value of what they hear and read.

The limitations of new knowledge, and the need for more studies, rarely make for exciting news. So parents are faced with figuring out which studies they should pay attention to, and whether they should alter what they are doing.

Most researchers have a different perspective, one that should be reassuring to parents. Human development is such a complex field that researchers typically become highly specialized in what they study. We look to our colleagues whose specialties complement our work and give it a broader context. In the last decade, there has been a concerted effort to bring scientists together to compare and integrate findings from individual studies that are often narrowly focused. This has led to a new synthesis and new types of interdisciplinary inquiry that benefit from the technology, theory, and advances of closely related fields.

We know that scientific studies invariably raise new questions even as they provide partial answers. That is the nature of research. We make strides by learning from our work in the context of the total and ever-changing collective body of knowledge in our field.

However, this broader perspective on infant development and parenting is not readily available to the general public when they read or watch a news account of a single study. As a result, new research can easily be misunderstood or misapplied. Consider the following:

CERTAIN FINDINGS MAY NOT APPLY TO ALL CHILDREN

Much of the research on infants and young children deals with those who are "at risk" or who have recognized special needs, such as premature and low birthweight infants, children with developmental disabilities, or children who have been abused. What is learned from research on these children may not apply to others. Special programs that boost their performance and improve their health may not be needed by children who are developing more typically.

INITIAL FINDINGS MAY PROVE INACCURATE OR INCOMPLETE

An area of research often starts with a small study or test to see if a new avenue is worth pursuing. Results of such early investigations are increasingly being reported by the media. However, early findings can be unreliable. Parents, like scientists, need to be both curious and skeptical when it comes to first-time reports.

COMPONENTS OF GROWTH DON'T HAPPEN IN A VACUUM

Almost all aspects of development are intertwined. For example, early mental achievements are closely linked to social and emotional development, and vice versa. Historically, many scientists tried to isolate individual elements of development to study them more fully. More recently, studies have considered infant development in terms of the everyday world and how the senses operate in a cooperative, synergistic manner. These extensions beyond the laboratory indicate that the rate and type of development in any area are strongly influenced by what happens in other areas. When new findings are reported, in this age of the sound bite, it is hard to convey their implications for a child's total development.

In short, it is not surprising if the practical meaning is not clear when you read reports of new discoveries. It is easy to miss the forest for the trees. And some discoveries are exciting simply because of what they reveal. They may not yet show what parents need to do. Remember that your infant's progress is the sum of many factors — some interdependent, some not, almost always a mix of biology and experience — placed in the larger context of a nurturing environment.

What Matters, What Doesn't

We have seen many "new" concepts in parenting over this century. Many were supported by some kind of scientific inquiry or clinical observation. Some were billed as breakthroughs. Unfortunately, many were later shown to fall short of their initial claims. Fortunately, they usually don't harm children. But they can cause unnecessary fuss or concern for parents.

Much-heralded breakthroughs can be either a new wrinkle in an established line of research or a new departure altogether. Consider the rise and fall of the following two "new concepts," from discovery and broad acceptance to challenge and revision:

SCHEDULED FEEDINGS

In the 1940s and '50s, strict feeding schedules for infants — no more than once every four hours or so — were widely accepted. They were supposed to help organize daily routines, build the infant's "character," and teach babies to fit into their parents' lives — not vice versa.

New information has pointed up the fallacies in this approach. First, newborns' stomachs are too small to hold enough milk to last four or five hours. Second, babies differ in how much food they take in and how well their digestion works. Third, withholding food for the sake of a schedule denies babies the chance to learn that someone cares when they cry and that their needs will be met. It also limits the frequency of close, caretaking contact with parents when lots of social and emotional communication occurs.

Feeding (along with most everything else about babies) doesn't lend itself to a "one-size-fits-all" solution. For example, there are big timing differences between breast- versus bottle-fed babies. So "demand" feeding is once again the recommended practice.

More good news. Demand feeding is not forever. Orderly schedules become part of most families' lives reasonably soon, without struggle or effort — a blend of baby and parent needs.

FREEDOM FROM LIMITS

In the 1960s, the theory circulated that if children were freed from adult constraints, especially rules and limits on their behavior, they would develop their creative capacities to the fullest. Adult interventions — even expectations or guidance — were viewed as constraints on a child's natural talents.

This theory, too, has been debunked. As these children were tracked over time, it turned out that an extreme lack of limits actually hampered development. Some of the children were less creative and inquisitive, not more so. They proved less confident and less secure in their relationships with others. Their sense of self-efficacy was impaired, not enhanced. And they behaved dreadfully. The scientific evidence about effective parenting styles indicates that the most successful one is authoritative — characterized by general consistency and certainty, without being rigid or authoritarian — and coupled with warmth and respect for the individual child.

These two examples only hint at the variety of new ideas that get picked up as "the latest wisdom." But they point up a number of cautions we would urge parents to follow as they track the latest developments from the research community.

Here is our short list of how to respond to reports of new findings. Remember that:

ONE FINDING DOES NOT WISDOM MAKE

No single study or discovery should prompt parents to change what they are doing (unless it sounds like fun for both babies and parents). Ideas that merit attention are those that have been tested in a variety of ways with a lot of participants, and whose results have been tracked over time.

DON'T TRUST JUST THE SHORT TERM

Some studies show results only over the short term — a few weeks or months. In many areas, it is well-established that short-term efforts to accelerate a single skill do not lead to any long-term gains. When children are progressing well and learning a lot naturally, parents should simply keep on doing what seems to work.

BE WARY OF FINDINGS TOUTED TO SELL YOU A PRODUCT

The baby business is booming. Nowadays, parents are willing to invest in their young children. Companies know this, and have profited enormously. If you want to try something, and have the resources to buy it, that's great. Just don't expect the promised results, or think that they cannot be achieved in many other ways without buying something special to "promote" your child's development. Suggestion: Check with your friends first; many will have these discarded baby "toys" in a closet to pass on for you to try.

ENJOYMENT FIRST

If a new idea doesn't sound like fun for your child or you (preferably both), don't do it. Many of the new programs for early learning are probably of marginal value, if that, and many are a crashing bore. Your family's enjoyment, on the other hand, is priceless.

RIGHT OR WRONG, SOME THINGS PARENTS DO MAY NOT MATTER THAT MUCH

What happened to all those millions of babies in the '40s and '50s who were schedule-fed? For the most part, they're fine. They are today's "boomers." So far, many scientific findings about normal development don't translate directly into practical applications for parents. Further, there is increasing evidence that children have tremendous adaptability, and there are many different routes to positive ends. This conclusion is supported by lots of scientific data. It's not just a "feel good" statement.

YOU KNOW MORE THAN YOU THINK

As stated earlier, this was Dr. Benjamin Spock's wonderful reassurance, first written for parents in 1945. Human beings evolved with lots of good sense, keen observational skills, and the ability to get by with a little help from their friends and other family members. When in doubt, follow your own instincts and listen to others who have suggestions to offer (even if you don't *always* follow them).

Science is a tough taskmaster, and replication of findings is the hallmark of good science. Because contemporary society is so dynamic — witness the changes in family lifestyles in the past thirty years — it is important that research stay up-to-date. An older finding is not necessarily to be trusted, or discarded.

Rather, we need hard evidence that the "facts" of yesterday's science continue to apply to today's situations.

Despite the caveats above, we have learned a great deal in the last few decades about how children develop and what fosters this development. Throughout this book we will describe what our discoveries show. Above all, the more you know about infant development, the more clearly you will see the wonders of childhood and the more you can celebrate the extraordinary events that enable your child to grow into a caring, good-natured, and capable being.

What Works/What Counts

To keep your focus on the forest, and not get lost in the trees of individual research findings, remember one guideline counts above all others:

The adult your child will become is shaped by the aggregate experience of daily life over the long term.

Lasting good effects are enhanced when supportive learning experiences start early, occur more often, and continue over many years. Numerous long-term studies involving thousands of children bear this out over and over again. This should reassure every parent. There is no "quick fix" that will guarantee a rewarding and fulfilling life for any child. There is also no short-term program which, if missed, will consign a child to the back of the pack.

Our research indicates that the essentials of a good foundation for life are similar for all children from all walks of life. The good news is that there are many different ways to provide these essentials. When children consistently receive high-quality care, affection, encouragement, and guidance, they thrive. When they don't get these essentials, for whatever reasons, they do not fare well. Worst of all, there is a serious and cumulative toll for children who do not receive these essentials for extended periods of time.

Our own research, as well as that of others, also confirms that a good start by itself isn't enough to provide lasting benefits. One way that early gains can be sustained — well into adolescence and adulthood — is if children continue to experience highly supportive environments at home, at school, with peers, and in the community. There is no simple inoculation for a good life. Good foundations must be followed by strong continued supports.

Whenever you read about a new discovery, keep these long-term trends in mind. This is especially true for research involving early learning.

Some new programs claim to promote language learning, prereading skills, and math concepts — but rarely are these for children under eighteen months of age. Many such claims have never been adequately verified. Even more important, there have been no long-term studies of the effects of systematic enrichment for normal infants from families that already provide a stimulating and responsive environment on a daily basis.

There are recent, long-term studies of young children who are phenomenally accelerated in some or many aspects of their development. These highly capable infants tend to have very positive home environments and capable parents. But their parents did not use special techniques or programs to push their children ahead. Instead, they tended to follow each baby's lead and respond in ways that encouraged and opened doors to continued learning that was well-matched to each child's readiness and interests.

The vast body of long-term research in child development is compelling. This research consistently shows that it takes a *lot of effort* over a *very long period* to produce lasting benefits. Children who do well have families and others who are continually thoughtful, responsive, and encouraging, and who teach in the context of everyday life.

Therefore, to enhance your child's development, your best bet is to focus on the everyday life your child leads. His future will be shaped, not by this or that educational toy or early learning program, but by the totality of his environment and experiences.

Windows of Opportunity

While we stress the totality of experience, we don't want to imply that timing doesn't matter. It does. There are "windows" of learning in early childhood — periods when particular experiences are especially important or when some skills are more easily developed. But these windows are typically moderate to long.

For example, children learn correct pronunciation of language better than adults do. But this window lasts until puberty — for about twelve or thirteen years. Even if this window is missed, people can and do master other languages. Students for generations have struggled through college French. Even though they probably won't speak with a perfect accent, they can emerge fluent enough to navigate Paris, conduct business, or read Dumas.

Media reports have covered some newly discovered early learning windows involving cognitive skills. But, once again, long-term studies are lacking. We don't know the long-term effects of early learning programs in any short-term "window."

But there are some windows that shouldn't be missed. If they are, the opportunity to learn can be greatly diminished. *Among the most important windows are those involving emotional and social development.* With all the attention on early learning, social and emotional development has received a disproportionately low level of coverage. This is particularly unfortunate because the need and opportunity for growth in these areas is so important during a child's early years. For example, it appears that if children don't learn how to trust at least one other person by the time they are three or four, chances are slim that they can ever gain this essential ability.

We now know that the entire first three years of life represent an extraordinary window for learning virtually everything. There are no proven benefits to picking specific activities for your child to do in designated months to take advantage of any short-term window. Instead, a balanced, enjoyable approach to parenting in all aspects over the entire three-year period makes the most sense for everyone.

A Balance of Assets

The two concepts we have discussed above reinforce each other in important ways:

- ❁ First, infants and toddlers grow in every way — physically, mentally, emotionally, and socially — at an astonishing rate.
- ❁ Second, how your child grows in all of these areas depends on the totality of experience.

Therefore, the total care your child receives in these early years will have deep and lasting effects on every facet of development.

As we have noted, it is easy to focus on physical growth or early memory skills. We urge consideration as well of social skills and emotional development, both on their own merits and for their impact on learning. As you learn more about how all aspects of your child's growth are linked, you will better understand the importance of social and emotional development and why your attention to these critical areas is central to your child's lifelong well-being.

In the following chapters, we will explain what is currently known about how normal, healthy children in supportive home environments develop, and what you can do to foster your child's progress. We will describe what works, what is irrelevant, and what can even be harmful.

In the process, you will see that *what we have learned does not change the traditional fundamentals of good parenting. It reinforces them.* It also explains why they work. Love and attention, play and encouragement, support and security — these are still the essential elements in raising happy, healthy children who grow up to be successful, well-adjusted adults. Increasingly, we are understanding why.

In fact, the newest research shows that the benefits of traditional good parenting are greater than we ever realized. It also shows that the ways to create wonderful results are as varied and individual as are parents and babies themselves. As we learn more about the complexity of the development process, two conclusions are inescapable:

- ❀ There is a wide variety in the "normal" ways and time frames for infant development to progress and for particular skills to emerge.

- ❀ Every child is unique from birth in the way he or she is likely to develop. Temperament, interests, and demeanor are as varied at birth and in the way they develop as are physical appearance and size.

The more you know, the more you can see and appreciate your baby's individuality and the wonderful opportunities that this individuality creates. With this information, you can learn to trust your own judgment more, to relax in your role as parents, and to enjoy your child to the fullest. ❀

CHAPTER 2

Wonders of
the Brain

Powering Up in Infancy

THE WORD "BREAKTHROUGH" DOESN'T BEGIN TO CAPTURE THE GAINS IN NEUROBIOLOGY — THE STUDY OF HOW THE BRAIN DEVELOPS. THANKS TO NEW IMAGING TECHNOLOGIES, WE CAN ACTUALLY LOOK AT THE BRAIN IN LIVING CHILDREN AND ADULTS. WE CAN SEE IT IN ACTION — HOW IT GROWS, ACTS, AND REACTS. WHAT WE HAVE LEARNED IS ASTOUNDING, AND THE IMPACT ON CHILDHOOD DEVELOPMENT HAS BEEN PROFOUND.

A few of the major findings are:

- The brain never stops changing; it continues to evolve throughout our lives.
- The most intense period of brain growth is the first three years of life.
- At age three, a child's brain is twice as active as that of an adult.
- How a child's brain develops is a complex blend of inheritance and experience.
- Each brain can develop in many different ways depending on many factors, such as genetics, experience, relationships, health, and nutrition.
- The quality of relationships and experiences in the first three years has a deep and lasting impact on how the brain gets "wired."
- The early wiring of the brain sets the foundation for development in every aspect of life.
- Brain development and behavior are bound together. They dynamically and continually influence each other.

Exciting material, to be sure. It can also be intimidating for some parents. It shouldn't be. Rightly understood, these findings are not a cause for anxiety. Instead, they can help make parenting more rewarding, enriching, and joyful.

A Head Start

At birth a baby's brain is already one-fourth of its adult size. It has roughly 100 billion nerve cells, called neurons. Most neurons have one axon that transmits signals to other neurons. Each neuron also has a number of fibers, called dendrites, that receive signals from other cells.

The brain cells at birth are plentiful in number and will not change much over the child's life. Yet a newborn's brain is incomplete in other ways. The cells aren't well-connected. The main task of the brain in early childhood is connection. Axons link up with dendrites forming trillions of connections, called synapses. When this wiring process is complete, a single neuron can be connected to as many as 15,000 others.

The result is a highly complex, efficient circuitry that carries all the impulses of the brain. These impulses control how our bodies function as well as everything from thinking and feeling to learning and memory. Impulses are helped in their travels by neurotransmitters, chemical compounds such as serotonin and dopamine, that enhance or inhibit certain activities.

According to research by Dr. Peter Huttenlocher of the University of Chicago, the young child's brain will form nearly twice as many synapses as will ultimately be used, reaching an estimated 1,000 trillion by age three. The ones that get used most will strengthen and last. Those that are unused or replaced by other pathways will eventually disappear (be "pruned," in neurobiological terminology). By the later teen years, typically half of the 1,000 trillion synapses of the three-year-old will have been discarded.

MEAN SYNAPTIC DENSITY OF THE HUMAN BRAIN — CONCEPTION TO ADULTHOOD

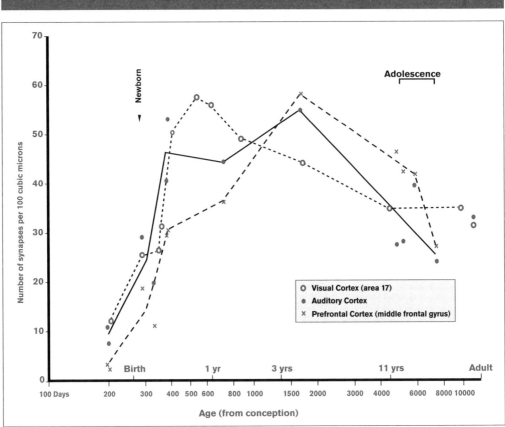

Adapted from "Regional Differences in Synaptogenesis in Human Cerebral Cortex," Peter R. Huttenlocher and Arun S. Dabholkar (University of Chicago), The Journal of Comparative Neurology, *Vol. 387, 1997.*

This goes to the heart of why early experience is so important. If a child gets too little stimulation, play, affection, discovery, language, and person-to-person contact, development of the brain *that depends on experience* will be slowed down or will fail to progress. The brain won't achieve its potential for complex, streamlined, efficient, and flexible functioning. Specialization and higher-order brain processes, especially those associated with reasoning, language, and solving complex problems, may be permanently limited.

But for most parents, the most important findings deal with the positive effects on the brain of children's relationships, activities, and emotions. Scientists have found new ways to measure the effects of different activities and emotional states on the brain. These findings have led to much of the current excitement about early learning and individual differences among children.

Each Brain, Like Each Baby, Is Unique

Researchers agree that there is remarkable variation in the details of each brain. We have every reason to think that this individuality is as great as the differences we see in people's appearances, temperaments, personalities, talents, and quirks. Researchers are now studying how brain architecture and functioning relate to early experience and to unique behavioral and social qualities.

Brains can also perform a given task in different ways. For example, there are many ways a brain can process, store, and retrieve similar information. These multiple pathways appear to protect and strengthen human capacity. Such findings underscore the value of cherishing your baby's unique capacity to be special and wonderful in ways that no one can yet know.

At the Beginning

The brain starts to form soon after conception when a single cell divides to create what will become the two hemispheres of the brain — the "left" and "right" brain. Over the next thirty-five to forty weeks, the brain develops *in utero* at a rapid rate, folding in on itself to create the many wrinkles and grooves of its more mature state. In what scientists call "equal potentiality," neurons start out undifferentiated. They are not yet specialized in what they do, or where or when they will do it. They soon migrate and begin to develop special functions that will define the major areas of the brain.

Early in an infant's life, neurons retain some of this original flexibility. This is one of the most remarkable findings of recent research. It is also one of the most important things parents should know. *There are many, many ways to obtain good outcomes in the brain.* Neuroscientists call this "equal finality." Other areas of the brain may come in to take over a function that would have been carried out by some part that was underdeveloped or damaged. However, equal finality doesn't last forever. Its course is now a matter of intense speculation and vigorous scientific inquiry.

This has wonderful implications for both medicine and parenting. The impact on medical care for young children has already been revolutionary. Many impairments to sight, hearing, motor control, and intelligence used to be considered unchangeable. Now we can lessen the impact of many such conditions, sometimes even preventing long-term consequences, if they are detected very early. Many more exciting studies are underway to help us further harness the natural compensating abilities of the infant brain to correct problems.

For parents, this compensating ability is great news. Children are naturally flexible in how they grow and learn. So are their brains. They arrive prewired with multiple opportunities for development. They are endowed with the ability to take advantage of many things in many ways. They also have large capacities to self-correct and rebound from problems, upsets, and injuries. They come into the world ready to absorb all sorts of good things and with a margin of error to absorb the bad. Infants need leeway in learning to be persons, and parents need leeway in learning to parent. In the adaptability of infants, Mother Nature has given us both.

Timing Counts

While brain development is flexible, there is, nonetheless, a general order to the way it grows and a logical sequence to that order. Dr. Harry Chugani has been at the forefront of developing new technologies to produce images of the living brain. Based on his pioneering work with positron emission tomography (PET) scans, he has documented the progress of brain function.

Not surprisingly, some of the most active parts of a newborn's brain are those that govern vital functions, such as breathing and heart functioning, as well as reflex actions, many of which are essential to survival.

But right alongside these functions are the senses. The newborn brain starts immediately to process "input" from the world through the senses, combining this input into perceptual patterns and interpretable events. Some interesting benchmarks include:

- **Three months:** The parts of the brain with the highest metabolic rate are those governing sight, sound, and touch.

- **Three months:** Some reflex reactions disappear, paving the way for more controlled movement of arms and hands, legs and feet, a precursor to greater physical exploration of objects and people. The brain also is ready for longer periods of sleep and extended alertness.

- **Six to eight months:** The front and rear lobes of the brain — those involved with reasoning, language, and vision, for example — become highly active. This is the time when infants reach for and manipulate objects, show stronger preferences for familiar versus strange people, and demonstrate more sophisticated comprehension of language.

The pattern of growth is to add both new skills and links between skills. For example, at around seven to eight weeks of age, your baby will turn toward you when you speak. Within a few weeks or a month, in addition to turning, your baby may smile and make sounds.

In general, the brain grows from inside out. That is, the outer layers of the brain, which are most closely associated with the higher cognitive, memory, and reasoning functions, start maturing later and will continue to grow much longer than the parts of the brain that control basic vital functions.

Researchers have begun to use various imaging technologies to document this growth pattern. For example, we can see the prefrontal cortex of infants seven to nine months old light up when they are engaged in simple problem-solving exercises. Younger infants, who are unable to do such exercises, don't show the same level of prefrontal cortical activity.

A number of researchers have identified windows of growth — periods when the brain is especially geared to developing a particular sense or ability. For vision, the period is six months to eight years, and for hearing, the period is the first four years. Again, this is now an area of intense interest and vigorous inquiry among developmental scientists.

Care, Behavior, and the Brain

New technologies are also helping us to see the effects on the brain of differences in how children behave and how they are cared for. For example, recent studies have shown the following:

TEMPERAMENT

Infants who act more confident, adventurous, and engaged show more activity on the left frontal side of their brains than children who are shyer, more withdrawn, and less apt to explore. Exactly what this means for later brain functioning is far from clear. But the results show remarkable individuality in how young children's brains process information and how they inform and guide what babies do.

MOTHER-CHILD ATTACHMENT

Infants who are separated from their mothers for even twenty-four hours (such as for hospitalization) show a wide range of effects, such as increased heart rate, blood pressure, interrupted sleeping patterns, and reduced responsiveness. Permanent separation is linked to greater stress for the child later in life. In turn, the biochemical stress responses, themselves, are thought to affect brain activity and development.

MATERNAL DEPRESSION

Infants in the care of mothers with severe depression show reduced brain activity and noticeable effects in the areas of the brain associated with expression and regulation of emotions. This may result from such mothers' inability to relate affectionately and responsively to their infants. The longer the mother's depression continues, the greater the chances that her baby will have later behavioral or emotional problems.

STRESS

When babies are hungry or don't receive other forms of necessary care, their levels of cortisol, a steroid hormone, rise. Cortisol has a number of functions, and it affects metabolism, the immune system, and the brain. Repeated excess doses of cortisol over a long period of time appear to make the brain vulnerable to processes that destroy neurons and weaken the brain's synapses. The magnitude of this effect may be small. But no one has yet studied these effects over the long term. However, studies show that children with chronically high cortisol levels have more developmental delays than do other children.

PARENTAL BEHAVIOR

The quality of early care has been shown to affect the amygdala, the region of the brain involved in regulating a host of important functions, including sleep, appetite, alertness, and emotional reactivity. The amygdala registers emotional input, which your infant comes to recognize as comfortable. Again, we don't know the long-term implications of early variation in the functioning of the amygdala, but some interesting ideas are being tested.

There are many unanswered questions about how and how much the brain is affected by the care that infants receive. But the collective body of evidence from studies, such as those cited above and many others, all point to the benefits of loving, attentive care for infants. Expect to see many more findings in the future on this exciting research front.

Bright Horizons

The more we learn about the brain, the more we appreciate how versatile, complex, adaptable, and powerful it is. The current focus on early learning greatly understates all of these. To channel the tremendous capacities and potential of the infant brain just into memorizing letters and numbers seems a waste to us.

For the most part, the more enjoyable an activity is for both parent and child, the more advantageous it is for the child's development. Such activities — reading a story, playing with water, singing nursery rhymes, exploring a found object in nature — engage many or even all of a child's sensory and learning capacities, far more than any early-learning memory exercise will.

As best we know, the principles of good parenting apply to *all* children and should help to improve the lifelong competencies and brain development of all children. However, it is important to adjust to each child's unique way of perceiving and responding to the world, and to the timing of your child's development.

In the coming chapters, we will show how your baby's many capacities are engaged and developed and how each is helped by the others. As you gain a scientist's eye view of these wondrous capacities, we hope you will want to do what we and most of our colleagues do with our own children: Forget the flash cards. Take your infant for a stroll or walk to explore and learn! ✿

CHAPTER 3

A Sense of the World

Tuning In,
Getting in Touch

BABIES ARE A LOT MORE RECEPTIVE AND AWARE RIGHT FROM BIRTH THAN WE USED TO REALIZE. NOT ALL THAT LONG AGO, MOTHERS WERE TOLD THAT THEIR NEWBORNS COULDN'T SEE, TASTE, OR FEEL PAIN — OR AT LEAST NOT MUCH. (DADS WEREN'T TOLD MUCH OF ANYTHING!) NOW WE KNOW THAT ALL OF THEIR SENSES ARE FAIRLY ACTIVE, RIGHT FROM BIRTH, EVEN THOUGH SOME ARE STILL UNDERGOING RAPID MATURATION AND WILL BE INFLUENCED BY EXPERIENCE.

The senses are a baby's means of tuning into, and out of, the world. Two of a baby's biggest tasks are to make sense of the world and to find order and regularities in the available sensations. As they grow, babies regulate sensation as they learn to discriminate, express preferences, and choose what, where, and when they focus their attention.

Thanks to new research, we now have a much greater appreciation of the role the senses play in infant development. We have learned much about the complex ways a baby's sensations of the outside world contribute to lasting human relationships and to active information processing.

The basic senses all work reasonably well from birth on. In fact, most were active prior to birth, when a fetus had many sensory experiences. The newborn's ability to detect and respond to sight, sound, smell, touch, and taste is remarkable. So is the infant's sensitivity to movement cues, from inside and outside.

Senses help babies learn. Their senses also help them attract attention and aid from others from whom they will learn even more. Not surprisingly, therefore, the earliest senses are intensely focused on people and long-term human relationships. Babies show a strong preference for human faces. Their ability to recognize their parents' faces and detect their parents' voices, smells, and touches help babies to differentiate the people they love and trust from others.

Even though each sense is distinctive and serves a unique role, the senses work together. Probably most senses work much better because of this synergy. The interplay between and among them makes it easier to translate information from one sense into responses that involve other senses.

Alert to the World

When babies are awake and alert, their sensory systems are functioning at their peak. The amount of time babies spend in this alert and aware state increases from only a few hours per day after birth to five or six hours per day by six months, and continues to grow well into childhood. Just as individual infants vary in their sleep–wake cycles and the amount of sleep that is optimal for them, so they also differ in their attention spans.

When awake, babies have biological cycles that influence their alertness and behavior. A basic rest–activity cycle (BRAC) was established even prior to birth, one that was closely linked to the mother's own BRAC. Over the first year, this BRAC changes dramatically, and corresponds closely with the times an infant actively participates in sensory and social experiences, providing more time and attentiveness to learn. This time period initially is fairly short, on average about forty-five minutes. By eighteen months, it will approximate the adult range of 90–120 minutes.

There are many patterns of waking and sleeping and being alert. Just before evening, for example, many babies have a somewhat fussy period. However, they also tend to have an extended evening period when they are alert — a convenient pattern for parents who are busy during the conventional work hours.

When your baby is alert, you will know it by the many cues she shows — eyes open and wide with a "bright" look, eyes that follow your movements, a head that turns and orients toward interesting things like sounds and moving objects and new smells, a change in body movements, and smiles and positive sounds that are signs of pleasure as she seeks more sensation.

SLEEP-ACTIVITY LOGS

Many parents find it helpful to keep a sleep-activity log for seven-day periods at different points in the first eighteen months. Simply record whether your baby was sleeping, awake and alert, feeding, fussy, or crying in approximate intervals of fifteen minutes.

This may sound difficult, but it is generally easy to remember what happened over a period of several hours. You may find it convenient to keep the sleep-activity log near the diapering area.

You will discover that your baby has a clearer pattern than you realized. However, in the first three to four months, these patterns may not match the time of day. This is because some infants have a diurnal cycle (a dark–light cycle) that is a little off from the twenty-four-hour clock. Your baby may have a twenty-three- or twenty-five-hour pattern, and may show regular patterns for a few weeks and, later, for a few months at a time. Appreciating this individual pattern often is a great way for parents to be sure they are available for their baby's "best times," and to anticipate when parents can have a little time for themselves.

After only a few months, your baby may begin to use more sophisticated signals — vocalizations, whole body movements, head orienting — to indicate she wants to see or hear something new or interesting, especially when she is alert and wants something beyond being held or left in an infant seat. Just as important, she will begin to let you know when she has had enough sensory stimulation and wants some peace and quiet, or sleep, or food (again). With each passing month, you'll discover some of the special sensations that delight your child — a musical toy, a special way of stroking, a favorite mobile or pattern to look at, a lullaby you hum, or silly words you say. The list goes on and on, and keeps changing.

Good Sense

Scientists have gathered a lot of information about how infants use all their senses to help understand the world around them. Sensory and perceptual development is closely linked to early learning.

SIGHT

The visual system has been studied in greater detail than any other sensory system. Like all of the senses, vision operates in conjunction with other senses. However, most of the evidence about infant visual development comes from studies that isolate discrete components, like contrast sensitivity, flicker resolution, grading acuity, and temporal resolution. These are important technical features that measure the performance of the visual system, but not ones we consciously perceive.

We have learned that the rates of development for discrete capabilities do not follow a constant time course. Some skills emerge rapidly, seemingly overnight, while others show more gradual, steady gains. At very early ages, some components function at nearly adult levels. Others are quite immature until six or twelve months, or even later.

We have also learned that the "average" age for certain capabilities is a poor indicator of when an individual baby first shows these skills. When many infants are studied, the "average" age can mask or distort the rate and pattern of change we see for individual babies.

This is another reason that parents should not be overly concerned with developmental benchmarks. Age norms should be used only as very rough markers as to when things might happen. Few children show a skill at the precise "average" age.

Changing your baby's mobile, pictures on the walls, or toys in an effort to anticipate weekly or monthly changes in visual acuity, for example, is probably unnecessary and not likely to be matched to your infant's development. Knowing that your baby has rudimentary color vision by two months does not mean you should only show black-and-white toys and pictures. However, very high contrasts — such as black-and-white stripes or swirls — are likely to capture your baby's attention. Most infants also like to look at the human face, and even at drawings of faces.

Right from birth, your baby's vision is ideally suited for social interaction. He can focus fairly well on objects that are eight to fourteen inches away — about the distance to the face of the person who is feeding him. As such, he has the vision he needs for one of his most important tasks — looking at you and establishing a close bond.

In the second and third months, a baby's vision improves dramatically. By this age, most babies indicate that they can tell the difference between red, blue, and green compared to white and other colors. Yellows and yellow-greens, however, are not yet recognized reliably. This is when brightly colored toys, books, and objects will attract your baby's attention. From now through adolescence, your child will be able to discriminate increasingly fine variations in color.

HIGH CONTRAST

Your baby's range of vision will improve to several feet at the end of the second month. By the end of three months, he will show interest in objects across an entire room.

Babies gain depth and distance perception more gradually. These visual components begin to operate reliably at about six months, just about the time that your infant will begin to crawl or scoot. Being able to guess what is nearby or far away, and where things are in space, is very useful at this point!

Dr. Davida Teller at the University of Washington has been a pioneer in infant vision. Working with an artist, she has helped to generate pictures designed to capture what the world looks like through the eyes of your baby. We include some of these images to give you a sense of what your baby sees. These may look fuzzy or out-of-focus to you. But to your baby, these images are not inadequate. After all, your baby has never seen the world any other way.

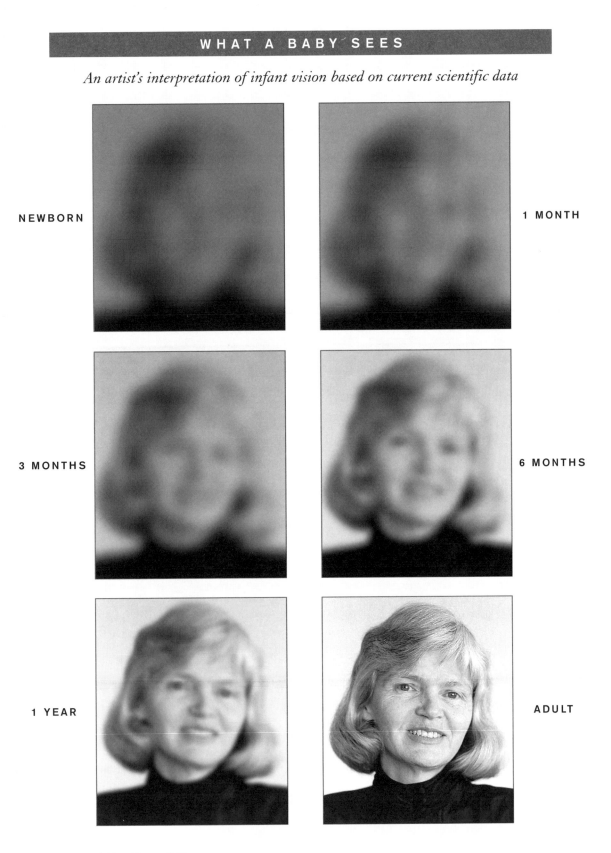

WHAT A BABY SEES

An artist's interpretation of infant vision based on current scientific data

NEWBORN

1 MONTH

3 MONTHS

6 MONTHS

1 YEAR

ADULT

©*Tony Young, 1998*

By two to three months, your baby will be able to turn both eyes inward (convergence) so that he can track an object that moves toward him. Before this, he would have seen two separate images, one in each eye. Combining focusing and convergence, your baby will start to perceive objects of different sizes and at different distances, whether they are still or moving. At about the same time, he will be able to track moving objects smoothly. You can encourage this skill by holding an object about one foot from him and moving it slowly from side to side.

What does the explosion of new knowledge about the visual system in early infancy mean for parents? At a practical level, it means we can accurately measure how well the baby's visual system works. Although most infants have normal vision, many have minor, potentially correctable, visual problems.

Failure to detect and correct these problems early may lead to lifelong visual problems that can only be partially corrected later on with prescriptive lenses. This is because the visual system in the brain has unique cells that respond to activation that occurs only through sight. For example, if a baby is not seeing certain angles or subtle variations, then later technical correction may not be effective, because the brain may no longer have the capacity for responding fully to the sensory input.

Only in the last ten years has the application of the new infant visual assessment techniques become part of the curriculum for optometrists and ophthalmologists. Now almost every community has at least one specialized professional who can check your baby's vision. This is especially important if the parents or grandparents have any visual problems, or if your child was very premature or has medical conditions that may be associated with later visual impairment.

On the lighter side, our new knowledge about infant vision has practical applications in the home. Now that we know what and how soon babies can see, there has been a revolution in interior decor. The bland nurseries of old have given way to colorful rooms and toys that are a delight to babies and parents alike.

The dramatic improvements in vision during the first three months provide your baby with a great view of the world. Beyond vision for its own sake is your baby's ability to explore and to discover. Looking is a way to learn about many things, from the different ways that people show emotions through their facial expressions to how mouths move when they make different sounds to how objects are transformed in size and shape as they move through space.

Clearly, the immediate visual world is fascinating for infants. But beware of television, videotapes, and computers. These are unlikely to offer the same natural variety and dimensionality as the real world. We can think of no reason to use these on a regular basis with young infants. In fact, many experts suspect these may create confusing and uninterpretable images in the early stages of development.

SMELL

A newborn's sense of smell is fully developed and very important. The sense of smell is connected to a part of the brain that is considered very primitive. Your baby will be able to distinguish smells from one another, and will show preferences for those she likes. In the first week, she will know the smell of her mother and strongly prefer her natural fragrance. She will also recognize the scent of her mother's breast pad from any other, and will prefer hers. We are not quite sure how to describe the mother's smell, but babies clearly know and recognize it.

The attraction of scent isn't a one-way street. Infants arrive with a wonderful "just born" smell. There is no other smell like it. It is delightful and downright intoxicating. Sniff your just-bathed baby and be prepared for a wonderful sensation. The scent is a lot like the traditional baby powder, but much better. In just a few months, it will disappear.

A basic fact of early life for mammals is that smell is an important way in which mothers and their young get and stay connected. Females in many species won't feed offspring other than their own. Smell is a key way they identify which young are theirs and which aren't. So the bond of smell is essential to survival for many young animals.

For humans, the attractions of scent create another avenue for bonding. The attraction of natural sweet scents helps both parent and infant want to be in close contact. Early on, babies do not like sour or bitter smells. This may be nature's way of protecting a baby from consuming dangerous or contaminated substances. As we discover more about the importance of caregiving to children's development, it is clear that a healthy future for them requires the kind of interaction that all these sensory bonds are designed to elicit.

Practically speaking, we guess that mothers and babies should stay clean and fresh and probably forget the use of perfumes and scented products, especially in the first few months of the baby's life. But to our knowledge, there has been no systematic research on this.

While the sense of smell is well-developed at birth, babies' reactions to various smells expand during the second and third months. As these senses mature, babies differentiate more between types and intensities of odors. A delightful pastime to try at various ages with your baby is to sniff bottles of herbs and spices, being careful to keep them at a safe distance. With increasing skills, you and your child can play games that name different types of smells — telling what you like best and what you don't like at all.

TASTE

For babies, as for adults, taste is closely linked to smell. A newborn has a well-developed sense of taste. Tests have shown that babies only a few days old can distinguish mild flavor differences and will show preferences, especially for sweets.

Infants soon show the ability to discriminate between the tastes of salty, sweet, bitter, and acidic. We still have much to learn about how individual differences in taste or smell function or the extent to which they contribute to whether a child is a "picky" or discriminating eater. Long-term studies do not confirm a lasting association between finicky childhood eating patterns and adult ranges of taste and adventure in food. In fact, parents report wide fluctuation over the early years in their children's willingness to try new tastes and textures.

For nursing babies, the smell and taste of mother's milk will vary based on what the mother has eaten. For this reason, some mothers choose to avoid heavily spiced foods, especially those heavy with garlic and onion. Try some variety and see what your baby likes and does not like. At the same time, breast milk introduces babies to the taste of the foods of their culture, albeit in a muted form. So there is no need to forgo your spicy favorites totally.

BREASTFEEDING AND ALCOHOL

Research has given us some important safety information for mothers who breast-feed. Among the most important concerns alcoholic beverages. Alcohol is transmitted directly through mother's milk into the baby's bloodstream in its original state. Babies cannot metabolize (break down) alcohol the way adults do. Infants can become intoxicated. But more important, regular exposure to alcohol can potentially disrupt normal brain growth and development.

Taste becomes a growing part of exploration as babies begin to mouth objects they touch or pick up. While infants can tell one taste from another, their desire to discover is so strong that even the most dreadful taste won't always stop them from ingesting something that looks new and interesting. This drive to discover will continue for many months. Therefore, it is essential that household cleaning products and other dangerous substances be kept out of your baby's reach.

HEARING

A newborn's hearing is well-developed, even though sounds are somewhat muted. Researchers have shown that hearing actually begins in the fifth month of prenatal life, when the fetus responds to a wide variety of sounds.

While newborns can distinguish changes in volume, they hear better those sounds that are somewhat higher in pitch. Most adults automatically speak in a higher pitch when talking to a baby, a seemingly intuitive behavior that matches a baby's preferences and capabilities.

Babies can clearly differentiate among voices. At birth, they immediately recognize and like their own mothers' voices best, which they heard many times prior to birth. This provides another link of familiarity that supports bonding. Soon they will also know and like the voices of their fathers and other loving and trusted caregivers.

Your baby's hearing becomes almost fully developed during the first three months. Using both hearing and his growing cognitive skills, he will be able to distinguish the sources of sounds and follow them. You will soon see that, when he hears your voice or footsteps, he will turn to watch you and follow you as you move about.

One fascinating finding about infant hearing is that babies can remember patterns of sounds, such as the rhythm and cadence of a story read over and over, or the melody and words of a song. Your infant may turn to familiar sounds, and may also be able to tune out or stop responding to bothersome, repetitive sounds, such as a ringing bell. Some babies seem highly sensitive to noise levels, while others appear less so. Observe your infant's responses to sounds, and particularly notice how your own voice, when you talk to your child, elicits positive responses. Your baby loves to listen, most of all to a voice from someone who provides lots of care, stimulation, and comfort.

TOUCH

A baby's sense of touch is well-developed at birth, and is the basis for a number of instinctive physical reactions. We know from many studies that physical stimulation of babies' bodies is important to their development. This is one reason they enjoy physical contact so much. There is, however, a lot of individuality in how and how much a baby wants to be held, stroked, and patted. Above all, timing of touch to the baby's state of alertness and responsiveness is key.

Touch is also an important learning tool for your baby. Her growing coordination during the first three months enables her to start taking advantage of this sense. Once she can grasp and hold objects, she can explore the way they feel against her hand, foot, or cheek. She will increasingly use her hands and mouth to explore surfaces and objects. You can encourage her by giving her toys and objects with different surfaces and textures and temperatures.

As her coordination grows, your baby will increasingly be able to control her hand and arm movements. Even at birth, she can bring her hand to her mouth and suck on her fingers or fist. This is a normal and important behavior, and it may be a helpful self-comforting or self-stimulating routine as time goes on. Soon she will be able to bring to her mouth anything she picks up. Her mouth is just as important as her hands in discovering the "feel" of her growing world.

Touching a baby can help to quiet her, to stimulate her or arouse her, depending on how you do it. Baby massage has been associated with positive outcomes in a number of studies. Dr. Tiffany Field of the University of Miami has shown that early infant massage is associated with positive mood and healthy weight gain. These good effects are probably due to both direct benefits to the central nervous system as well as to the more positive parent–infant interactions babies experience when they are massaged.

Massage may inhibit the release of stress hormones, such as cortisol, and increase neurotransmitters (chemicals that affect the activity of neurons in the brain) associated with pleasure, such as dopamine. More research is needed on this topic, including studies of the ways that parents naturally stroke and massage their babies in the course of everyday caregiving.

It is important to remember that much of this research on infant massage has been conducted on infants with special needs (such as low birthweight infants) or other risk conditions. Some parents are now scheduling their babies for special infant massages. We doubt that this is beneficial, and it certainly is not needed. Above all, having someone else massage your child denies both of you the special warmth and intimacy that come from the gentle skin-to-skin contact during massage.

It All Adds Up

Over the first year, your baby's growing memory enhances the power of basic sensing and perceiving. Right from birth, babies distinguish many things that are familiar and others that are new. But parents can greatly enhance the learning power of the senses by providing a certain amount of continuity, predictability, and pleasant comparisons.

When babies' senses, as well as their minds, experience similar sensations, activities, and routines over and over again, they come to know what to expect — what things go together, when some things happen (and don't happen) and when someone is likely to appear (or disappear). As part of their everyday tuning in to the world around them, infants notice and remember similarities and differences — a form of discrimination that is vital to many learning activities, social exchanges, and emotional well-being.

For almost all of the senses, it is thought that there are periods during which an infant's brain is especially receptive to, and positively influenced by, stimulation of that sense. It is likely that these periods include multimodal or multisensational experiences, as well.

Unfortunately, precise timetables for each sense have not been established, partly because most infants receive the varied types of sensory experiences they need in the course of their normal care. Studies of extreme deprivation, often isolated clinical cases or research conducted in orphanages, provide important clues about the consequences of inadequate stimulation or total absence of certain forms of stimulation. Yet these studies are not definitive.

Recent research indicates that an infant's capacity to detect subtle differences in highly similar sounds "drops out" in the first year when the sounds are not part of a child's everyday language world. Such detection improves for sounds heard frequently. In the coming years, expect to hear much more about new research findings that connect infants' early sensory experiences with brain activity and the development of special perceptual and behavioral competencies.

Because of the powerful interplay among the senses, lack of experience in one or more may affect development in others. Too much stimulation, especially when it is not positive or not developmentally appropriate or interpretable, may also have negative effects. Remember that your baby needs "quiet time," just as you do. Quiet time is part of the natural flow and rhythm of human experience, especially early in life. Even sleep is considered biologically vital to the learning process overall.

Finally, as described in detail in the next chapter, babies should not be totally passive and dependent beings for very long. Active engagement of their senses and use of their growing skills are essential to their development. As they grow, they will spend more of their time and attention on self-initiated or self-regulated experiences, which involve different levels of brain activity than those needed for passive experiences.

The senses quickly become an avenue for activity that babies can control, marking another milestone in growth. Infants as young as eight weeks old who were given an opportunity to influence the world (such as by head turns that electronically controlled mobiles over their cribs) showed much greater visual attention, smiled much more, and vocalized lots more, compared to babies who simply watched the same turning mobiles but could not control them. More on this in the next chapter.

Working Together

In sum, the vast body of research on the senses shows how important these "windows on the world" are right from birth in forging bonds to parents, and opening the pathways to virtually all aspects of growth and learning. A mix of different ways to sense the order and diversity in everyday life appears to ensure vigorous development of young children's brains, as well as their competence and their enjoyment of life. Babies are wired to experience the world in multiple ways, and they clearly delight in the pleasures and information that their senses receive and convey. ✿

CHAPTER 4

Cause and Effect

*The Basis for
Learning and Trust*

AUSE AND EFFECT. ACTION–REACTION. EFFORT–REWARD. I CAN DO THINGS. PEOPLE CARE ABOUT ME. THESE ARE SOME OF THE MOST IMPORTANT, ENGAGING, AND LASTING LESSONS INFANTS LEARN.

From their earliest moments, babies make big strides in understanding when, where, and how they fit into their world. They continually look, listen, and touch to figure out how the things and people in their world work and operate. What they discover lays a broad foundation for their initiatives, their expectations, and their accomplishments in the years ahead:

- How can I make interesting things happen?
- How can I learn to do things myself?
- Are other people caring or indifferent?
- Does it matter whether I respond or not?
- Are my achievements important?
- Does paying attention and trying hard pay off or not?
- Which actions of mine win positive results? Which don't?
- Who are the people I can trust to help me and teach me?

The answers to these questions are a vital part of children's learning and the formation of their attitudes toward life. The answers come from their experiences, day by day, week in, week out. Your actions and reactions, your words and responses to your baby's vocalizations, your teaching, and your celebration of what he has learned are the most important gifts you will ever give him. As his sense of self develops, so does a structure of beliefs about how capable and worthy that self is.

Infants learn soon whether and how much they can contribute to their everyday experiences. "Quality time" is not optional, no matter now busy parents may be. It is a daily parental responsibility. For babies, "quality time" is what everyday life is all about. "Quality time" is when babies experiment with life — learning about how they are an active, not just a passive, participant.

Children whose needs and activities have been responded to right from birth learn more — more about people, things, language, and ideas. They learn to interact playfully and cooperatively, and they know they can trust others to care. Young infants whose accomplishments are celebrated become willing to try new ways to solve problems and to exert effort to learn more.

The best of learning in infancy, and throughout childhood, is fun, rewarding, interesting, and always relevant.

Who Notices Me? Who Cares About Me? Do I Matter?

For normal growth and development, young infants, right from birth, need to learn that they can cause good things to happen on a predictable basis. In child-development jargon, this is called positive response-contingent stimulation. It means that what happens to babies depends on what they do: When they do things, the people around them notice and respond. Response-contingent stimulation is not mechanistic or formulaic. It is a natural, often spontaneous, form of give-and-take between your baby and the world.

As with everything else we discuss in this book, balance is important. Too much and too little responsiveness both miss the mark. Historically, many parents feared that if they were overly attentive or responsive, their child would become demanding, self-centered, or spoiled. Excessive indulgence over the long term can, indeed, produce unattractive behavior. But in the early months of life, parents cannot spoil their children! Positive response contingency does not, however, require that parents notice every action, respond to every sound, or never allow their infant to experience the world alone.

Response-contingent experiences, in fact, do not always require a parent or adult to be the responder. Many toys and objects provide a rich array of response-contingent feedback. A rattle makes sounds when a baby shakes it (loud ones or soft ones, short ones or long ones, depending on what the baby does). A ball rolls when a baby pushes it. A sound is heard when a baby claps her hands. Together, these and many other experiences help build a child's repertoire of self-initiated behavior.

At the other extreme, young infants who are routinely ignored fail to learn the value of positive human transactions. They cry more and show signs of distress — at least for a while. Babies were not designed to be neglected or to be passive. Later, such infants stop crying, and they also have reduced opportunities to learn and grow.

When infants experience the world around them as unresponsive or chaotic, they show dramatic delays in their natural learning and loving. They also lack the broad, engaging, and adaptable social repertoire that infants who have a richer response-contingent environment gain. This can lead to developmental problems and a failure to thrive as an active, learning child.

Babies flourish when their needs get well-timed, trustworthy, positive responses. Response-contingent feedback is, therefore, another way in which the totality of daily experience builds your child's foundation for life. A response-contingent world does not produce a self-centered, demanding child. To the contrary, response-contingency is a key element in fostering inquisitiveness, stimulating learning, and showing a child how to be responsive, considerate, and caring.

Wired for Action

The great Swiss biologist and child development specialist, Jean Piaget, was a pioneer in systematically observing and explaining how young children learn about, organize, and adapt to their world. He identified the onset of symbolic thought early in infancy. He also recognized that an infant's early actions and responses, including the cause-and-effect activities we are discussing here, are the building blocks for more sophisticated cognitive functioning.

Dr. Robert White of Harvard University also provided extraordinary insights into the world of infants. Babies not only are able to learn, he said, but they have a curiosity drive and a need to learn. His classic paper on infant curiosity was considered radical stuff in 1959. But his position has now been extensively confirmed.

Prior to White's hypothesis, most learning theorists viewed organisms as driven only by basic survival needs, such as hunger, thirst, and safety. The idea that a curiosity drive could be as biological and as basic as these other needs truly revolutionized the field of learning and subsequent research. White described an "effectance motivation," which is closely related to the many forms of cause-and-effect relationships described in this chapter.

When infants are deprived of response-contingent experiences for long periods of time, such as in severely understaffed orphanages, the lack takes its toll in many ways. After a while, most babies cease to cry or to elicit adult attention. Rather they become listless, passive, disengaged. Sometimes they self-stimulate (something all babies do to some extent) to excess, engaging in repetitive but nonpurposive behavior, reflecting the lack of stimulus in their environment.

Most tragically, their behavioral repertoire does not expand, their language development is markedly retarded (or nonexistent), and their sense of self may fail to emerge. Their rate of brain growth appears to slow down, keeping them in an immature state — a terrible cumulative toll of their sensory and social deprivation.

These behavioral and biological losses may be irreversible. Although our own research has demonstrated that these children are capable of later learning and can benefit from subsequent enrichment and response-contingent stimulation, it may be impossible to completely "catch up" or compensate for their early neglect.

Babies are not wired to do nothing for long periods of time. There is extensive evidence from many sources that infants are acutely aware of their environments. They are also highly sensitive to the quality and quantity of response-contingent experiences. Research confirms these findings in numerous studies of children reared under very different conditions, ranging from highly enriching to abusive, erratic, or neglectful.

Studies we conducted show how dramatic the effects can be. We examined failure-to-thrive babies between six and twenty months who were strongly suspected of severe maternal deprivation. These infants were extremely small and undernourished, apathetic, and lethargic. They were not prone to explore visually or manipulatively. They simply lay passively in their cribs for hours on end and stared blankly ahead.

Clinical tests scored all of these infants as functionally mentally retarded, even though there were no prior signs of brain or other organic malfunction. Their overall development was so delayed, and their condition so potentially life-threatening, that they required hospitalization.

In subsequent laboratory work, we were able to show the benefits of enriching these infants' lives by providing response-contingent experiences. The benefits of response-contingent opportunities included:

- Increased alertness and more vigorous activity levels
- Spontaneous expressions of delight and surprise
- Increased and more diverse vocalizations
- Subsequent, much-needed weight gain

In later research with typically developing infants, we affirmed the importance of early response-contingent experiences. Infants who received extra opportunities to cause positive reactions from people or objects or both showed increased attention to external stimuli. They also showed more interest in what their own bodies could do — looking at and exploring their hands, for example. They became more aware of their own sensory-motor capabilities. Most dramatically, these infants showed frequent signs of glee, joy, and wonder directly related to learning about themselves as active agents in life.

One of the most important findings was that young babies who had more frequent and positive response-contingent learning opportunities later showed greater willingness to learn other new things, and to actively explore the external world around them. *It is undeniable: Learning begets learning.*

These and literally scores of other studies clearly show what is and what is not good for babies. Especially in the first eighteen months of life, extended periods with little or no opportunity for response-contingent exchanges are harmful:

- ❀ Do **NOT** park an infant in front of a television, even when child-oriented, "educational" programs are on.
- ❀ Do **NOT** leave a child where he may be ignored for long periods of time or where there is no one to play and speak with him.
- ❀ Do **NOT** subject an infant to situations in which the sights and noises are overwhelming and insensitive to his needs.

Remember that *basic care* for babies includes responding to their curiosity drive and their need for stimulation and learning opportunities, just as much as their need to be fed, diapered, bathed, and protected from physical harm. Parents cannot be too caring or too vigilant about the quality of their child's everyday experiences.

Settings where stimulation is woefully inadequate eventually teach babies to be passive. At the outset, babies who receive inadequate care cry and fuss. Soon, however, after their cries are ignored, they are likely to become very quiet. They may appear to be occupying themselves or to be content doing nothing. In fact, the situation may be much more serious. They may be learning that human beings are not responsive, caring, or helpful. Such children may come to believe that they are incapable of being effective agents. They also may not feel connected to, or trusting of, others.

If these feelings of passivity, inadequacy, frustration, and disappointment recur often, they can drastically limit a child's potential for learning. Very young infants have relatively limited mental capacity or motor control to create active learning situations on their own. They must depend on others to provide such situations for them. They also don't yet have a vast store of remembered ideas and experiences that they can think about. Babies and young children must rely on others for stimulation — the right kinds and amounts.

During the first eighteen months, your baby learns cause-and-effect relationships by mastering a number of response-contingent stimulation associations. This basic understanding is of enormous developmental importance. Once the idea of causality forms in a child's mind, it sets the stage for more sophisticated and nuanced understandings of her relationship to the world. Your baby's growing cause-and-effect repertoire, coupled with an expanding capacity to recognize and to recall past individuals, actions, and events, lays the foundation for a new stage of consciousness, including a sense of self and mind.

In the latter part of the first year, a curious and exploratory infant will invent a host of variations on the cause-and-effect actions he knows. Two patterns are particularly profound. Both deal with gradations of effects produced by a child's actions. One deals with proportionality and the other with behavioral timing. In the case of proportionality, infants learn that more vigorous behaviors generally produce bigger consequences. For example, the harder he bangs a drum, the louder it sounds.

Behavioral timing refers to when the effect produced by an infant's action will happen and how long it will last. The younger the infant, the more immediate the effect has to be in order for a learning connection to occur. Most infants younger than nine months, for instance, cannot make a cause–effect connection if the effect takes two seconds or more after the child's behavior stops. Thus, for young infants, *consequences have to be almost immediate to be effective.* But as infants grow, they can learn from consequences that take longer to happen.

This is apparent when games like peekaboo or hiding objects can be extended. A number of mental operations are presumed to undergird the shift in behavioral timing. Most parents seem to know that very young infants require instantaneous feedback or responsiveness, and that older ones can wait a few more seconds. Observe your infant. You will learn quickly what timing is just right for each stage of your child's development.

Many activities are complex, teaching a child how multiple actions affect one another. Push-pull toys are a good example. A child quickly learns the different effects of pulling slowly or fast, this way or that. Musical toys with different color keys and pop-up objects are another example. Busy boxes and puzzles all teach children about multiple dimensions and how their own behavior influences the outcome. Even mirrors provide learning opportunities long before your baby knows she is a separate person with a unique identity.

The Joy of Effect

The central players in your baby's world of cause and effect are people. Nothing can take the place of people in teaching your baby about causality. All the games you play, as well as your responses to your baby's coos and gurgles, will be among her major sources of pleasure and learning.

But objects and toys are wonderful teachers, too. A voice-activated mobile or tape recorder can provide much delight. So, too, can special baby equipment, such as controllable jumpers (your baby's leg movements will help her "jump" up in the air, safely). But toys and equipment need not be elaborate. Simple rattles, ankle and wrist bells, and squeeze noisemakers are just a few of the many things babies can learn from.

Your baby will appreciate variety. Be prepared for your child's individuality to express itself here, as everywhere else. A toy that is one child's absolute favorite may never be interesting to your child. And last week's favorite toy may hold no interest this week. (Just wait and try again in a month or two. At a later age, your child may be delighted by a once-discarded toy.) Also remember that learning occurs from touch, taste, smell, and movement, not just looking and listening.

An inventive and insightful parent can introduce just enough variety in the toys and social interchanges to provide a great deal of enjoyment. Many of us who study child development believe such enjoyment indicates a very important kind of learning, one that is key to the development of a child's understanding of self as a separate being.

We believe that a new concept gets formed and routinely validated when children think about their actions as having consequences in the external world. In this view, children show a developmental variation on the famous maxim of the seventeenth-century philosopher René Descartes: "I think, therefore I am."

Ah-Ha and More

In the first year of life, your child will show many "ah-ha" reactions — a clear sign that he has made a new connection in his brain. Every time this happens, it is an all-consuming moment of joy, wonder, and appreciation. His delight and surprise are contagious. They are also a tribute to your good parenting. In these moments of discovery, your child shows how a complex set of mental and perceptual processes come together with active interpretation, reflection, and emotional response.

These wonderful moments of insight are important precursors of what's to come by around fifteen to eighteen months — the sense of self as a thinking being. After this will follow the evolution of thinking about thinking, a whole new level of cognition that is the foundation for understanding, creating, imagining, solving problems, and pondering.

When we write of an infant as able to cause things to happen and to self-occupy, we do not mean to imply that babies are "in charge" or really independent. Quite the opposite. This emerging sense of order in the external world and the ability to contribute to what happens are the foundation for interdependence.

The back-and-forth interplay between an infant and the people and objects in the surrounding world reinforce your child's role as a player, both a contributor and a responder. Your baby is not learning to rule the roost, get her way, or be dominant. Rather, your child is sensing a new kind of voluntary control. This is part of what makes each individual special.

We now know that infants who are more socially engaging — skilled and responsive in their interactions with others — are especially likely to be sought out and played with by adults. Their learning opportunities will be many and varied, which in turn help to advance their behavioral and mental competence. This creates a positive spiral of social engagement, learning, and mutual enjoyment.

The Comfort of Relief

Both people and objects can provide pleasure and learning. But only people can offer the other half of cause-and-effect teaching in infancy — relief from distress. While a young infant can increasingly learn to soothe himself, important problems require outside aid.

Whether he is hungry, wet, tired, or in pain, only another person can help. And it is from these interventions that your baby begins very early to learn *two of the most important lessons of life*: *to trust others* and *to know that one's own needs matter.* These are crucial elements in every person's ability to work with and relate successfully to other people.

If both lessons are learned early, they provide a solid foundation for a healthy self-image and strong socialization skills. If that sounds like a tall order to come from things as simple as learning cause and effect from a rattle and peekaboo, and to trust that caring adults will help when help is needed, it is. But this is just one more way in which seemingly small things in infancy, repeated over time, can have profound and lasting effects.

This is also why the totality of experience is such an important concept. It is not the learning of any particular cause-and-effect relationship that is crucial. Rather, it is the learning about the idea of cause and effect. As a child comes to know that she can count on some things to happen, to have her everyday needs met in a responsive way, she also comes to have more of her waking hours available for other types of experiences.

For babies, learning is not a chore. There are no tests, no grades, no negative judgments to face. Instead, learning is simply what occurs when one tunes in with full attention to what is going on, and when one is willing to try out new behavior and see what happens: Can I reach the toy? Hold the object? Drop the object? Get my father to retrieve it? Get my mother to smile and laugh?

Once upon a time, parents were told, "Babies sometimes just need to cry so they can exercise their lungs." We know of no support for this. Even more strongly, we cannot think of any reason why a baby should learn to get used to discomfort or distress, to simply endure something unpleasant to prepare her for the fact that "You won't always get your way in life."

Such lessons of life will be learned in constructive ways at later ages, when the opportunities arise naturally. Young infants cannot engage in the type of emotional and behavioral self-control that older children can. This is beyond their mental capacity. To expect such behavior, or to try to teach "the hard lessons of life" to an infant is improper, a waste of time, and highly ineffective. Moreover, it produces a poor outcome. Parents who consciously ignore their infant's cries or signs of distress are teaching a child that adult love and attention come only after pain and neglect. Such behavior can never engender healthy trust and respect.

Shifting Gears in Learning

Infants differ in how much time they like to spend in various activities, whether in direct face-to-face interaction, playing with objects, or observing the world on their own. The first indicator of how much response-contingent experience a child wants or needs can be gauged by the child's emotional response to what Dr. John Watson of the University of California at Berkeley called "the game."

Watson regarded early social response-contingent exchanges as truly priming the infant for learning. This is because a very young infant's motor skills are immature and require an observant and socially engaging parent to help prime the child to detect "if this, then that," response-contingent relationships.

Even very young children smile, coo, or laugh when mastering a new cause-and-effect activity or a variation on a familiar one. This reaction normally energizes and sustains parental engagement. During these times of active infant learning, parents are learning, too — about their child's level of perceptual awareness, voluntary motor control, and likes and dislikes. As many great teachers have remarked through the centuries, teaching itself has many rewards, and the teaching process — like parenting — changes the teacher.

Reading the Signs

A good guideline for parents is to stop a particular activity soon after a child begins to signal a lack of interest. Parents' ability to read the behavioral cues of their young child is an important developmental milestone in parenting. Young children, just like adults, use a variety of facial expressions, hand movements, body positions, and sounds to convey important information about their emotional state.

If parents underestimate their child's capabilities, or do not learn to read their infant's cues well, they may wrongly assume these gestures are without meaning. Nothing could be further from the truth. Even very young infants are capable of expressing emotions, interests, individual preferences, and changes in their state.

Parents are frequently reminded how important it is to learn their child's cues for interest and disinterest, but what are they? An infant's lack of motor control has a big impact on which cues convey interest or disinterest, pleasure or displeasure.

Infants, like adults, vary widely in the vigor, style, and predominant display of their signals. But most infants' cues are distinct. Dr. Kathryn Barnard and her colleagues at the University of Washington have developed a system to describe in precise terms the nuances of parent–infant exchanges. While these cues are taught to infant specialists, they seldom make their way into parenting books. But they are easy for attentive parents to learn and use.

It's easy to pick up on the signs that your baby is interested when you are playing or teaching — gazes, smiles, babbles, and the like. But you might miss some of the more subtle cues of interest, such as a raised brow, open hands with slightly flexed fingers, and a brightening face.

Many "I want to quit" signs are also easy to spot, such as crying and fussing or pushing you away. Most parents also pick up on the precursors to these, such as whimpering or a grimace. But the earliest stages of disinterest are easy to miss. These include an averted gaze; a frown or lowered brow; putting a hand behind the head, ear, or back of neck; joining the hands or extending fingers; kicking the legs or straightening the legs with tension; looking away; puckering the face; turning the head; wrinkling the forehead; or yawning.

When your baby shows signs of disinterest or distress, we strongly suggest that you *stop whatever you are doing*. Many parents assume that if their baby is not paying attention or is fussing, they should try a little harder! When your baby loses interest, take a break. Stop what's not working. Your baby may want some quiet time. Maybe she wants to shift activities. Let her cues guide what to do next.

Once you know the cues, you can then observe what tends to provoke a particular response from your baby. You can become adept at predicting how much stimulation will get your baby to smile or laugh, and how much is too much. You will also learn what causes your baby to fail to meet your gaze, when she is out of sorts, when she wants to be left alone or just held, and when she wants to try something else.

When your baby does any or a combination of the above, follow her lead. Often you will have a sequence of exchanges that seem to flow effortlessly. Other times you will need to pause, rest, or move on to something else. If your baby does not respond positively to a new or continued activity, give her some quiet time. This is actually a hard lesson for some parents to master.

While you are learning your baby's cues, she is learning yours. Over time, the interaction of these social skills results in an ever-increasing social competence — what Dr. Evelyn Thoman of the University of Connecticut has called "the dance." This is the elaborate, reciprocal system of social interchange that resembles a sophisticated tango, which holds delight and meaning for both partners.

In the first year, you will see that your infant may "dance" somewhat differently with mother than with father, or siblings or grandparents. This indicates your baby's sensitivity to each person and that person's own style.

Having learned the importance of stimulation, some well-intentioned parents overdo it. Remember that your baby is absorbing and learning a great deal during these early months and years. As with anyone who is intensely learning something new, your baby's attention span may vary, and he will need "down" time, just as you do.

She will learn better and enjoy more if you are sensitive to her preferences. Trial and error are part of learning, for both parents and babies, but frustration is not. Avoid it! When things are not working, don't keep trying the same thing. You may even find you enjoy the opportunity to become an observer yourself, while someone else plays with your child.

Early Memory

Memory is the key to much of what your baby learns. He is building both the capacity for memory and a personal encyclopedia of people, objects, events, and dynamic relationships (patterns of cause and effect) actually stored in memory. Both will play valuable roles in the areas of development we will discuss in the next few chapters on language, social and emotional development, and intelligence. To give you a better understanding of how all these developments occur, the rest of this chapter is devoted to what we know about memory and how it develops to allow nearly every other aspect of growth to occur.

By the time your baby is eighteen months old, it is estimated that literally hundreds of thousands of bits of information will have been learned and stored, from simple discriminations to much more sophisticated concepts. Babies learn which people do what things, and do not do other things; which toys and objects are best for which times and places; that people show different feelings on their faces, in their speech, and in their behavior; that babies, themselves, can contribute to what is happening in ways that make things better; and that each day there are likely to be some events (sights, sounds, smells, tastes, actions, sequences, words, etc.) that are new and not yet fully understood — ones that warrant being checked out in anticipation of fun, joy, and new information and eventually placed into a symbolic mental framework in the brain for future reference and use.

The study of memory was once limited to that of toddlers and older children. In recent years, researchers have developed new and innovative ways to study what very young infants can remember. Babies can't tell us directly what they recall. But we have learned that highly distinctive and unusual patterns, sequences, and behaviors are noticed and remembered from even the very first few months of life, lasting for six to twelve months or longer. It seems remarkable that adults remember little or nothing of their infancy. This may explain in part why adults find it hard to believe that young babies can remember so much, including small and detailed things.

There are many ideas about why this is so. One is that memories that are stored before a fully developed symbolic system, such as language, is in use may be encoded in different ways. These early memories may be stored in different places than later memories that will belong to a dominant symbol system. Another theory is that infant memories become subsumed under early childhood memories and remain more as primitive traces than a set of logically stored information. Yet another explanation is that there may be little reason to use these memories, since so many other events and experiences replace those of infancy and afford much greater continuity to later events. Finally, before a true sense of self fully emerges, the memories may be less connected to the child's sense of individuality, and therefore may be encoded and retrieved in very different ways than after the sense of self has matured.

Even though we don't know why most infant memories aren't retained in consciousness, infant memory processes are very active and serve many purposes. Remembering both reflects and helps to advance an infant's mental functions. It also facilitates social and emotional connectedness.

A young child's memory is impressive. Parents are rightly amazed at the things their babies remember from so long ago. Memory is a clear indication of how much the child is noticing and actively processing. An active memory reminds others that what happens has effects that last longer than just a moment or two.

Memory for adults is largely influenced by language and labels, as well as sophisticated visual organizers and referents. For infants and young children, memories may include much more information about sensations, from touch, smell, taste, movement, temperature, sounds, and sights. But there are many unanswered questions about how infants' memories operate. Virtually nothing is known about the actual brain activity during infancy that corresponds to different types of learning and memory. This is likely to be a very exciting area for scientific breakthroughs in the coming years.

Most important, these infant memories help guide young children's choices, preferences, and feelings about repeating some activities (but not others), and their degree of interest in new activities. Generally, infants prefer things and activities with some elements of the familiar and others with some degree of novelty. If something is too familiar, with no variation, it can be boring. It won't hold a child's attention and encourage exploration and interaction. If something is too unfamiliar, too complex, or too difficult to be interpreted in a meaningful way, it will also fail to hold the child's attention.

This situation was recognized and described by Dr. J. McVicker Hunt of the University of Illinois as "the problem of the match." Hunt hypothesized that there is an optimal discrepancy between what the child "knows" and what the child "can learn" at any moment in a given situation. He showed that a skillful teacher who knows the child well can exploit the "problem of the match" to aid the child's development.

As babies are able to engage in more complex activities, so the adult-mediated learning opportunities change to match the child's readiness level. Repetition and review are not to be ignored. They are features of good learning, and allow a child to experience repeated successes. But success without being challenged becomes boring and meaningless.

Activities that are a good match provide many different ways for young children to learn. These forms of learning emphasize discrimination learning, response-contingent stimulation, observational learning, imitation, concept formation, and use of symbolic communication to learn the basic concepts and skills for social interaction.

What Should Parents Teach?

In light of the new evidence about how much children can learn and how able they are to learn even in early infancy, parents often ask two questions: First, "What do we need to teach our child — and when?" Second, "How do we know if our child is learning enough?"

In terms of *what* children need to learn, there is no scientific evidence that suggests parents should launch into systematic teaching regimens or provide highly structured learning situations. Rather, *infants learn best in everyday encounters around creative caregiving.* This means parents should be interactive, playful, affectionate, and responsive to the infant's cues of joy and distress. The important thing is to be sure that infants are consistently cared for by loving, responsive adults.

When young children are cared for in groups, however, we believe that an educational plan with appropriate materials is a practical necessity if every child is to receive appropriate and individualized attention. In Chapter 9, "The Many Worlds of Infancy," we offer guidelines to help parents select high-quality care whenever a child is regularly in nonparental care, whether at home or away.

What is most important is that adults who care for young children have the skills to help them learn. These adults need skills that are specialized to the age and stage of the child in their care. The educational strategies recommended for professionals in early childhood development are ones that parents themselves will acquire and should look for in others who care for their child.

In answer to the question "Is our child learning enough?" we do not know how much infants should be learning or when, particularly for optimal brain growth and development. Studies of young infants and toddlers indicate they learn at phenomenally high rates when they receive the natural attention they require and have an array of everyday opportunities to learn.

We doubt that there are many absolutes for how much a baby should learn at any given age. Rather, what needs to be learned are the features of one's culture and family, the patterns of everyday activities, and how to communicate. This is another instance of "parents know best." No formal measuring stick is needed or desirable. Rather, it is your child's engagement in life and daily enjoyment that will be your best guides.

Accelerated Learning: A Good Idea or Not?

Accelerated learning in any specific content area, like recognizing colors or shapes or letters, is likely to be of dubious lasting significance for infants. Instead, parents should provide activities that are interesting and that show basic, orderly relationships. Games like pat-a-cake, rhymes accompanied by touching or swaying, saying words in connection with their meaning (like swinging a baby "up" and then "down" or touching objects that are "soft" versus "hard" and "smooth" versus "bumpy"), and introducing hide-and-seek games when a child is ready are all forms of very active and very effective parent teaching.

Reading offers many different opportunities for teaching, as does storytelling. Dozens more ideas are contained in the second half of this book. But none are intended specifically to accelerate or speed up learning. Instead, they are to provide the natural loving supports, learning, and limits appropriate to everyday development.

As important and true as it is that "parents are children's first and foremost teachers," you also are parents who have lots of other things to do, including taking good care of yourselves and others in your lives. It is through love, caregiving, and everyday encounters that you will teach your best, often with little or no conscious awareness of what or how much you are helping your child to learn.

Even early on, parents can share their own favorite things, their cultural traditions, and their values and priorities with their babies. These are all conveyed through parents' words and actions. Babies will learn and remember in ways that match their perspectives on life at each age and stage of development.

Throughout history and across cultures, widely differing specific child-rearing practices have flourished. On the other hand, never before in history has there been such wide endorsement for the goals of universal literacy and the dream that our children will be able to adapt to the rapid, often unpredictable, changes in the world.

Perhaps the new era in parenting — this information age — will require new kinds of teaching to prepare children and parents for becoming citizens of the world. Only time and careful research will tell us more about what, when, and how much babies need to learn. Fortunately, there are many children thriving now — without being pushed in any way.

All the special events and the things you go out of your way to teach your child will benefit and be enjoyed by both of you. But remember that the most profound teaching your child receives is the aggregate experience of everyday life with family and friends, at home and outside, receiving and giving to the world. Special things help to fine-tune this aggregate experience, but they can't replace or counter it. The love, affection, and stimulation your child receives day in and day out are the core of your child's learning experience. ❀

CHAPTER 5

People Skills
in Infancy

Social and
Emotional Development

SOCIAL AND EMOTIONAL DEVELOPMENT OFTEN GETS LESS ATTENTION FROM PARENTS AND THE MEDIA THAN OTHER ASPECTS OF GROWTH. SEVERAL REASONS FOR THIS ARE LIKELY. FIRST, OUR UNDERSTANDING OF GROWTH ON THESE FRONTS IS RELATIVELY NEW. SECOND, IT IS EASY FOR PARENTS TO FOCUS ON FIRST WORDS, FIRST STEPS, AND OTHER EASY-TO-SEE ACHIEVEMENTS, AND PAY LESS ATTENTION TO THE MORE SUBTLE GAINS OF SOCIAL AND EMOTIONAL GROWTH.

Third, parents may think that not much is happening on the social and emotional fronts until a child begins to manifest what adults would consider social and emotional behavior. For example, they may believe that social development doesn't really begin until a child is able to talk, move about, and "socialize" in the sense that adults do. They may also think that emotional development doesn't require attention until the emotions begin to mature and require guidance.

Nothing could be further from the truth.

Once again, research findings are telling. They show that social and emotional skills develop apace with other skills, such as sensory, motor, cause-and-effect, and language. The foundations for social and emotional skills are built through an infant's everyday interactions with other people.

Infants quickly come to understand and express emotions, and to be highly engaging, competent social partners. Consider some recent findings:

- As early as one month of age, infants display emotions that indicate they are closely tuned in to what's happening around them.

- By four months of age, infants can recognize differences in joyous, angry, and expressionless faces. Even more impressive, they will vigorously try to change their parents' facial expressions to be happier.

- Laughing shows how smart a baby is. At first, simple touch and gentle tickles will make babies laugh. But only a few months later, infants laugh in response to social games *they understand* and when *they figure out* how to create delightful "events."

- Positive emotions do more than reflect how content a baby is. They help babies learn better because babies who feel good are more alert, attentive, and responsive. When babies learn without experiencing obvious distress or fussiness, they remember better, too.

- Soon after toddlers develop a true sense of "self" at around fifteen to eighteen months of age, their range of emotions expands to include new "self-conscious" ones, such as pride, embarrassment, shame, and guilt. These complex emotions reflect the strong link between thinking and feeling, and they can be influenced by parental behavior.

What Is Social-Emotional Development?

Social-emotional development covers a broad array of feelings and skills people use to understand and interact with others. Emotional and social skills can be looked at separately. But they are linked to each other as well as to many other aspects of development. Once again, there is compelling evidence that biology and experience combine to build human competence.

Socialization is an important aspect of social development. It is the process of introducing children to the values, rules, and expectations of their family and culture. Beginning in infancy, parents socialize their children to become good citizens. This involves much teaching, and differs widely across cultures and over the generations. This is because the world in which we live is changing. Also, the behaviors we consider important, acceptable, normal, and desirable also change in response to the times and the contexts in which we live, work, and play. Good socialization is essential to every child's future as an accomplished adult with a full and rewarding life. And it passes on to the next generation as well.

EMOTIONAL DEVELOPMENT

Healthy emotions enable people to express and constructively manage the full range of human feelings, to postpone gratification, to find constructive outlets for negative emotions, and to understand and appreciate how others feel. With healthy emotions, people also learn about the many ways to experience joy, amusement, and satisfaction at the good things in their lives.

Emotional development begins right from birth as infants learn to trust and enjoy their parents and others who care for them. They also learn the basics of regulating their emotions as they remain attentive to things that interest them, as they discover ways to occupy themselves, and as they explore what works best to elicit their parents' loving responses. As toddlers acquire a sense of self and new language skills, they begin to relate feelings to their unique self, and to label their feelings. They increasingly comprehend how their emotions are connected with their actions, as well as the actions of others.

From the first few days of life, your baby attends closely to your face, already able to read and respond to positive and negative expressions as well as subtle differences in your voice. This keen connectedness helps form the earliest kind of love. He is also acquiring an early form of empathy when he reads and responds to the cues of others, showing clearly that he cares about others and their feelings.

In the first year, infants come to feel and express a sophisticated range of emotions. These coincide with changes inside themselves (internal cues and states) that help them know what to approach and what to avoid, which people and events make them feel good and which do not, how to show their delight and make others happy, as well as how to get help to relieve distress that is beyond their young ability to fix.

SOCIAL DEVELOPMENT

Social development covers the broad range of skills people use to relate to, play with, learn from, and teach others. Social skills are important for survival and for a good life. They also are a way to show a person's individuality. The judgments of others about us are based largely on our social skills, including our adeptness at expressing ideas, our concern for others, and our ways to solve or prevent problems. In this sense, social development will be as vital to your child's success in school, in friendships, and in work as any IQ-test score, perhaps even more so.

An infant's social skills influence what people do. From early on, some babies seem like real "people babies," wanting almost constant time with others. Others like more "alone" time. Some babies smile and laugh more than others do. As far as we know, such differences affirm individuality. They may also be linked to genetic propensities. Fortunately, there are many ways for infants to become socially and emotionally adept and to fit into their social worlds well and with ease.

As with emotional skills, social abilities develop right from birth. Beginning with an infant's emerging sense of self, social skills grow to include trusting others, gaining self-confidence, having a good self-image, playing happily with siblings and other children, sharing, getting help from parents, acting within prescribed limits, cooperating, respecting authority, and respecting the rights and needs of others.

As social skills are refined over time, they enable us to develop a social identity and social effectiveness that extends to all facets of our lives. School-age children with good social skills are able to engage more help from their teachers, withstand extremes of peer pressure, make good judgments in choosing and keeping friends, and succeed in pursuing their interests and developing their talents. Adults with strong social histories and skills are better able to love and trust others, to build and enjoy lasting friendships, to work effectively in their careers, and to be caring and responsive parents — all key to personal fulfillment.

Clearly, social and emotional health affects every other sphere of a child's development and an adult's life. Research increasingly shows how soon and fast many of these essential skills begin to emerge. Happily, this research also shows that you can best help your baby develop these skills by being responsive, tuned in to your child's cues and individuality, and genuinely happy and interested in life yourself.

A Logical Extension

With our growing understanding of brain development, it is logical that social and emotional growth occur apace and in response to many other dramatic aspects of growth. Another logical extension is that parents can help to shape their child's social and emotional competence.

Many people are excited about the idea that we have "emotional intelligence" and "social intelligence." We can't really test a person's social or emotional intelligence yet. But everyday behavior reveals that, just like academic smarts, some people have more of these types of intelligence than others do.

Parents can be highly effective in helping children gain social and emotional skills. The goal is not just to make a child "popular." Rather, it is to help a child make sense of a complex social world and have the skills to join in successfully.

But there is another powerful reason to be interested in an infant's early emotional well-being and social growth: Deviations in these areas of development may have profound and lasting consequences. The resulting problems can be exceedingly difficult and troublesome to correct.

There is increasing concern that some infants may not be receiving enough of the good old-fashioned attention and love that is so essential to healthy social and emotional growth. Two profound changes in the last generation are affecting the way many infants are cared for. These are the explosion in the use of nonparental care during the first two years of life and the large number of children who grow up in single-parent homes.

These dramatic changes give reason for concern about whether infants and toddlers are getting the consistent and personal attention they need for positive social and emotional development. Researchers are increasingly studying the effects of such population and lifestyle changes on young children.

In Chapter 9, "The Many Worlds of Infancy," we report in detail the results from a new, long-term national study on the effects of infant daycare. Here, we simply share the good-news side of the story. Many children receive excellent, supportive care from nurturing, knowledgeable people who are *not* their parents, and these children fare very well. They are close to their parents and they also develop positively in all other areas. Other studies affirm that many dedicated, mature single parents do a terrific job parenting. Indeed, in many cultures, child-rearing is an activity shared far beyond the nuclear family, with parents drawing help from extended kin, friends, and even professional caregivers.

Not all children in single-parent homes or in full-time, nonparental care, however, are so fortunate. Then, too, not all married families or families where mothers stay home are optimal either. Substandard care in any environment is clearly associated with a wide range of developmental problems, just as good care can clearly come from many sources and be beneficial. *What counts in your child's social-emotional development is the totality of experiences.* Brief periods of distress or difficulty will not permanently harm a child; prolonged periods should be avoided at all costs.

The Links Between Learning, Social Skills, and Emotions

A great challenge for researchers has been to disentangle mental or cognitive development from social and emotional development. Many researchers today agree that this cannot, and need not, be done. There are indisputable links among them.

An infant's ability to think and understand is closely tied to her emotional development. Her social skills also reflect a combination of mental operations, motor control, feelings, and what others around her do. All of these dimensions of development show an orderly progression. They also fluctuate from day to day, hour to hour, due to an infant's state of alertness and comfort, just as they do for adults.

When babies are alert and feeling good, they are more likely to observe, explore, play, show sustained attention, experiment with people and objects, and learn and remember new things. Positive emotions can also motivate babies and give them tools to let others know what is going on inside them.

Negative emotions, on the other hand, alert others to a baby's needs. When responded to quickly and effectively, these negative emotions can be kept to a minimum and serve as constructive forms of communication. Quick relief also frees up more waking hours for more interesting and fun things. The fact that babies cannot learn much that is new or helpful when they are experiencing negative emotions is protective.

Sadly, some babies learn through repeated experience that they cannot count on others to notice them, help them, reduce their distress, or teach them. Even without overt abuse, chronic neglect of a young infant creates a negative spiral, limiting an infant's opportunities to learn and to love.

The links work in the other direction as well. Learning can bring out positive emotions and complex social behavior. Infants show their delight in figuring out what is going on in the world, and in noticing interesting things. When they are exploring, discovering, and learning, they are feeling lots of positive emotions.

Emotions and Their Role

There are many important debates about infant emotions, and they are far from resolved. These debates focus on how to classify discrete emotions, how to measure when each is present, and the origins of emotions. Researchers are using new techniques to measure how much an infant's external behavior corresponds to internal feelings. They do this by monitoring physiological changes in heart rate, cortisol levels, and brain activity. Researchers are looking into whether basic brain mechanisms may account for the behavioral changes common to many infants, such as the peaks in irritability and crying around two months of age or the expression of anger by four to six months of age when an infant cannot get a desired effect.

It is clear that emotions become more differentiated during the first eighteen months of life. However, classifying emotional expressions continues to be a daunting task, although much progress has occurred on this front. Dr. Paul Ekman of Stanford University and Dr. Carroll Izard of the University of Delaware have made pivotal contributions to the classification of emotions.

Dr. Joseph Campos of the University of California at Berkeley and Dr. Michael Lewis of the Robert Wood Johnson School of Medicine have expanded the list of fundamental emotions to include pride, embarrassment, and distress or pain. Other variations include empathy and envy. However, there is broad agreement that these emotions appear in all cultures, although in widely varying levels. There is also broad agreement that the brain actively controls emotion.

FUNDAMENTAL EMOTIONS

A basic list of "fundamental emotions" includes:
- interest
- joy
- surprise
- sadness
- anger
- disgust
- contempt
- fear
- shame
- shyness
- guilt

Many infant researchers treat "showing feelings" and "having feelings" as equivalent. They can tell a lot about what a baby is feeling by changes in facial expression, posture, movements, and vocalizations. They study patterns of internal states and external actions in the context of what is happening in the environment.

There is much to learn about how the brain processes emotions. But receptors in the central nervous system may help distinguish different emotions. As with the basic senses, babies are likely able to have multiple emotional experiences together or in close succession, adding more nuances to their emotional life.

We have feelings all the time. Mostly we pay attention only to the real ups and downs or shifts in our feelings. But emotions serve three very important functions: biological, communicative, and motivational.

BIOLOGICAL

Emotions help connect inner feelings to external movements, especially facial expressions. When we are happy, we smile. When we are angry, we scowl. Some aspects of emotional expression appear to be prewired. These show up before an infant fully understands the meaning of the emotion, as with smiling, for example. Other aspects acquire an individuality, giving each baby some special ways of showing feelings. Many biological needs, including curiosity and the drive to explore, are associated with emotional states.

COMMUNICATIVE

How well we signal what we are feeling, and how well we "read" and respond to each other's cues are central to both emotional and social development. Based on what we see, we adjust our behavior to acknowledge what is occurring and to establish and maintain good relationships. People who are good at picking up cues quickly and responding constructively are likely to fare better in all types of relationships.

MOTIVATIONAL

Emotions, and the brain chemicals they trigger, are powerful motivators, propelling us toward some people and situations and away from others. Along with memories of past experience, they lead us to want to extend or end activities, to try or avoid something new, and to make us better or less able to remember what we have learned.

Researchers believe all three aspects of emotions relate to physiological and biochemical changes. Scientists watch how a child's heart rate and blood pressure vary in different situations; how stress hormones increase or decrease as a result of certain interactions; how brain impulses change during times of positive, pleasurable experiences versus times of distress or anxiety.

The Progress of Emotional Growth

The emotions of infants are thought to be fairly basic, probably highly connected and integrated, and not finely differentiated at first. Two big types of emotions dominate: positive versus negative.

Over the first eighteen months, an infant undergoes rapid and major changes involving all aspects of emotional growth. In just this short period, a normal infant will become a sophisticated and discriminating individual capable of showing far more precise ways to display feelings, and will become much more aware of other people's feelings as well.

Babies start out with very easy-to-read types of emotions. Over time, these become more subtle, complex, and varied in response to what is occurring. For example, the primary negative emotion in the first month is distress or a response to pain. An infant soon shows different behavior for sadness and disgust — more differentiated types of negative emotions — along with continued pain and discomfort responses. By the end of two months, anger appears. By three to four months, sadness emerges. Next comes fear, which becomes more apparent in six- to nine-month-olds, as they understand more about the objects, people, and events around them.

While the word "negative" connotes unpleasant and undesirable feelings, such emotions are natural and necessary. What's important is that parents keep negative experiences brief and infrequent compared to periods of positive emotions.

Positive emotions at first are mostly interest and some joy or simple pleasure, perhaps in response to internal states. The list expands to include more distinct and responsive forms of happiness: a true social smile, showing joy, surprise, and focused interest. Many parents are surprised to learn that interest is considered an emotion. It is, and a highly important one to infants. Interest typically promotes and sustains positive social interactions. Through expressions of interest, infants learn that they are able to contribute in important ways to a social relationship. Expressions of interest invite others to play, to talk, to hold, to smile.

While the infant's expression of interest brings out positive behavior from others, the emotion of joy also appears to enhance the infant's information-processing ability. This means there is an extraordinary and delicate interplay between emotions, social exchanges, development, thinking, and learning.

An alert infant is ready for love and learning, and for developing bonds with others that will elicit good care and appropriate stimulation.

The "stranger anxiety" that many infants show between six to eight months is a good example of how emotions relate to attention and cognition. When children make greater distinctions between people, they become warier and often distressed when strangers approach. We now know that such anxiety builds gradually. However, it sometimes looks to parents as if this new behavior erupted overnight.

A partial solution draws on the positive parent–child bond. A child's anxiety can be minimized if the stranger first talks to, and playfully interacts with, the parent before trying to play with the child. Scientists call this "social referencing." The infant uses the trusted adult as a reference point for deciding how to react. The parents "tell" their infant how to behave by their own gestures and words, including introducing the new person. These reassurances make the person less "strange" and intimidating, and more a part of the familiar world.

Are Emotions Catching?

Smiles seem contagious. Babies in the first few weeks of life smile almost reflexively when an adult smiles. Later, such smiles seem more genuine. But babies show other forms of what is called "emotional contagion" in relationship to other babies in two predictable situations. This seems amazing and may be a primitive form of empathy.

Empathy Crying: When one baby begins loud and extended crying, other babies who hear it soon join in with their own crying.

Gleefulness: When infants laugh and make happy sounds, other infants respond in kind.

Similarly, adult playfulness and open expression of happiness invite imitation from an alert, nondistressed baby.

These early forms of empathy differ from the more mature form that appears toward the middle of the second year. In this later version, a child shows understanding, sensitivity, and caring toward the plight of another. For example, he will show unhappiness if someone else is hurt or upset. But the early emotional contagion is an important precursor to this more mature form.

Just after eighteen months, when a child better understands "self," he develops new awareness of others. He will begin to label others' emotions, feel something like these emotions inside himself, and then show that he cares. Later, empathy may sometimes involve external emotion matching.

Children also can show empathy with words and acts of kindness or support. This corresponds to a greater awareness of self and a more sophisticated understanding of how inner feelings are displayed. It also shows that emotions can, to some degree, be under the child's control.

There is a lot of speculation about the role of trust and empathy in children who later commit crimes of violence or torture. Case histories of these children show that they lack empathy for their victims or remorse for their actions. Clinical experience strongly suggests that these children had very poor (at least disrupted and uneven) relationships with family members beginning as early as infancy. However, more research is needed to confirm a cause-and-effect relationship.

Others speculate that individual differences in temperament contribute to these cases of violence and social aberration. Dr. Bruce Perry of Baylor University has even suggested a brain development model to account for the likely relationship between lack of trust and empathy and various criminal behaviors.

The Emotional Environment

Researchers are also studying how much infants respond to the emotions around them, even before they can label them and interpret the meaning of what they see and hear. For example, babies are much more tuned into the emotional well-being of their parents than we used to think. Because babies are, from birth, especially sensitive to facial expressions and changes in facial cues, they are primed to receive information from these complex expressions.

What a parent feels can, and does, affect an infant. Recent research suggests young children are aware of, and affected by, parental discord, depression, and anxiety. These negative emotions affect babies' physiological and behavioral responsiveness.

Babies also become fussier when parents argue. Research indicates that infants in homes with greater marital discord may cry more or be harder to console. This is probably the case for several reasons. First, their parents' sounds, touches, and facial expressions are not the way they usually are. Second, the infant is less likely to receive the same type of attention during periods of parental discord. Sometimes the infant may be ignored, undermining the trust and security that has been established. Or the infant may be overly attended to without allowing the child to have time alone or adequate rest.

In short, too much negative emotion by people in an infant's environment is harmful. Such disruptions are distressing because young children need continuity and predictability in their everyday exchanges.

It is a good idea to protect children from their parents' ups and downs, at least during the first few years of life. Children of this age are unable to understand mood and behavioral shifts that are disturbing to them. When parents disagree or are under stress, it probably is best not to express this in front of infants.

This may sound old-fashioned, but it is a safeguard worth taking. Parents need not worry that this will overly protect their infants, because even the most responsible parents will show some range of emotions in front of their young children. Remember, as we have stressed many times, it is the totality and the patterning of an infant's experience, not the occasional deviation, that will shape your infant's development and security.

Shaping Healthy Emotional Growth

There are two essential ingredients to building a healthy emotional foundation for your child: encouraging joy and relieving distress.

Throughout the first eighteen months, your baby should have ample opportunity to feel joyful. Your play, games, songs, readings, and conversations are the basis for her growing expression of positive emotions, both of different types and at different levels.

She also needs many experiences in which her negative emotions are relieved by your help. Comforting your baby quickly not only provides needed relief, it also strengthens the attachment between you. This is a crucial issue in socio-emotional development and essential to later growth and functioning.

It is too early during the first eighteen months to teach the need to control or delay the expression of some types of emotions. There will be plenty of learning opportunities for this later.

Extensive research confirms that highly responsive parents who can read their own babies' cues will have children who are more social, more appropriate in their interactions, and more empathetic. These foundations for a socially and emotionally competent child and adult are being laid in the early years through parents' efforts to show their infants that feelings are important to well-being and to social interaction.

The better you are at reading your child's cues, the sooner you can intervene to lessen negative emotions and elicit positive ones. As with much of parenting, you will learn what works by trial and error. The good news is that, in this first year and a half of his life, you can trust your baby to tell you what he is feeling by his facial gestures, sounds, and body and hand movements.

At the same time, even the youngest infant needs an emotionally responsive person to be with and learn from. When exposed to a quiet and unresponsive face, babies react negatively. Why? What does this signal? This reaction indicates that infants somehow "know" that they need to be with someone who gives clear cues, especially smiles and coos, on a regular basis.

Since almost all learning occurs within a social context in early life, this inter-connectedness in thinking, feeling, and social development is reinforced as a firm part of your baby's foundation for life.

It is important to recognize that different cultures have different practices and beliefs about the extent to which certain emotions are preferred or acceptable in various situations. These cultural norms, like basic rules of emotional regulation, can wait for elaboration and parental guidance until later. However, during the first eighteen months, parents' own behavior will help set the stage for an infant's understanding of how others behave. Parents will use both actions and words to convey what they feel.

Social Development and Its Role

Social development goes along closely with emotional maturation. In part, it involves how we manifest the emotions we feel in the presence of others and how we act on the emotional cues we read from others. In the larger context, social skills involve the totality of how we relate to others in all facets of our life.

Relating to others begins with early bonding with parents, not just in the first few minutes or hours, but over the entire first year. The importance of this bond has been established beyond a doubt by extensive research. Important findings by Drs. Alan Sroufe and Byron Egeland at the Institute of Child Development at the University of Minnesota confirm that when the attachment between mothers and babies can be described as secure and supportive, the babies fare better in almost all areas of development.

Parent–infant interactions are the raw material of bonding. These shape and strengthen or weaken the primary attachment relationships. From these interactions, infants learn about their inner feelings and about how their feelings relate to things that happen in the outside world.

Research confirms that infants discern differences in how their individual parents interact with them. We think this is healthy. It promotes skill in playing and interacting with others. Babies notice lots of things, like the differences between parents' voices (pitch, volume, direction, timing), their faces and facial expressions, and the ways they like to interact — from fun routines to the "dance" — the system of social interchange involving cues, sounds, expression, and movement.

There is evidence that babies who do not establish any close bonds may have long-term difficulties in social and emotional development. These children have not learned that adults are trustworthy and responsive, because they haven't experienced such trust and responsiveness. Fortunately, such extreme cases are rare — often a product of poor institutional care that children receive in times of disease, famine, war, or other dire events.

A central part of your baby's early social activity will be the "dance" we described above. This is the ongoing pattern of interaction made up of sounds, expressions, and movements. The analogy of a dance is useful, because the infant has a chance to learn how to be a good partner. At first, infants mostly follow. Soon they help contribute to the dance itself, taking it in new directions parents could never anticipate.

To lead in this dance, and then to encourage your baby to take a more active role, you need to be good at reading your child's emotions and cues. This ability equips you to be supportive and to foster healthy social and emotional growth. Most parents are actually very good at reading their own child's emotions accurately, even if they can't describe in great detail the components of each one.

There is wide variation in the early relationships infants build, based in large part on how they are cared for. We now have strong scientific evidence that the actual quality of the early parent–infant attachment affects what happens later between children and their parents. These bonds also influence many other aspects of young infants' development, from language and cognition to emotional expressiveness and behavioral adjustment.

Compared to children in anxious or avoidant relationships, or neglectful or abusive situations, children with secure, responsive, stable, early relationships are more likely to show better social skills, fewer behavioral problems, more positive peer relationships, and better school adjustment.

The Progress of Social Development

As with emotional skills, social abilities develop right from birth. Aspects of social development are captured in the imitations and responses that occur — back and forth, often dynamic — between an infant and others. These form the basis for the ability later to build friendships, to share, to be kind and fair in dealings with others, to be willing to learn through observing and listening to others, to cooperate and compete in ways that are mutually satisfying. Ultimately, good social behavior and good socialization involve behaving within prescribed limits, promoting the well-being of others, and contributing some novel or creative behavior.

From the early hours of life, babies associate pleasure and discomfort with what is happening outside. Their natural, strong preference for the human face as something to gaze upon contributes to early social success. Your baby will look directly at your face. As such looks become more sustained, so will the feelings of mutual love and attachment.

Your baby can mold his body in response to yours. He can even imitate some of your facial and hand gestures. He shows a behavioral readiness to trust you, to follow and copy you, to learn from you. Much of what is learned in your baby's first year deals with who is special, how they treat him, what happens when he lets his needs be known.

There is a fairly well-mapped course of social awareness, social responsiveness, social cautiousness and selectivity, as well as social imitation over the first eighteen months of life. Smiling and laughing within the first two to four months start the sequence.

This is followed by obvious signs of pleasure and a preference for being cared for by certain people. Midway through the first year there is a period of delightful openness and friendliness. This evolves into more selective social imitation, especially beyond the infant's familiar, positive everyday social experiences.

Infants of this age can differentiate among many people. They are beginning to come to grips with issues like constancy and continuity. From a child's viewpoint, some people often appear to be bombarding them in ways that seem unexpected and undesirable. At the very least, many stranger "assaults" (overly active or abrupt greetings and contact with babies) are intrusive, and do interrupt other things. From this perspective, it is amazing that infants are as playful and friendly with strangers as much as they are.

In the second year, you can begin to teach winning social behaviors — saying "please" and "thank you," hugging and kissing, and sharing. As these behaviors win smiles and recognition from others, your baby will take another step in the "dance," understanding a new level of how his actions cause others to approve and respond well to him. His growing repertoire of these behaviors will be the foundation for his maturing social self.

Shaping Healthy Social Growth

You shape your baby's socialization right from birth by the aggregate pattern of your daily interactions with her. As you learn her cues and understand how sophisticated even her earliest responses are, you can encourage the most positive social growth.

It is important not to underestimate your child's abilities in this regard. For example, infants expect words and actions to go together, and they can detect when these are not well-matched or synchronized. This shows a fine-tuning of the infant's nervous system to integrate information across the senses and to interpret this information in a social context.

Children are also surprisingly sophisticated partners with their parents and siblings. They love to observe and imitate behaviors that get positive responses. This opens the door to teaching good manners and polite behavior, which are extremely valuable in expanding a child's socialization.

Be aware that your baby needs, and should have, a social life beyond the immediate family. She should be exposed to a larger social network of people on a regular basis — children as well as adults. It is through expanding interactions that her early, positive behaviors will be reinforced and strengthened.

There is no basis for thinking there is one best way to socialize a young child, other than to avoid extremes. An infant spending all her time with only her parents would be unnatural. On the other hand, having little predictability in whom one spends time with — an absence of positive, familiar social partners — would be extremely problematic.

Babies need the same sense of order and comprehension in their social lives that they need for their sensory and perceptual worlds. They also need the very same cause-and-effect, response-contingent experiences discussed earlier, which teach an infant to be a player, to be responsible as well as responsive. Babies who have more social response-contingent experiences are healthier and happier.

To nurture social development, do what you enjoy most — play, talk, be affectionate, prompt, and pay attention to your baby in ways that feel good to you. Most of all, make parenting a reflection of all you are, through your everyday activities and your own style. This is a wonderful way for you to enjoy parenting to the fullest and for your baby to get a great start in life. ✿

CHAPTER 6

The Magic and Power of Words

Language and
Communication

Lack of speech is a key feature that sets infants apart from the rest of humankind. The word "infant" comes from Latin and means "incapable of speech." Yet from the first months of life on, infants are highly communicative beings. They are intimately tuned into speech, gestures, and taking turns, all of which are important in learning and using language.

The transformation of language ability in the first eighteen months is truly remarkable. By the end of this period, your infant will understand perhaps hundreds of words and expressions. She will also have developed an especially effective form of communication with you as a parent — a multifaceted system of sounds, syllables, words, phrases, gestures, signs, tones of voice, and invented words or silly sounds that will convey great meaning. She is also likely to enjoy sounds and words unto themselves, both for their sheer sensory delight, as well as for their use as tools of social exchange, emotional expressiveness, and learning. By eighteen months, many of your child's utterances are likely to be understood not only by you, but by other adults as well. A lifetime of conversation will have begun.

Elements of Language

Language is a remarkably complex system, one we continue to learn throughout our lives. It is also essential to many aspects of learning and socialization. As a result, the study of the emergence of language during the early years of life has yielded a fascinating body of new knowledge. Today's research has given us fascinating insights. To start, researchers look at three broad and somewhat different aspects of language:

- 🌸 **Receptive language:** This is what infants understand from the language of others.

- 🌸 **Expressive language:** This is how they communicate to others through increasingly sophisticated speech and expanded vocabulary.

- 🌸 **Pragmatic language:** This concerns all the subtle facets of language — facial expressions, body movements, tone, volume, inflection, ideas about when to speak and for how long. These additions are the amplifiers and fine-tuners of communication. They help infants and all of us to better express what we mean, and to understand what others are telling us.

We have learned that infants vary greatly in their linguistic styles and how they learn to receive, use, and even invent language.

HISTORY OF LANGUAGE STUDY

For many years, the study of language focused on its origin — whether language was biologically predetermined or learned. Now, these views have been replaced by an interactionist approach, articulated well by Dr. Elizabeth Bates of the University of California at San Diego. She reminds us that language is a process that starts very early in infancy, perhaps even prior to birth, and depends on vital inputs from sensory perception, cognition, motor development, and social exchanges. Language is much more than the mere acquisition of words and rules. And multiple types of learning and experience complement the brain's natural capacity to use language as an integral part of our behavioral tool kit.

Prespeech Communication

Infants are born with the ability to discern all the sounds that make up human language around the globe — from trilled r's and guttural consonants to clicks and diphthongs. Moreover, they are more sensitive to the nuances of these sounds in the first ten months of life than they will ever be again. This is why babies can learn to speak the language or languages of their environment "like a native."

Researchers have documented that infants concentrate selectively on the sounds they hear. In a classic case of "use it or lose it," they lose their sensitivity to sounds they don't hear. Moreover, this is apparent by nine or ten months of age, before most babies say their first word.

Even in the first few weeks after birth, infants are good at speech perception in a number of ways. They can distinguish everyday speech from nonspeech sounds. They can differentiate between the speech of men and women. They even know the voices of their own mothers from other women. Specific mechanisms or structures in the brain likely make these distinctions possible. How and when these brain bases develop most likely depend on both experience and maturation, as do most developmental processes.

We also know that early language involves more than just hearing a language spoken. It is influenced by the context in which it is heard, and even by what we see. Drs. Patricia Kuhl and Andrew Meltzoff of the University of Washington demonstrated that infants as young as three to five months can lip-read. Even at this tender age, they can tell the difference between mouth/lip patterns associated with sounds like "ooo" and "eee." If they hear a sound that does not match the expected lip movement, they may actually "hear" it differently. This is another example of how the senses work together to help us understand the world.

Infants become adept at expressive communication long before they speak. For instance, they use movements and sounds to let you know what they want or don't want. Fussiness is one early staple of infant communication. So are happy gurgles and giggles. When your baby wants food, rest, to move away from someone or something, a clean diaper, or relief from general discomfort, these needs will be communicated. Pleasure, surprise, and appreciation for your good care will also show — increasingly in ways that are under voluntary control.

Signs and Gestures

Infants, whether hearing impaired or not, typically have a sign language of their own. They use body language, facial expressions, and reaching and touching to convey what they want to say. Increasingly, their gestures and signs occur with accompanying sounds. Soon the sounds will grow more differentiated, becoming wordlike, and then turn into words or phrases.

Yet not all sounds and gestures are meant to communicate something specific. They can be part and parcel of how your baby will explore and enjoy sensations — the fun of making sounds and hearing one's own sounds. Then, too, sometimes they just happen — an outburst combining reflex action and voluntary movement.

Pointing to things occurs very early in life, although it doesn't become intentional until around eight or nine months of age for most babies. Initially, such pointing is like many other forms of behavior that begin as more primitive dispositions to move certain ways or do certain things. Over the months, these behaviors evolve to become intentional, controlled, and useful.

SIGN LANGUAGE FOR BABIES

A major scientific advance has been to document, understand, and enhance the natural use of signs and gestures by infants with significant hearing impairments. If they are encouraged by parents who communicate with them using a formal sign language, these infants begin to use gestures earlier and more regularly than children with normal hearing. With a continuing responsive communication environment, later aspects of their language and mental development are remarkably normal and accomplished.

Gestures are central to language. Since imitation is a big part of learning, young children are quick to pick up the moves for "wave bye-bye," "come here," "pat-a-cake," "clap hands," and "peekaboo." As with words, your baby's repertoire of gestures will grow as he learns. He also will try to imitate your adult mouth movements, particularly when you make certain sounds that come from different movements of your mouth and face.

Vocalization skills change rapidly during the first year. From the communicative power of fussing and cries, infants move to a wider range of sounds as their emotions become more differentiated. By two to three months of age, cooing emerges. Soon thereafter, full laughs appear. These sounds reflect an infant's growing capacity to feel and express enjoyment. They also appear to be precursors to infants' use of more varied speech sounds and speech "play." By five or six months, infants attempt, and sometimes succeed in, making sounds of the consonants in their language.

First Words

Within a few months, babies begin to make consonant sounds more clearly and repetitively. Scoring high on the proud-parent scale are repetitions of sounds such as "da" and "ma." Parents are rightly pleased at these, sometimes assuming they mean more than they do. But it won't be long before infants' growing skills allow them to attach meaning to sounds they make such as "Da-da" and "Ma-ma." This new achievement can occur anywhere from eight to fourteen months.

But it is important to remember that there is a wide range of normal with respect to milestone attainment. Moreover, earlier or later attainment of language milestones is not necessarily predicted by when a child says her first words. New findings indicate a complex pattern of associations among the many different components of language, such as syntax, vocabulary, grammar, and mean length of utterance.

As the early variations show, language development can happen in different ways over a long period of time. Some infants seem to speak in sentence-like phrases before words, although the individual words may be indistinguishable. This often has a singsong quality and many characteristics of adult speech, but without the clarity. Linguists sometimes call such children "intonation babies" because they are tuned in to the ups and downs of tone. These curves of intonation by themselves convey meanings, such as whether a response is expected or not.

For other infants, their love of individual words dominates. They seem to learn language in a more orderly, word-by-word manner. Linguists call these children "word babies" because of their preference to use individual words for their meaning. Some of these children seem to be perfectionists in their pronunciation, while others are less so.

Both of these approaches are perfectly normal, and each offers some advantages. There are many good routes to mastering language. Few other aspects of your child's development will be as engaging, delightful, and even frustrating (when you just cannot figure out what your eager or determined child means).

Almost all children appear to make a jump from a few, well-used words in their vocabulary — often ones noticed, shaped, encouraged, and celebrated by their parents — to a word explosion, usually about midway through the second year. It's amazing that infants can learn so many words so well and so fast!

Infants have an explosion in vocabulary. Research findings by Dr. Janellen Huttenlocher of the University of Chicago show that this growth is clearly linked to the extent that their parents converse with them.

EFFECTS OF MOTHERS' SPEECH ON INFANT VOCABULARY

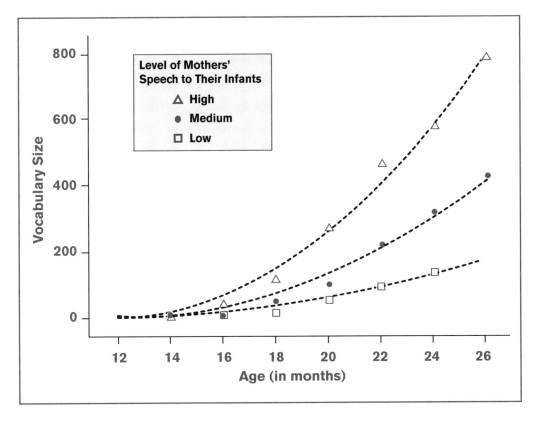

Janellen Huttenlocher, Wendy Haight, Anthony Bruk, Michael Seltzer, and Thomas Lyons (University of Chicago), "Early Vocabulary Growth: Relation to Language Input and Gender," Developmental Psychology, *1991, Vol. 27, No. 2.*

Invented Language

Children's own invented words or idiosyncratic language have been studied less than other aspects of language. Yet these delightful creations charm families for years. Many parents and grandparents, brothers and sisters talk about how a baby made up a word that they all now use. Often babies give new names to their relatives. In many families, parents brag that their child speaks an extra language — "Melissa-ese" or "Joshua-ese." They are right. Get out your baby record book and write down your favorites.

Some invented words recalled to us by proud parents include: "Pop pop" for grandfather, "Mom mom" for grandmother, "buckabuck" for milk, "toot-neen" for train.

Words that Work

That language depends on, and benefits from, the development of other systems is important to the everyday care of infants. Audible language with no social and personal meaning is neither useful nor relevant to an infant. Conversations that an infant hears or sees but does not participate in (such as on radio or TV) are not sufficient as sources of language learning.

To gain and sustain your baby's attention, *speech must happen in frequent, conversational, person-to-person exchanges.* Ideally, these exchanges should be pleasurable. They should also have the right mix of predictability and novelty. Talk to your child in a positive context, using both familiar and novel words and sounds. This will hold your baby's attention and encourage the desire to communicate more often and more clearly.

Taking turns is a cardinal feature of language. It is essential to learning language as well as to skilled social interaction. When your baby coos or gurgles, be sure to listen. Then respond. Even playing peekaboo games is now considered by language scientists to be a way parents teach some fundamentals of communication.

Some infants are obviously enchanted with speech early on. They delight in spoken language as well as the diverse uses of language, such as in songs, rhymes, and games. Others may appear to have less initial interest in language, especially in becoming adept speakers themselves. This may be due to a greater temporary focus on other aspects of their world and development.

Children sometimes learn words, but then stop using them or even seem to forget them. This often coincides with mastery of a new skill in another area which captures the child's attention. For example, a child who has just learned a new motor skill may babble or talk less while he practices that new skill.

Conversely, new words may cause an active walker to slow down or stay seated while he practices new words or phrases. We don't know the reason for this developmental fickleness. But it is common, generally transitory, and often charming. As an attentive parent, you will have continuing cause to marvel as your child masters one new skill after another. Please do not worry about temporary pauses or "backward steps" in development.

Encouraging Words

Mental or cognitive development can parallel and probably influence language development. As the prominent Russian developmentalist, Dr. L. S. Vygotsky, is reputed to have said, "Language and thought may be separated, but, in reality, they rarely are."

Generally, infants who are exceptionally precocious in language are bright children. But there are many highly intelligent children who were not particularly precocious in their early language development. Early first words, by themselves, are not highly predictive of above-average intelligence. Should you actively promote language acquisition and help to shape its development? The answer is yes and no.

Yes, because language provides a wonderful way of connecting with people. Yes, because language is both efficient and enjoyable. Yes, because, when your child shows she is ready, she will enjoy being taught in appropriate ways. Remember that the most effective learning results when children are motivated to learn. If talking, songs, rhymes, and word games are relaxed and enjoyable, your child will want to learn more because she's having fun and she's playing with you.

No, because there is no evidence that structured teaching is the best way to have children learn language. No, because focusing too much on one aspect of development may have negative consequences for other areas of development. No, because parents function best when they are natural teachers and share what they know, rather than when they follow prescribed lessons.

A Word of Caution

As in all aspects of development, there are notable differences in children's rates and levels of development. The one area that produces the greatest alarm for parents is speech and language. Remember the complexity of what is involved. Your child is not only hearing, learning, and memorizing sounds and meanings. His entire vocal structure, and the central control of the brain over this structure, need to develop to give him good control over producing sounds that match what he intends.

Rarely is there a need for special interventions or speech therapy, or even systematic teaching of aspects of language, in the first few years of life. But parents who are genuinely concerned about possible delays should seek professional advice.

Be aware, however, that there is some evidence that excessive attention to very mild speech delays or problems may create other difficulties. To date, we don't have adequate information about whether there is any benefit to very early therapy for children who are developing typically. Moreover, the possibility that such therapy could interfere with or inhibit learning has not been ruled out.

Given the limited evidence of the value of intervention for very mild or "suspected" language problems, we think parents should rely on the advice and observations of others they know and trust, including other parents, grandparents, pediatricians, and trained childcare providers. Above all, we advise parents to keep on doing all the wonderful things they have been doing with their children. They should not focus excessively on minor errors and problems in early language.

Keys to Teaching Language

Most parents naturally show remarkably sophisticated knowledge of the principles of effective teaching. The keys are to:

- ❀ Speak close to and directly facing your child, with frequent eye contact (although this may vary from one culture to another).
- ❀ Use other cues and gestures to increase meaning and enjoyment.
- ❀ Use "parentese," especially in the early months. This is speech with a singsong or up–down quality and a slightly higher pitch. Speak a bit slower. These attributes will help make language especially engaging to your baby.
- ❀ Simplify your speech. Shorten your sentences. Use lots of repetition. Refer to concrete objects and specific events — things your infant can understand. Make sounds that are easy to understand.
- ❀ Expand on what your child says. When your child says something simple, such as "Throw ball," you can respond with "Throw (your child's name) the ball." "See car" can be expanded to "See the car go by." "Go bye-bye" can be transformed into "Mom (or Dad) and (child's name) are going bye-bye." You may be surprised how naturally you do this.

If you are inexperienced around babies, you may feel self-conscious about using "parentese" and not inclined to try it. Go ahead anyway. It can be fun, and it does grab and hold your baby's attention longer than plain adult speech.

Dr. Phillip Dale of the University of Washington has been studying children's language for many years. He has an astute observation for parents:

Talking in baby talk to a child for the first five years of life would surely hinder his (her) learning, but so would speaking in the language of an encyclopedia or a diplomatic treaty.

Words for a Lifetime

The beginning of true conversation just as infancy draws to a close should be very rewarding for you. Through language you will get an even clearer understanding of your child's uniqueness and charm. Be willing to follow your child's curiosity and learn new words about new interests. How many parents have become experts in trucks, flowers, dinosaurs, birds, or seashells because of their child! But don't forget to introduce your child to your favorite things and words as well. Pretty soon, you will be discussing philosophy and values and all sorts of fascinating things. ❀

CHAPTER 7

Learning and Intelligence

What Is Intelligence?
Can We Change It?

O F ALL THE ASPECTS OF HUMAN POTENTIAL, NONE IS MORE HOTLY DEBATED THAN INTELLIGENCE. FOR MANY PARENTS, THEIR CHILD'S INTELLIGENCE IS OF PARAMOUNT CONCERN: "IS MY CHILD 'SMART' ENOUGH TO DO WELL IN SCHOOL? TO GET INTO A GOOD COLLEGE OR A UNIVERSITY? IF NOT, CAN I HELP MY CHILD TO BE 'SMARTER' OR DO BETTER?"

"School Smarts"

You undoubtedly care about the total range of your child's interests and abilities — creativity, social skills, problem-solving ability and so forth. But, like most parents, you are probably especially concerned about the skills that will enable your child to do well in the classroom — from learning to read and then memorizing Shakespeare to learning arithmetic and then mastering geometry. Here is some of what we know:

- In the care and education they provide and arrange for their children, parents are the keys to intellectual development for almost all children. The research literature is filled with studies that underscore the links between parental involvement and young children's assessed "intelligence." This finding is one of the most robust in all of the scientific developmental literature.

- By two years of age, many of the intellectual foundations will have been laid to support a lifetime of learning.

- No single, *short-term* accelerated learning program in the first three years that concentrates on a single aspect of development has been shown to have lasting benefits.

- Instead, a child's intelligence is shaped and influenced by his or her cumulative experiences over time.

- There is no reasonable doubt that nurturing has a profound effect on intelligence. The nature-versus-nurture debate is wrongly framed and has been strongly criticized for over two decades. Biology matters. So does experience. Intelligence does not develop in a vacuum.

Your child's intelligence is being shaped, challenged, and expressed every day by experiences with people, objects, and events — especially when he is an active participant. These experiences are the raw "ingredients" of intelligence.

Here's more good news. These same ingredients nurture many different facets of a child's intelligence, such as the creative, the musical, the interpersonal, and the logical, as well as the Shakespeare-memorizing and geometry-learning kinds.

How do we know this? Through an enormous amount of research over the past thirty years. The vast majority of this research deals with what scientists call at-risk children — those who are severely deprived in one or more ways. Some are in woefully understaffed orphanages. Others come from homes that, for a variety of reasons, are extremely neglectful and unsupportive. Still other children have biological risk factors, such as prematurity and low birthweight.

The research you care about concerns the children who were helped — those whose scores on intelligence tests were raised. We have conducted a number of such programs involving thousands of children and families. These studies and many others have identified important ways to give lifelong developmental benefits to children. Studies such as these provide valuable material for much of the information and advice in this book:

- **The Abecedarian Project, a multidisciplinary program to enhance the intellectual and social development in at-risk children. The Project, now in its twenty-fifth year, provided extensive early educational intervention to infants and their families. The Abecedarian Project continues to track the effectiveness of those interventions, which proved both substantial and long-lasting.**

- **Project CARE, a program that compared two different development-enhancement strategies. The program was given to children from both at-risk and supportive environments.**

- **The Washington Family Behavior Study, a long-term study of 400 families that provided an in-depth look at changes in the American family and how values influence parenting strategies and children's outcomes through the adolescent years.**

- The Infant Health and Development Program, an eight-city program designed to prevent developmental and learning disabilities in premature and low birthweight infants.

- The Romanian Project, which provided intensive learning and social enrichment to infants and toddlers in orphanages, demonstrating the extent to which young children can "recover," and the areas in which they cannot, from severely deprived early experiences.

- The National Transition-to-School Demonstration Project, the largest study ever conducted — involving more than 8,000 children nationwide from kindergarten through third grade — documenting how children's school success depends on the multiple investment of families, schools, and communities and identifying what types of parent involvement really make a lasting difference.

These show that substantial, early educational intervention can make a positive difference in children's intelligence. The at-risk infants in these studies received direct and intensive early education. These children showed significant gains in intelligence-test scores.

But far more important, children from the *least* stimulating home environments benefited the *most*. They showed *lasting gains* associated with real-world competencies. For example, they were more adept in interactions with their mothers when they were young, and they became more skilled in learning in new situations. Later, they did better in school, where they had greater reading and mathematics skills, and fewer children had to repeat a grade.

So what does this mean for your child? We suggest there are two answers that really matter:

- First, we don't know if children who are already thriving can have their IQ's boosted. No one has adequately studied this. The reason is simple: When children are already thriving, there seems no need to change things. (Also, as we said earlier, results from studies of special populations, such as at-risk children, don't always translate well to normal children from supportive environments.)

- Second, the studies with at-risk children have reinforced the *importance of the aggregate of daily experience* in shaping a child's intelligence. The gains in intelligence-test scores for the children in these studies were achieved only by transforming *a significant part* of these children's lives for *many years.*

An interesting sidelight from Project CARE: The program was also given to middle- and upper-middle-class infants. They, like the at-risk children, thrived in the educational enrichment program. But carefully matched middle- and upper-middle-income comparison children *not* in the program also thrived, whether they were cared for by their mothers or enrolled in other high-quality programs. Children in both groups had IQ's well above average. These not-at-risk children showed *no extra boost* in their intelligence-test scores. Why? Because they were already getting lots of well-timed and individualized stimulation at home and elsewhere. But the programs were a good complement to their home environments, and these children certainly learned and enjoyed themselves.

Much other research also shows that early experiences are critical to the development of normal intelligence and competency in social, emotional, and everyday situations. Can intelligence be modified in the early years of life? We believe this crucial question *has been settled scientifically.* The answer is a resounding *yes.*

No one can deny, however, that there are profound individual differences in children's intellectual profiles. They have different strengths and weaknesses, even in the same family, even when they receive consistently high-quality nurturing and stimulation. There is still much to study and resolve in discerning all the factors that contribute to such variation in human competence.

Many important issues remain to be addressed. We predict that this area will be a "hot" scientific field for the foreseeable future. Expect to read a lot more about how genes and experience work together to shape the brain and intelligence.

What Is Intelligence?

For many years, most researchers accepted that intelligence is what an intelligence test measures. However, these tests tap only a portion of the broad range of human capabilities. This is not surprising, given the history of the intelligence-testing movement. Such tests came into use in the early part of the twentieth century to identify or predict which children would not benefit from traditional schooling. Therefore, they tended to measure those aspects of human performance associated with doing well in traditional school systems. Thus, for some purposes, standardized tests of intelligence can serve a useful purpose.

But there are also serious weaknesses in such tests. These tests have been seriously misused for educational, political, and social purposes in ways that have been harmful and inadequate for many children. Keep in mind a basic point about standardized tests of intelligence: They are *designed to discriminate* among individuals. Some people will score higher and some lower. Items for such tests are selected precisely because they discriminate, not necessarily because they measure an important or theoretically justified aspect of intellectual functioning.

Items which discriminate among individuals sufficiently well are kept in the overall test. In the process of *standardizing* the test, items are summed and the overall scores are made to fit a norm to optimize the test's discriminability. The test then becomes a test of "intelligence" because the test makers call it that, *and* because it correlates well with other tests constructed using similar procedures.

The range of items sampled, the format of the testing situation, the time limits, etc., constrain the types of information that can be collected. Great pains are taken to keep test questions secret. If they become known, test takers can learn the correct answers, and the items lose their ability to discriminate.

This is why there is such furor in academic circles about "teaching to the test" — structuring school curricula around what teachers think is likely to be on standardized tests. If a good theory of intelligence guided test construction, and if the cost-driven constraints on intelligence testing were loosened, the criticism of "teaching to the test" would likely subside.

Excellent critiques of standardized intelligence tests have been written, such as Dr. Stephen Jay Gould's award-winning book, *The Mismeasure of Man,* which was recently updated, and Dr. Stephen Ceci's book, *Intelligence:*

More or Less. Dr. Robert Sternberg of Yale University is the editor of *The Encyclopedia of Intelligence,* an extraordinary reference on the topic.

The most ardent critics of intelligence testing point out the many limitations in the design and refinement of intelligence tests. They also identify inadequacies in studies that claim to show a strong relationship between intelligence, or some of its components, and overall achievement and success in life.

These critics charge that intelligence tests often become self-fulfilling prophecies in places where such tests are used to decide who will or will not be placed in more advanced or resourceful learning environments. Critics also point to the links between a child's intelligence and his or her family's socioeconomic status as evidence that factors other than pure intelligence are contributing to the long-term success of more "intelligent" children.

Measuring Intelligence in Infancy

When it comes to measuring intelligence in infancy, there has been serious investment over the past fifty years in how to detect differences in intelligence that will be sustained into toddlerhood and through adulthood. Historically, these measures have had limited ability to predict long-term outcomes accurately.

One notable exception is the ability to detect infants with serious developmental delays or deficiencies. For these infants, tests usually are not needed to reveal that there is a problem. Rather, the tests are useful in confirming the extent and nature of a child's delays or differences (assuming the infant can be tested on the standardized tool). Under current educational law, such tests are used to decide who is eligible for publicly paid developmental therapies and services that go by the label of early intervention.

Dr. Michael Lewis of the Robert Wood Johnson School of Medicine edited a landmark book on the origins of infant intelligence. In his introduction, Lewis identified some of the key issues that, to this day, remain central to the field of infant intelligence. These include:

- Many behaviors "tested" on infant tests do not have a direct counterpart at later ages.

- Some important dimensions of intelligence in older children or adults may not be expressed during infancy.

- Individual rates of development, or the age when a child first shows a skill, may not always correspond to how capable a child will be later in that same skill.

- Factors relating to the testing situation may limit the accuracy of measurement. For example, not all examiners are equally skilled in bringing out a child's best performance, an explicit goal in the test session.

- Some so-called limits of infant intelligence tests may reflect that intelligence is not a fixed entity that be can measured with great precision at one age and expected to remain essentially unchanged thereafter.

The theme in intelligence research for more than three decades has been one of both *continuity and change*. Some aspects of a child's skills are visible early on and continue, while others fluctuate or emerge later.

We have proposed that a new type of infant intelligence test is needed — one that simultaneously measures a child's competencies in many different areas and also considers the child's actual learning opportunities and the quality of the child's total environment. Such a new type of infant assessment would be far more useful in understanding the differences in children's rates of development and each child's individuality.

The Many Sides of Intelligence

In our opinion, the most advanced theories of intelligence today endorse a multifaceted view of what intelligence is. Dr. Howard Gardner of Harvard University and Dr. Robert Sternberg of Yale University have been true pioneers and ardent researchers in this field. They and others see intelligence as comprised of many dimensions. They further postulate that most people are more skilled in some areas than in others. Rarely is a child or adult uniformly capable across a very broad array of skills and talents.

The chart below shows how seven types of intelligence identified by Dr. Gardner are manifested. Dr. Gardner has proposed up to three other types of intelligence — naturalist, spiritual, and existential.

INTELLIGENCE TYPE	HOW YOUNG CHILDREN MANIFEST THIS INTELLIGENCE
Interpersonal	Noticing and distinguishing other people's moods, style, motivations, and intentions, and using this knowledge to guide actions.
Linguistic	Being sensitive to the sound and meaning of words; mastering syntax; appreciating the many ways language can be used.
Logical-mathematical	Knowing about objects and symbols and the types of actions that can be performed on them; knowing how to abstract, identify problems, seek explanations, and discover logical solutions.
Bodily-kinesthetic	Using one's body in skilled ways to achieve goals or express feelings; being able to manipulate objects skillfully.
Spatial	Skillfully perceiving the visual world; performing transformations in perceptions; and creatively expressing visual experiences.
Musical	Recognizing individual tones and phrases of music; understanding how to combine tones, phrases, and rhythms; being aware of emotional components of music and sounds.
Intrapersonal	Recognizing one's own feelings and emotional life; using one's own emotions to guide and understand one's behavior and one's self.

Adapted from the work of Howard Gardner, first described in Frames of Mind, *New York, BasicBooks, 1993.*

This type of broader construct of intelligence is now widely accepted. In addition, most developmental scientists have abandoned the simplistic view that intelligence could be described by an algebraic equation using genetic factors (or inheritance) and environmental influences.

Another matter of debate concerns the raw material of intelligence versus how it is used. Scientists and practitioners once strove to separate "potential" or "ability" from "performance" and "learning." We doubt that this can ever be practically achieved. No children develop in isolation and without learning. Nor do all young infants have the same learning opportunities.

Even more fundamentally, we have learned that the use of intelligence or skills can vary greatly in different situations. As Dr. Edward Zigler of Yale University showed many years ago, a child may not show his skills to the same degree in all settings for a variety or reasons, including a lack of motivation to do well.

Types of Learning in Infancy

It is also important for parents to appreciate the many types of learning that each child masters. Most of these complement and reinforce one another. As you will see, these types of learning are not limited to infancy. They continue throughout our lives.

How infants and young children learn also depends on many features of the learning situation itself. Location, timing, prior experience, and post-learning activities can all influence how much is learned and how much is retained. There is a wealth of evidence that intelligence or infant competency is responsive to immediate and contextual cues, and that success or failure in one setting or on one day is not always a good indicator of what will happen in a different setting on a different day.

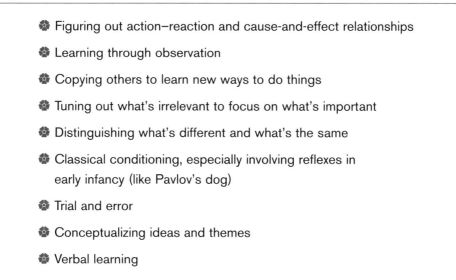

TYPES OF LEARNING IN INFANTS

- Figuring out action–reaction and cause-and-effect relationships
- Learning through observation
- Copying others to learn new ways to do things
- Tuning out what's irrelevant to focus on what's important
- Distinguishing what's different and what's the same
- Classical conditioning, especially involving reflexes in early infancy (like Pavlov's dog)
- Trial and error
- Conceptualizing ideas and themes
- Verbal learning

The Partnership of Intelligence and the Brain

A great deal of research has focused on finding the precise qualities that account for individual differences in overall intelligence that show up in a broad test of performance. Factors such as the amount, rate, and quality of attention, information processing, responsiveness to novelty, and memory capacity have been studied. The results are interesting, but they don't give a straightforward picture of what accounts for individual differences.

Four decades of scientific findings from basic developmental neuroscience, clinical studies of people with various brain abnormalities, and studies of extreme rearing conditions (such as severe, early, and prolonged deprivation in orphanages) indicate that two major principles are operating:

Responsiveness to environmental inputs. What happens early in life helps direct and refine subsequent development. We see this in everything from the most basic to the most complex aspects of central nervous system functioning and brain growth and development. Virtually every interesting aspect of neural differentiation and specialization is affected by early and cumulative life experiences relevant to different areas of the brain and how they function.

Plasticity of the brain. Because the brain is remarkably malleable and responsive, there are many ways it can develop. Not all brains operate in the same way, even when the external sensory, perceptual, or behavioral functioning looks identical. The probability of any two brains being identical — even those of identical twins — is near zero.

We want to underscore the significance of these two sweeping conclusions. Early experience is extremely important to ensure that the brain develops functionally and to enable different human brains to find different ways to achieve approximately the same outcomes. These statements may appear to contradict each other. On the contrary, these are worthwhile principles for parents to appreciate as they observe, nurture, and seek to enhance their child's course of early development. What happens in one area of experience and brain development almost always impinges upon and influences other areas.

How Do We Measure Intelligence?

Every item on every intelligence test has always required test takers to do at least one of two things:

- Display specific information that they previously learned, or
- Apply previously learned rules or principles to a new situation.

As a result, intelligence tests can never be content-free. Therefore, creating a "culture-free" or "experience-free" test is unlikely ever to be accomplished. In our opinion, given the integral role of experience in intellectual development, the attempt to create such a test is misguided. Ideally, we would have good tests for assessing many dimensions of intelligence, including those that are highly valued and encouraged by different cultures.

Intellectual assessments generally presume typical or "normal" sensory, perceptual, and motor functioning. Impairments in any of these present serious challenges to accurately assessing a person's intelligence. Any such impairment needs to be taken into account to arrive at a meaningful test result. Parents whose children have any such impairments should be cautious in accepting conclusions or recommendations based on standard intelligence tests. Almost always the bias is toward underestimating the child's intelligence rather than overestimating it.

For example, the Bayley Scales of Infant Development and the Stanford-Binet Intelligence Scale, widely used tests for young children, assume normal vision, hearing, and motor skills. In our opinion, these tests have not been adequately adapted for children with sensory-motor impairments.

Also, test norms change over time. The method used for norming is like grading on the curve. This limits the number of children who can be very smart and guarantees that some children will always fail miserably. What was needed to score 130 on an IQ test in 1950 is not the same as what's needed today.

In spite of all these limitations, intelligence tests are still widely used. So what exactly do they tell — and not tell — about a child's mental performance? What are the origins of the skills they measure? What do test scores tell us about how well a child will perform later in school and in life as an adult? What factors — personal, family, and cultural — are associated with variations in intellectual status? Which of these factors can be changed, and which changes alter intelligence? These are profound questions. They have broad implications for both personal use and for social and government policies. These implications help to explain why the field of intellectual development has for generations been so controversial and acrimonious. So much is at stake, philosophically, scientifically, and practically.

A key subject of debate is the degree to which intelligence is determined by factors prior to a child's birth and how much it can be altered. This debate is far from settled.

What Parents Should Do

There are two broad recommendations we offer to parents:

- ❧ **Work to ensure that your child's natural abilities are encouraged and not compromised during these critical early years of life. All the information and suggestions in this book are designed to help you nurture your child's many talents and interests.**

- ❧ **Look to the breadth and depth of human performance as we are describing it. Don't focus on the narrow slice of your child's total capacity that is measured by standardized IQ tests. They ignore many domains of intellectual performance. They focus on cognitive-academic abilities to the exclusion of many other capacities.**

Intelligence, by its very nature, is developmental. What constitutes intelligent behavior for a one-year-old is vastly different from what we expect to see in a three-year-old. As Dr. Robert McCall of the University of Pittsburgh has shown, when a child is tested repeatedly, his or her IQ score typically *varies by over 20 points* before reaching maturity. Very few parents or educators know about this important finding!

There is a vast amount of research using children of different ages that shows predictable patterns of association between various family, social, and cultural factors at particular points in development. Not surprisingly, children who come from homes that have the behavioral and emotional advantages of competent and caring parents, as well as increased financial and physical resources, tend to do much better than those from lower-resource homes.

But income and social status alone do not determine a child's intelligence. Many long-term studies are now underway to relate changes in family, social, and cultural forces to changes in intellectual performance and brain functioning of infants and young children. These studies will likely revolutionize our understanding of intelligence, especially when combined with what we are learning about developmental genetics from the gene-mapping work in the Human Genome Project.

Can We Change Intelligence?

The question of whether we can change intelligence has intrigued us since the time that we were first exposed to the idea of intelligence as an area of scientific study. After having thought about the topic for almost forty years, we have come to several broad working assumptions:

- ❀ Because human intelligence changes in its manifestations during development, we prefer to reframe the question as follows: In what ways and to what extent can the developmental course of intelligence be altered in positive ways by modifications in experience?

- ❀ Framed in this way, a clear course of scientific inquiry is implied: Alter experiences for some children for some period of time and compare their intellectual development to initially comparable children who do not receive the altered experiences. Although this type of research is more easily conceived than carried out, its logic is clear and compelling.

- ❀ To us, intelligence is a large, multifaceted concept that is relevant to everyday functioning and typical people. Intelligence is almost universally desirable and applies in adulthood to artists, lawyers, mechanics, chefs, professors, physicians, musicians, and newspaper writers, to name but a few. For certain, intelligence applies to parents.

- ❀ Within each of these examples, some people are seen as more intelligent than others. Yet the behaviors that result in judgments about intelligence across professional categories are diverse. That is why we, in principle, endorse the theoretical idea of multiple intelligences advanced by Dr. Howard Gardner.

- ❀ The scientific task is to figure out how to sample all the relevant contexts and behaviors so that we can determine the structure of intelligence and how it changes over time. This would require a very ambitious research program, one that has not been even remotely approximated to date.

- ❀ We do have assessments of children that have been validated to some extent against school performance and one another. This is useful, but only a narrow slice of relevant performance. Therefore, the kinds of tests used to sample "intelligence" limit how well the results can be extended to all of "intelligence."

❀ We find it not useful to speculate on issues about intelligence that are not yet scientifically resolved. The complex issues surrounding this critical subject need further study. Such study is important and eminently feasible.

Given these basic assumptions, there are two types of research strategies that we regard as the gold standard with respect to studying changes in intelligence:

1. **Longitudinal studies of identical twins reared apart and in significantly different and documented environments**

2. **Randomized, controlled trials of systematic and documented interventions or educational programs**

Other research strategies can give us useful information. These include comparison of siblings and studies that correlate factors associated with variations in intelligence at particular ages.

All other research strategies that we know about are less powerful and clearcut than when the two gold standard strategies are used at a high level of technical adequacy and completeness.

The Many Facets of Your Child's Intelligence

All these points and findings boil down to one thing: Your child is not just a single number — not an IQ score, or a score of any kind. Your child is unique and wonderful in so many ways, and the paths to growth are numerous and varied. Your challenge is to draw out your child's many intelligences, gifts, and capacities, to encourage and celebrate all talents, interests, explorations, quests, and achievements. This is the adventure that parenting should be, one that builds not only an intellectual foundation, but the basis for every other facet of your child's total being. ❀

CHAPTER 8

Love
and Limits

*Foundations
of Character*

O F THE MANY ADVANTAGES PARENTS CAN GIVE BABIES, SETTING REASONABLE LIMITS IS NEAR THE TOP OF THE LIST. LIMITS ARE PART AND PARCEL OF SOCIALIZATION — KNOWING WHAT KINDS OF BEHAVIOR ARE EXPECTED AND ACCEPTABLE. THEY ARE KEY TO A CHILD'S SAFETY. AND THEY HELP TEACH CHILDREN HOW TO USE GOOD JUDG-MENT LATER ON WHEN ADULTS AREN'T AROUND TO SUPERVISE THEM.

Reasonable limits, consistently maintained, promote four things that help children learn and enjoy life the most: safety, predictability, an engaging personality, and a foundation for more active learning.

SAFETY

Of course you will set limits to ensure safety. However, you might not realize that even common safety limits are important beyond your child's physical well-being. In the first eighteen months of life, your child will not yet understand independently the reasons behind the safety limits you set. Later, however, your limit-setting will be a basis for continued trust between the two of you.

PREDICTABILITY

Predictability is comforting to people of all ages. Your child should come to trust two aspects of predictability of limits. The limits you set should be consistently applied, at least almost all the time. And specific behaviors that conform to or deviate from these limits should produce predictable responses from you (and ideally, from others as well).

ENGAGING PERSONALITY

A child who respects others and who has a warm and positive disposition is a delight to have around. Such a child is also a magnet for others, both adults and children. The behaviors you teach in your child's first eighteen months will be a good foundation for all the socialization skills to come. A well-socialized child with a rich behavioral repertoire has the keys to open many doors. This social repertoire will help your child to understand and fit into many different social situations, as well as to be a valued contributor.

FOUNDATION FOR ACTIVE LEARNING

The safety and predictability of limits free a child to explore with confidence and with less active supervision of every single behavior. When children feel safe and trust how people and objects in their environment work, they are free to use their energy to play, explore, and learn. With a pleasant disposition, children will make friends easily, giving them a whole new environment for play and learning. Over time, the limits you set will help teach your child to use good judgment when facing new, unexpected, or potentially dangerous situations, or to seek the opinions of others who are more experienced when facing new challenges and uncertainties.

The Process of Setting Limits

Limits and their enforcement should evolve gradually over time in a child's life. Limit-setting is a cumulative, long-term teaching process, one that grows and changes in level and complexity. In this process, each new step should match the child's readiness. It is especially important that each new step be tuned to a child's language and cognitive skills. In this sense, setting limits is an integral part of effective teaching, the same teaching you provide in the context of everyday care and play.

Little formal limit-setting should occur in the first eighteen months. However, many things you do in this period build a very important foundation for the limits you will set later on. The cumulative progression of steps is as follows:

- ⚙ **From birth:** The attachment you build with your infant by your responsiveness and affection shapes trust in your teaching and the desire to do what you say.

- ⚙ **From birth:** How you care for your baby and how you behave with others will make powerful impressions of behavior to copy.

- ⚙ **Six months and on:** Visibly showing pleasure and verbal praise for your child's good behavior is a highly effective way to create more good behavior.

- ⚙ **Eleven to fourteen months:** By setting a few, very simple limits and consistently guiding your child gently away from off-limit sites or objects or unacceptable behavior, you teach your child what limits are and the response you expect. However, punishment is not appropriate at this age, except for mild withholding of your approval.

- ⚙ **Fifteen to twenty-four months:** As your child's language and cognitive skills grow, you can slowly add new limits, especially to ensure safety. You can also teach manners and good social behaviors, praising your baby when new skills are learned and used. Prompting is often the most effective technique for bringing out your child's best behavior. In general, punishment is still not advisable. You can use your baby's desire to please you much more effectively than punishment in eliciting the behavior you want.

- ⚙ **Two years and on:** You will gradually add new limits for both safety and social appropriateness. Time-outs and other noncorporal responses may be used. But if you have followed the steps in the earlier stages, you won't need to use them very often because your child will be naturally cooperative and trusting most of the time. Instead, your best ally in guiding your child's behavior will be your verbal and emotional approval or disapproval.

As this progression indicates, timing is very important in teaching and guiding your child. Parents are often warned of the problems they will encounter if they wait too long to start setting limits. But the problems can be just as serious, sometimes more so, if parents set limits too soon, especially if they punish children before they are able to understand what is happening to them. Punishment used too early can lead children to become timid and unwilling to explore and learn for fear of reprisal. Just as important, inappropriate punishment or excessive disapproval can cause children to become passive and to feel confused.

For limits to be effective (and humane), a child must be able to understand and remember three things: that there are such things as limits in life; what the limits in his or her life are; and why those limits exist. Cognitive and language skills aren't strong enough for these three ideas until a child is well into the second year and acquiring a clear sense of self.

The Basics of Limits

There are two aspects of guiding behavior:

Discouraging undesirable behavior: Over time you will need to identify clearly which actions are not allowed in certain places, times, or situations. Throughout this period, the best way to teach is a gentle "no," followed by distraction. Turn your child's attention to a safe and acceptable alternative. If necessary, gently remove your child from situations when behavior becomes dangerous or inappropriate.

Reinforcing good behavior: First, set a good example with your own actions. "Please" and "thank you" are the types of good words your baby should hear early and often. Second, express your delight and pleasure when your baby's behavior is good. Acknowledge and applaud actions and words that are polite, kind, and caring.

You can use what you are learning about infant development to your advantage. This is one of the many gains from all the research on how infants grow and learn. For example, you will find many ways to put your child's desire to please you to good use. You will understand the importance of providing safe areas where your child can play and explore without a need for limits. You will understand what limits make sense and why at each stage of this first year and a half of your baby's life.

For most of this first year and a half, children are not willful or looking to disobey. They are not having a contest about who can win or be in control. They are not intentionally thwarting you. They have no understanding of ownership or value of objects. They aren't mature enough yet. They are simply delighting in the world that they are increasingly able to explore.

There are three keys for success in the world of limits:

❀ **Set limits when and where they really matter.**

❀ **Enforce them in a timely and consistent manner.**

❀ **Set only those limits that your child can understand.**

It makes no sense to set limits a child has no ability to comprehend. It makes no sense to punish a child for something he could not understand was wrong. As with every other aspect of parenting, the key is appropriateness — setting limits when your child is old enough to understand and when natural opportunities arise. Understanding your child's comprehension, abilities, and natural curiosity can help you provide the guidance he needs, as he needs it, and in a way that he can understand and learn from.

A great deal of clinical observation shows that children aren't happy or good learners if there are too many or too few limits. If there aren't enough, children don't feel secure, and they are easily distracted. On the other hand, too many rules can also be counterproductive, restricting the most natural and productive curiosity and energy. The goal is to have a reasonably child-friendly home with a reasonable set of limits.

Your home should be inviting to everyone, children and adults alike. There is no need to turn the entire house over to your baby, nor should you restrict him to a small portion of the home. Everyone's preferences can be accommodated. Your baby should be reasonably free to be in most of the home. But he should also have some spaces where he can play without danger to himself or the room.

Routines at bedtime, mealtime, and play allow everyone to coexist peacefully. Endless battles are disruptive to you, no benefit to your child, and will only escalate if not checked.

Maintaining Limits

Enforcing limits is a subject of heated debate in some quarters. Parents may hear or read advice suggesting — incorrectly — that the only way to enforce limits is to use corporal punishment, such as spanking, or worse. Put off by such suggestions, some parents may prefer to avoid limits altogether rather than subject their children to such harsh measures.

Happily, there is ample evidence that corporal punishment is less effective in maintaining limits than more supportive approaches. By building a solid foundation of trust and care in the early months of your child's life, she will be naturally responsive to your wishes and cooperative most of the time. In these early months, one primary tactic will be to distract your baby — switching her attention to something else and away from dangerous or unacceptable behavior.

Throughout these first eighteen months, it is important to keep in mind what your baby understands and means by her actions, and what she doesn't. Most things your baby will do that you don't want are a product of her natural curiosity and enthusiasm, or her biological needs at the moment — like discomfort or hunger. It is important to understand your child's motivation for her actions. Even routine errands take your child to places that abound in new colors, shapes, and smells that are powerfully enticing to a young explorer. Your child will likely want to reach for bright new objects. Plan ahead. Bring a favorite toy or allow your child to play with a safe, nonbreakable item from the place you are visiting.

When Should Parents Start to Set Limits?

The most common problem with limit-setting occurs when parents assume their baby is acting intentionally long before their baby is capable of such intentionality. Appearances can be deceiving. It sometimes seems as if a baby does something to slow parents down just when they are rushed, such as waking up, going to sleep, fussing, wanting to eat or play, or dirtying a diaper. Or a child may act demanding, insistent, or uncooperative just when his parents are especially tired. On the positive side, just when a parent wants everyone to admire a baby's latest accomplishment, the baby won't say the new word or show the new skill.

If such occurrences make you wonder if you should exercise more control with your baby, *STOP*. Take care of yourself. Find ways to make your life smoother and less stressful.

In the first year of life, your infant cannot purposefully try to make you miserable or disappointed. If you have such feelings, get to their root causes. Do not try to force your child to fit in and "behave properly" before he is able to do so. Soon enough, your child will be ready. He will also likely be quite skilled at learning the right types of limits.

Sometimes parents are so zealous in their desire to have a well-behaved or respectful child that they begin too early or too harshly. This is unfortunate. Here are examples where limit-setting is mismatched to the child's development. Please do *not* do these things with your child:

- Parents may want to start early to teach their child not to interrupt or bother others when they are doing something important. Such parents may have seen rude three- and four-year-olds, and they do not want their child to turn out the same way. Therefore, when their child is only four or five months old, these parents start to ignore "attention-getting" behavior whenever they are on the phone or visiting with others. When this does not work, they speak sharply and loudly, telling the child, "Stop it," or "Don't interrupt when I am busy. Pay attention!"

- Parents understandably want their child to learn not to break things or touch things that do not belong to him. So when their child starts to crawl, they say "no" when their child moves toward something breakable. They say "no" again, very emphatically, whenever he reaches for a breakable object. They may even hit the back of his hand if he reaches out after being told to stop. To reinforce their point, they pick their baby up, look directly at him with a stern and angry face and say, "Don't ever do that again!" If this causes their child to cry or fuss, they are confident they have made their point.

The assumptions behind these actions are wrong on several counts. First, the parents have incorrectly assumed that their child is able to differentiate between situations or types of objects. In fact, babies cannot do so yet. A four- to five-month-old baby cannot tell when parents are really busy and do not want to be bothered. Moreover, a baby of this age should be encouraged — not discouraged — to communicate her needs. When parents cannot be interrupted, they need to enlist the help of others or wait until their child is sleeping.

In the second example, parents hope that if they tell their baby often enough to stay away from certain things, their child will eventually learn which things can and cannot be touched or played with. However, an infant who has just learned to crawl is not yet able to differentiate between breakable and nonbreakable objects. Moreover, an infant does not understand the concept of ownership. A child who is repeatedly stopped when crawling or reaching toward interesting objects will become less interested in the world, more passive or disengaged, and less apt to actively explore objects. This stifles natural and invaluable curiosity and early learning.

Discipline with Forethought and Kindness

One of the most important things parents can do is decide what is really important to them. Remarkably, there is no uniform code for what constitutes safe, socially acceptable behavior or flat-out objectionable behavior. (This should be apparent by observing how parents themselves behave!) Therefore, when children are very young, we encourage parents to talk a lot about their dreams for their child, including their images of well-adjusted and well-behaved children. Parents might ask:

> ❀ **"What are our priorities for do's and don't s at different ages in our child's life?"**

- "Which social behaviors do we want to promote? Which really distress us?"

- "What manners do we agree are important and helpful to children? Are there some we think are unnecessary or outdated that no longer need to be taught?"

Our society is diverse. The norms also vary widely from place to place, even neighborhood to neighborhood.

- In some areas, children address adults respectfully but use their first names. In other areas, this is considered rude and inappropriate.

- In some cultures, for a child to interrupt adult conversation, even with an appropriate question or comment, is viewed as a sign of the child's precocity and interest in adult conversation. In other places, children and adults alike may be expected to wait until another person has completed speaking before they talk at all.

- Some families teach a complex set of table manners, including a request to please be excused before leaving the dining room table. Other families never eat at a dining room table and have different manners.

- Cultural and religious institutions have different standards as to when children may participate and how they are expected to behave.

The list goes on and on. Such behaviors are part of socialization.

Expected norms also change over time. Just think back a generation or two about what was considered "proper" and "improper." From a global level we can see that many important rules of human conduct are arbitrary. Nonetheless, they are important to the people within a given culture. Even signs of social regard can differ dramatically. In some cultures, people have much physical contact, stand close to one another, and look directly into other people's eyes. Elsewhere, greater restraint is the rule.

As parents of a very young baby, this is a wonderful time to plan how you will socialize your child, how you will initiate him into your very special world. You want your child to know the right rules and the subtle cues to be successful. You also want your child to be able to think on his own, with his own ways to demonstrate love, interest, sharing, cooperation, initiative, creativity, and responsibility. Not all good behavior is rule-bound or formulaic.

Be prepared. Parents differ. You may need to compromise. You might also want to consider the values and practices of grandparents, other relatives and close friends, and your community. When children are older, they can even learn more than one set of rules and limits. For example, there may be important things to do or not do at grandparents' homes that may not apply or be essential at home, such as being very quiet, or not running too fast, or speaking slowly and clearly.

With forethought and planning, limit-setting can be reasonably pleasurable and highly effective. If you ignore this until you have to think about it, it may already be after some bad behavior cycles have gotten underway.

Limits: An Essential Part of Love

For all the reasons above, we encourage parents to set and keep sensible limits as soon as their babies become mobile, but not before. Limits become more important as babies' mobility, language, and cognitive abilities grow. The point of introducing this subject early, however, is to alert you to the initial behaviors that signal the onset of more independent thought and action. If you recognize these behaviors for what they are — a combination of curiosity and a growing desire to assert independence — you won't be surprised when they are more fully expressed. If you build a good foundation for setting limits, you will have a much easier time establishing and maintaining them. And if you maintain them consistently and lovingly when you do put them in place, you will have a much easier time as your child grows.

When boundaries are set and maintained this early, everyone wins. Babies are safer. They feel secure. Their trust in you continues to grow. They will be happier and more enjoyable. And their relationship with you and other members of the family will be off to a strong and healthy beginning. Indulge your babies with your affection, with play, and with games. But don't deprive them of the essential support that limits provide. ❀

CHAPTER 9

The Many Worlds of Infancy

*Good Times at
Home and Beyond*

THE WORLD SEEMS TO BE CHANGING BY THE HOUR, AND NOWHERE ARE THESE CHANGES MORE EVIDENT THAN IN FAMILY LIFESTYLES AND APPROACHES TO PARENTING. MANY FAMILIES LIVE VERY DIFFERENTLY FROM THE WAY THEIR GRANDPARENTS DID. THE SHIFT OF WOMEN INTO THE WORKPLACE, FREQUENT TRAVEL, THE HIGH INCIDENCE OF DIVORCE AND REMARRIAGE, AND THE RISE OF NONPARENTAL CARE OF YOUNG CHILDREN ARE JUST SOME OF THE PROFOUND CHANGES IN THE ENVIRONMENTS IN WHICH CHILDREN GROW UP.

What hasn't changed is what's important in the lives of young infants:

- **The nature of their home and family environments**
- **The overall quality and quantity of stimulation they receive, both at home and elsewhere**

What adjustments should parents make in these new environments? How can they provide and arrange good childcare? This chapter makes no attempt to provide comprehensive answers to these questions. In part, this is because of the complexity of the issues — and the fact that many topics have yet to be studied scientifically.

Instead, we share some recent findings that may help you to better understand, assess, and respond to specific aspects of your child's world, at home and away. We hope this information will help you incorporate current knowledge of young children into your everyday lives and routines and all the changes that are part of today's world.

The World at Home

THE "RIGHT STUFF"

A tremendous amount of scientific inquiry has focused on the quality of children's home environments. There are many ways to measure these environments, depending on the child's age and level of development. Some aspects of the environment predict development and achievement later in life.

The findings are both impressive and unsurprising. Infants whose home environments have more of the "right stuff" do markedly better later in intellectual, linguistic, and social-emotional development. What, then, is the right stuff for very young infants? And to what extent should parents be sure that all of this is present in their children's lives?

Pioneering work on this topic has been led by Drs. Bettye Caldwell and Robert Bradley of the University of Arkansas at Little Rock. Their observational scales for the home environments of infants are the most widely used in the world and have offered clear guidance to a generation of researchers. Drs. Caldwell and Bradley have demonstrated that there are at least six dimensions to home environments of infants that are powerful predictors of cognitive and social growth.

SIX DIMENSIONS OF HOME ENVIRONMENTS

- Social responsivity
- Absence of punishment
- Organization of the environment
- Availability of appropriate books, toys, music, and games
- Involvement of mother and father with the child
- Opportunity for variety in daily experience

These dimensions are important in virtually all cultures that have been studied and for families from all walks of life and social and economic circumstances.

A CHILD'S EYE VIEW

There has been a revolution in the way researchers study the lives of infants and children, one that may help you better understand the environments and guidance you provide for your baby. Scientists have learned the importance of seeing a child's environment from the child's vantage point. They look at an infant's continuous, cumulative experience, which is how children comprehend what happens to them. Then they assess how the child interprets and is affected by that experience, taking the child's capabilities and perspective into account.

Older research, however, was based more heavily on parents' accounts, which reflected the parents' perspectives. We have learned that an adult's view of what is happening may inadequately reflect how things are actually experienced by a child. For example, many studies have shown that parents are not highly accurate in reporting what they do with their infants or how often they do things. Their knowledge is even less reliable when their infant is in someone else's care. Here are some examples that describe how this revolution in thinking changes the way developmental scientists measure and evaluate young babies' experiences:

- The number of books, music tapes, or compact discs in a baby's home are measured best in terms of whether they are appropriate to the child's stage of development and whether they are actually available to, and used with, the baby. It's not enough to know simply whether books and tapes are present in the home.

- A father's contribution to his child's development is best indicated by whether he engages in regular everyday activities, like sharing meals on a regular basis and playing with his child, rather than the amount of time he spends at home.

- For a baby to have a sense that he has a special place in the home and family, there need to be visible signs that he can see and touch. His first scribblings, photos, and special acknowledgments need to be where he can see them, not relegated to places where only adults can appreciate them.

❀ **Babies need to be included in conversation, not just hear discussions between others. They need compliments and celebration, even before they speak or understand much. This is part of what makes a stimulating home environment.**

What counts is that the child actually experiences things. What is potentially available isn't the same thing as what actually happens. This is true of objects as well as people. That is why pots and pans are as good as expensive, but unused, toys, and why a designer nursery without a loving and knowledgeable adult is potentially no better than an understaffed orphanage or a poor-quality childcare center.

As these examples indicate, the collective research shows that love and care are meaningful to an infant only when they are expressed in ways that the infant can feel, see, hear, and understand. Love and care also need to be shown often and in many predictable ways, not erratically or in ways unrelated to the infant's own behavior. Quality time is important. But so, too, is the overall quantity of positive and developmentally appropriate experiences.

Periodically take stock of how your child is likely to see and experience her environment. Check out the rooms in your home from her eye level. As she grows, reexamine what she can and cannot reach or get into. Look again at where her creations or favorite things are placed in the house. Periodically rearrange the photos and mementos on display to keep them current, especially as your child's memory builds so that she can remember outings or events that are captured in the items or pictures. Keep up with her growth and interests in every way you can.

A PARENT'S EYE VIEW

Behavior occurs within contexts, usually ones that we help to create. Social psychologists have known for decades that our environments include both physical (actual) and psychological dimensions (that is, the ways in which we think about our environments). Often, our interpretation of our world and our perception of its adequacy influence our behavior as much or more than actual events or circumstances do.

In our own research, we have discovered families with similar living environments who describe them quite differently. Some are pleased, others less so. We have also found families that are remarkably alike with nearly identical incomes, in the same neighborhoods, who describe the adequacy of their incomes quite differently.

We recognize that parents differ in the circumstances and surroundings they believe they need to be good parents. We also know that parents' perceptions have a direct bearing on how they behave. It is behavior that is important to the infant — not another's perceptions, because an infant is too young to understand such an abstract concept.

It also matters to children if parents are unhappy. It makes sense, therefore, for parents to do all they can to ensure that they, too, are as satisfied as possible with their arrangements and with the changes in their home and life that are brought about when a child arrives on the scene.

That said, there are some basic standards that seem to work well for many families. In our observations, these tend to be to the advantage of both the parents and the child, a big plus for overall smooth family functioning.

Organizing family life: Having a reasonably well-organized home is an asset for many reasons. First, the logistics of infant care — feeding, diapering, bathing, and sleeping — require a lot of juggling with supplies and equipment. Organization helps. To the extent that the home environment is well-thought-out, well-supplied, and easy to negotiate, parents are likely to feel good and not hassled, and are likely to have the time to be responsive to their infant. Also, an organized home with interesting things to look at, listen to, and play with helps make everyday caretaking more fun for the baby and parents, and provides the openers or props to start a "conversation."

Home for everyone: A home environment that is welcoming to both parents and babies is likely to work the best. In some families, the balance seems to tip so that the baby or children dominate the household. This can wear on the adults, and it rarely helps prepare children for being part of — rather than the center of — an environment. Parents in such child-centered homes may also be at risk for neglecting their own interests and friends, not to mention their relationship to each other beyond their new role as parents.

On the other hand, a home with few adaptations for an infant, other than a new baby room, is also not balanced. Children are part of the home, and need to feel that they fit in and are part of what happens throughout the house, not just in separate baby places. Each family, of course, has to find the right mix. But we encourage parents to give serious thought to the arrangement in their homes and to experiment to find what works for them.

Keep up with your own interests: We see too many parents who feel that they must sacrifice their own favorite pastimes and hobbies in order to give their undivided attention to their children. First, this just isn't so. Second, it can make parents resentful. Third, it can keep couples from enjoying interests they share, interests they should pursue to keep their relationship strong.

You can, and should, find ways to include your child in almost all of your interests. When you are doing things you like, you invariably enjoy yourself. When you are having a good time, your child will especially enjoy being around you. And children love to do "grown up" things. They love to do what you do. Young children are highly imitative. Involving your child in your projects and hobbies is a great learning experience and fun for both of you.

When your baby is very young, talk to him and describe what you are doing as you sketch, build a model airplane, take a bubble bath, watch a baseball game, or plant flowers. Take your baby with you and point out all the neat things at car and boat shows, flea markets, sporting goods stores. As your baby gains dexterity, there are many safe ways for him to join in as you cook, wash the car, listen to music, or read magazines. The list is endless. As your child grows, the common interests you have developed are likely to continue to be a wonderful, enjoyable bond between you.

Whatever your interests, keep up with them. Everyone in the family needs to have "a life." That includes you. Your interests are part of what makes you the unique person you are. They are central to your enjoyment of life. Pursuing them is also an important way for you to be the best parent possible.

Network of care: Ideally, every baby should receive lots of love, care, and stimulation from at least two caring and knowledgeable adults who are part of the child's everyday experience. This social network can include family, friends, and other stable caregivers. In most societies, the care of infants and children has always been provided in a social context that is more than a mother alone with her baby for hours and days on end. Such arrangements provide social experience and learning for the child and an important change of pace for parents.

Safety: This is a very big issue. Parents need to carefully evaluate each and every room, hallway, nook, and cranny for potential risks, especially for an active, exploring infant. The American Academy of Pediatrics has an excellent checklist in its book, *Caring for Your Baby and Young Child: Birth to Age 5.* For young babies, topics include automobiles, bathing, changing, fire, falls, poisons, sleeping, toys, firearms, and water, among others.

Between Home and the Outside World

For families today, this in-between zone is one where much time and energy are spent, and sometimes this contributes to fatigue, frustration, anxiety, or anger. Much of the problem is due to the hectic pace or unpredictability of many parents' lives.

Many babies and young children have trouble with sudden, abrupt change — some children more than others. As you have read throughout the earlier chapters in this book, babies are absorbing and processing enormous amounts of information when they are awake. Therefore, most babies will be happier with gradual transitions to new places and new people.

Whenever possible, plan to allow a little extra time for transition. This allows you to move at a more leisurely pace as you prepare yourself and your baby. Babies quickly pick up on whether you are harried. If you are, they may become a bit edgier and fussier.

Guests: If guests are coming to your home, you may establish some routines that your baby will learn to associate with visitors — including talking about who is coming. If your baby is shy or showing extra sensitivity to strangers (including family members he doesn't see often), have guests greet you first and interact with you before they approach and play with your child. This is true for both visitors and babysitters.

Help them to respond to your baby's cues. If your baby is overwhelmed, provide some quiet time or extra comfort. This can be difficult with proud grandparents and close friends, but visitors will usually appreciate what you are doing. If you are leaving your child in the care of a sitter, a gradual rather than very sudden transition may not eliminate a crying bout, which is normal at some ages for babies, but it can help immensely.

Going out: If you are taking your baby out on errands, for a visit, or to a childcare center, the same advice about a gradual pace works best. If your child regularly spends time in out-of-home childcare, you can establish routines for leaving. Some special play or reading time in the morning is great, if everyone is awake.

Arrival: When you arrive at someone else's home or a childcare center, spend a few moments with your host or child's caregiver. As with guests in your home, let your baby see you interact pleasantly with these "new" people. If you are going on errands, spend a few moments letting your child "take in" the new surroundings at each store or place.

Departure: If you have spent some time with those who will care for your child after you leave, whether a sitter or childcare-center teacher, don't drag out your departure or trick your child. When it's time to leave, hug and kiss your child, say good-bye, promise that you will return, and then go. Don't keep saying you are going to leave, and then hang around. This makes the transition more anxiety-producing for the child. As soon as you are out the door, your child is free to go onto activities with others.

Never, never slip out while your child isn't looking. This may avoid a scene for you, but the sitter or teacher gets the full brunt of the fear and anxiety produced by your sudden "disappearance." This undermines the trust you are working to build in your child. But if you tell your child straight out that you are leaving and will come back, you reinforce trust by your behavior. When you go, promise to return. When you return, point out to your child that you have come back as you said you would.

In the car: For most families, a lot of time between home and outside is spent in an automobile. Some parents and infants spend a considerable amount of time each day commuting. If this is true in your case, we have a few tips.

First, you need a vehicle that will accommodate your infant, an age-appropriate safety seat, a well-stocked diaper bag, and some safe toys. In the first few months, you will get used to traveling like a nomad with your belongings, even if you were formerly a "one small suitcase" world traveler. Believe us, we know, as do all experienced parents, that it is better to be overprepared than to run out of diapers, plastic bags, wet wipes, books, or toys just when you really need them.

These are a few "tricks" to car travel that can make it more pleasant:

- Drive extra carefully. Good driving skills also make for a smoother ride for your baby.
- When you travel without another adult, allow more time to accommodate getting in and out safely.
- Carry some of your infant's favorite tapes or CD's. Those with children's stories, nursery rhymes, and soothing music are usually a hit.
- Safely secure soft cuddly toys to the car seat.
- Talk to your baby as you drive. Describe what you are seeing in an interesting and conversational way.
- Try, try, try not to be in a hurry all the time or to pride yourself on your split-second efficiency. Remember, with babies' schedules, pride goeth before the fall!

The "Right Stuff" Beyond Home

Two areas we want to address in this section deal with the many places children typically go these days and out-of-home childcare.

OUT AND ABOUT

Young infants and children today routinely go to many places where children were almost never taken one or two generations ago, such as the supermarket, shopping mall, or nice restaurants. It is wonderful to see how many such establishments have become "family-friendly," accommodating children in all sorts of ways.

At the same time, parents should understand how children "see" these places. Some children can be overwhelmed with the new sights, sounds, and smells. For most children, however, they offer a whole new world of things to explore. This means wonderful things to touch, feel, grab, drop, and play with. Hence, a trip to the store can easily exasperate the most patient of parents.

However, as you understand how naturally perceptive and curious your child is, you can turn many errands into outings that your child will enjoy and learn from. Many smart store owners offer lots of help. They offer child play areas to occupy children while parents shop. They provide miniature carts so children can shop along with mom or dad — a big treat!

Be choosy about where you take your child to shop, visit, and dine. Patronize establishments that provide for a child's needs and interests. If your child's enthusiasm is more than you might wish for, you can adapt your routines in the future. At least you will understand that the enthusiasm is a testament to your child's drive to learn and explore.

CHILDCARE OUTSIDE THE HOME

The central place where many infants spend a lot of time is in a preschool or childcare center. With sixty-two percent of mothers now in the work force, alternative childcare is a national way of life.

As a result, out-of-home childcare has become a major national issue, hotly debated and politically and socially charged. The center of the controversy is:

Is early childcare by someone other than the parents harmful — or helpful — to young infants?

Given the intensity of the issue, it is remarkable how few careful, scientific studies have been conducted that offer relevant answers to this vital question. Most research has been limited by many factors, and much of it is outdated. Earlier findings presented a conflicting picture about whether nonparental care in the first two years of life had either negative effects or virtually no detectable effects on the social, emotional, and mental development of young children.

Parents turned to pediatricians for advice on early childcare. Yet pediatricians rarely were trained in this area and typically offered their own personal opinions rather than scientifically justified advice.

A new congressionally endorsed national study, funded by the National Institute of Child Health and Human Development, has addressed this important issue. Now in its seventh year, this study is being conducted in ten cities, and it has provided the most compelling findings to date. These findings, not surprisingly, are complex, but tremendously useful to parents.

Since 1991, this study has tracked some 1,300 children in ten locations across the country. These children are from various ethnic and cultural groups, they come from a broad range of family structures in all walks and most circumstances of life, and they are cared for in a variety of settings:

- **Full-time care by their mother**
- **Part-time care by other family members**
- **Part-time care in another home**
- **Part-time care in their own home supervised by a nonfamily caregiver**
- **Part-time care in a child center or preschool**

The average child in the study who was in alternative care spent thirty-three hours per week in such an arrangement. The results consistently make the point that what counts is the *quality of care* a child receives. The report states:

> The **quality** of child care over the first three years of life is consistently but modestly associated with children's cognitive and language development. The higher the quality of child care (more positive language stimulation and interaction between the child and provider), the greater the child's language abilities at 15, 24 and 36 months, the better the child's cognitive development at age two, and the more school readiness the child showed at age three.[1]

For cognitive and language development, the source of the care appeared to be immaterial:

> In terms of cognitive and language development, researchers found no benefit for children in exclusive care by their mother. Among children in care for more than 10 hours per week, those in center care, and to a lesser extent, those in child care homes, performed better on cognitive and language measures than children in other types of care, when the quality of the care giver–child interaction was taken into account.[2]

However, for *mother-child relationships,* the source of the care did matter:

> An increased **amount** of child care was modestly associated with less sensitive and less engaged mother-child interactions.[3]

These results are important for what they tell us about nonmaternal care. They also underscore the importance of the care given to every child in the first three years. What happens to children in this critical period — in or out of the home, with parents or other caregivers — is profoundly important in shaping how children turn out.

---

[1] The NICHD Study of Early Child Care, National Institute of Child Health and Human Development, April 1998.

[2] Ibid

[3] Ibid

FINDING GOOD CARE

The NICHD study shows the benefits of good-quality care. But it also points up the dangers of poor-quality care. Unfortunately, many children are in care that is, at best, neutral in its effect, and many others are in care that is considered actively harmful.

Yet virtually all parents believe or want to believe that their children are receiving good care. Clearly, many of these parents are wrong. Their children are at some degree of risk, and the parents are unaware of the problem or deny its existence. Perhaps they have made the best arrangements they can and don't wish to acknowledge the possibility that those arrangements aren't good enough.

One major problem with much of childcare is financial in origin. Inadequate funding leads to marginal facilities, less than desirable teacher–child ratios, and childcare workers who are often undereducated, undertrained, and seriously underpaid. The result is that overworked or underattentive caregivers don't provide enough responsive one-on-one stimulation, communication, and encouragement for each child.

Other problems with childcare relate to convenience, such as closeness to your home or work, days and hours of operation, policies regarding care of sick infants, and whether meals are provided. As important as convenience factors may be, please do not forget that the quality of care is the most important thing for your child. This is a case where your extra investment in time and money are truly worthwhile with a lifetime high yield.

In Chapter 4, dealing with cause and effect, we discussed at length the essential need for positive response-contingent experiences for healthy development. Without enough such experience, brain development in babies slows and can suffer seemingly irreversible damage. Babies don't have the cognitive skills and stores of memories to occupy themselves on their own for long periods of time. They need others to stimulate, teach, respond to, and guide them. If your child is at a poor-quality center, do all in your power to move to a higher-quality one. If you can't, have your child spend as little time there as possible while you continue to look for a better arrangement. If need be, take sick leave or vacation time to take care of this.

Parents need to know what to look for to ensure that the care their child gets is, at the very least, not harmful. To do this, parents need to take the time to see how their child is treated. It isn't enough to visit a center during an open house when special efforts are taken to put on a good show.

What to look for: The quality of childcare your baby needs can be met in a variety of settings. But the elements you should look for include these:

- Energetic, well-trained, friendly, and child-oriented teachers
- Low child-to-teacher ratios: not more than four-to-one for infants
- Timely and sensitive responses to infants' needs and preferences
- A program that builds a strong and balanced foundation of emotional, social, cognitive, physical, and language skills for each child
- Encouragement of each child's natural curiosity and creativity
- Activities designed to meet the needs of each individual child, with a way to note special requirements
- Developmentally appropriate materials and equipment
- Daily reports for parents about each child's activities, participation, and progress
- Flexibility of schedule to meet families' needs
- Regular quality-assurance inspections and parent surveys
- Open to parent visits *at all times without notice*
- A safe, clean facility with good security procedures governing on-site care and picking up the child at the end of the session
- Cheerful and bright surroundings for play inside and out
- Quiet areas for sleep and rest

Your child's teachers should want to know as much as possible about your child's preferences, needs, and cues, and you should give them all the information you can. You should also tell the teacher each morning about anything that would help the teacher to be as responsive as possible to your child. For example, let the teacher know if your child had a restless night, learned a new game, didn't eat breakfast, or has grandparents visiting.

WARNING SIGNS

There are a number of clear "red flags" in childcare. If you spot any of these, take action immediately and confidently in the knowledge that your child's best interests are at stake.

You are asked to call before you come: If a center requires you to call ahead before you visit, something is wrong. If your child is in such a center now, we strongly urge you to start making unannounced visits. Walk right in. See what's going on. Even if you are told the caregivers are "on a break," see if your child and others are being held or attended to. Is your child crying or happy? Bored or enthusiastic? What about the other children? If you don't see interaction or find a sense of joy, you should be seriously concerned that your child is not receiving quality care.

The place stinks: This is almost always the telltale sign of poor hygiene. Good childcare smells good.

Babies cry too much: If you see babies who cry a lot and the caregivers describe them as "naturally that way," this means the caregivers don't want to attend to such children. So what happens when your child is crying?

"Same old, same old": If your child is involved in exactly the same activity every day at pick-up time, this can mean insufficient variety. Your baby needs variety, both for joy and learning.

Teacher turnover is high: Whatever the reason, this is not a good sign for your child's developing sense of trust or social predictability. Do staff seem to be complaining and unhappy? If so, there's probably good reason.

In sum, nonparental childcare can be wonderful for you and a benefit to your child. *But only if the quality is high.* If such care is not available or affordable, then it is worth reassessing your options. The quality of care your child receives will affect many aspects of your child's future. Good effects will last a lifetime. Ill effects are hard, sometimes seemingly impossible, to undo.

As you gain experience in negotiating the outside world with your infant, you will become more skilled in being prepared and knowing what to do when your child does not adjust well. Success as a family includes being able to go many places and be with other people. Just as important, parents need to be respectful of others, so that a distressed baby or overly active child is not disturbing, such as at movies, restaurants, and concerts. Explore the world openly, ready to adjust or make last-minute changes. Relax and have fun! ❀

CHAPTER 10

Seven Essentials

*Guiding Principles to
Help Your Baby Every Day*

Thischapter summarizes what really matters — everyday activities for parents and children that have been proven to work. The facts that support these Seven Essentials are not based on one or two studies, and they do not promote one person's philosophy or some company's products. They are based on scientific evidence from over a thousand papers and articles. These studies involved many infants and parents in many settings and circumstances, and they used multiple methods and techniques to prove their accuracy. These are not opinions, fads, or maybe's. To the best of our knowledge, *these guiding principles represent a true synthesis of what is really known.*

Most researchers stay focused on their work. But we felt the new scientific findings are so compelling that they needed to be shared with parents in a useful way. Parents need practical advice that capitalizes on these findings.

We began work on the Seven Essentials over a decade ago. The first round produced some sixty distinct requirements — hardly a user-friendly list in that form! As we reduced the list, time and again, we worked to ensure that the research evidence remained strong enough to justify inclusion.

To claim that this chapter synthesizes all of the important scientific findings is a tall order. Undoubtedly, many different ways and words could capture the most important and most certain of the research advances. But we have used these Seven Essentials for over ten years, and parents have consistently found them helpful.

We acknowledge the important contributions of our colleagues, many of whose contributions are mentioned in the reference section at the end of this book. We know we must accept responsibility for how we have translated major findings into practical application. We may have left out some useful information, but we are confident that these recommendations are sound. Using them, parents can be certain that they are doing a great job building their child's foundation for life.

Some words and common sense things may appear to be missing, at least at first. There is nothing that says directly "Love your child every day." This is not because love is not important. Rather, it is because there are so many different ways parents can show love, or feel love, that to instruct parents to love their babies doesn't really say much.

Moreover, research does not connect love per se with positive child development outcomes. Instead, studies show that love must be translated into positive, nurturing actions to really count for a baby. The Seven Essentials focus on specific actions to do just that.

Can parents really do all of these things? You probably are (or will be) doing them naturally and spontaneously. Moreover, many of these essentials occur in a single exchange. As you help your baby explore, you are likely to teach (mentor), and probably also celebrate new behavior and help to practice new skills, often using words to guide and reinforce your infant. That's five of the essentials. If you also protect your child from harm and inappropriate disapproval, as well as provide useful limits, then you've done all seven.

These practical suggestions are not *just* for parents. They are every bit as applicable to grandparents, aunts and uncles, older brothers and sisters, special friends, and anyone who is entrusted with the care and guidance of young babies, whether for a few hours to many days, weeks, and months.

How to Do Everything You Can for Your Child

Our best advice to parents is twofold:

First and foremost, continue to care about being good parents, trust your own instincts, listen and learn from others, and be open to trying new things.

Second, these are guiding principles you can learn and apply every day. Yes, these are probably worth memorizing. And yes, we really do mean every day!

Think of these Seven Essentials as developmental "vitamins and minerals" that every infant needs daily. There are many different ways to provide them. Most are lots of fun, easy to learn, and natural for parents and others to do. None require buying anything. All can be done anywhere in the world, almost any time.

Personalize them. Let them reflect your own interests, personality, culture, values, and traditions. Be creative. Be relaxed. Rest assured you can and will be exactly the best kind of parent you always have dreamed of being.

These Essentials will help in all walks, ages, and stages of life. And their value extends beyond the first eighteen months. Keep adapting them to your child's development and readiness for new advances and new stages of growth. Note that the word "parent" comes from the Latin root, *parens,* meaning "to bring forth." These Seven Essentials will help you to truly *bring forth* the best in your child.

THE SEVEN ESSENTIALS

1. ENCOURAGE

Encourage exploration with all the senses, in familiar and new places, with others and alone, safely and with joy.

2. MENTOR

Mentor in basic skills, showing the whats and whens, the ins and outs of how things and people work.

3. CELEBRATE

Celebrate developmental advances, for learning new skills, little and big, and for becoming a unique individual.

4. REHEARSE

Rehearse and extend new skills, showing your baby how to practice again and again, in the same and different ways, with new people and new things.

5. PROTECT

Protect from inappropriate disapproval, teasing, neglect, or punishment.

6. COMMUNICATE

Communicate richly and responsively with sounds, songs, gestures, and words; bring your baby into the wonderful world of language and its many uses.

7. GUIDE

Guide and limit behavior to keep your child safe and to teach what's acceptable, and what's not – the rules of being a cooperative, responsive, and caring person.

1. ENCOURAGE

Encourage exploration with all the senses, in familiar and new places, with others and alone, safely and with joy.

You should actively promote curiosity and exploration. Help your baby to seek new experiences, new information, new forms of stimulation. It's not enough to simply let your baby explore, although self-initiated exploration is very important.

Encourage your baby to use all of the senses, alone and in combination. Show how you look, listen, touch, smell, or manipulate things so that you can experience something new, different, surprising, or delightful. Your encouragement can be shown by nodding your head, smiling approval, placing your child in the right place to make exploration easier. For instance, just holding your two- or three-month-old infant in an upright position activates the visual system and increases visual exploration. As your child's comprehension of words increases, use words to foster exploration. Show how checking things out leads to delightful surprises and reveals new information and the yet-to-be-discovered side of things.

Use any and all senses plus your baby's improving gross and fine motor skills. Babies do delightful things to appreciate shapes and textures. They like to explore new objects with their mouths or gently bump into objects or push them around to see how they feel. As adults, many of us tend to limit our exploration to the world of language and sight. Be adventuresome yourself, and get in touch with all of your own senses!

Why is exploration so important? Exploration captures the dynamic interplay between the world of senses and learning. Without exploration, some learning can and does occur. But the learning that appears to be the most robust, the most long-lasting, the most versatile, is the learning that is connected to self and to self-initiative. By encouraging exploration, you are setting the stage for a lifetime of constructive curiosity.

Our world is rapidly changing, and to enjoy true success throughout childhood and well into adulthood, one must become a lifelong learner.

SAFETY

The more childproof your home, the easier it will be to encourage exploration. If you have stairs and they are gated, you don't have to worry that your child will tumble down them. Place locks on cabinets and drawers that contain things that might hurt your baby. Put window rails on upstairs windows and guards on your stove and oven knobs so your child can't turn the heat on or grab pots on the stove top. Cover unused plug outlets. Keep long cords from window blinds, telephones, lamps, and other appliances out of your baby's reach. Get toilet locks for all the toilets once your baby can pull to standing. Keep breakable objects, sharp edges, and pet-food bowls out of your child's ready reach.

When your house is safe for your child, you can relax and encourage active exploration. (But with young babies, for the full first eighteen months of life, always remain in the room while your child is awake even after your house is childproof.) We strongly urge all parents to get a good book that covers all the basics about safety and childproofing. In some communities, there are now childproofing experts who will evaluate your home and recommend or install everything you need, usually for a modest price. Don't worry. Your house will not always be like this, and you will adjust surprisingly quickly to the little everyday accommodations needed to open and shut things, etc.

This underscores the importance of being open and willing to explore, to check things out, to consider things beyond what one already knows and has mastered. Above and beyond these sound reasons for encouraging exploration, we know that exploring itself can be joyous, interesting, and fun.

Exploration contributes to, and is part of, alertness and attention. With increasing capacity, infants expand how and how long they will take in information from the world. Try not to be too restrictive in guiding your baby's natural curiosity. You must guard your baby's safety. But don't worry that your baby will be overly curious or socially inappropriate. In infancy, there is no reason to worry about too much curiosity or a baby being "nosy."

There are lots of reasons to be concerned about safety. Thoughtful adults need to structure the outside world — from furniture and toys to people and places — so that children won't be in danger when exploring their world. When you see possible risks for physical well-being, quickly and gently move them or your infant. But be careful not to admonish or convey that something is wrong with being curious and checking things out. As we discuss in Essential 5, below, you should protect your child from inappropriate disapproval, teasing, or punishment for doing things that are perfectly natural and normal at this age.

More ideas for encouraging exploration. Touch an object, feel its texture, its warmth or coolness, its hardness or softness, its size. With your child, discover if something can tickle (a feather) or make a noise (clapping hands). Look at something together, and move it around (right-side-up or -down, front or back, moving quickly through space). Look at many things, and people, too, under bright lights and in shadows. When you walk down a hall or into a room, take a tour of the "gallery" on the walls. Look under and inside things. Cover something up, then uncover it. Watch bubbles appear, move, burst. See their many colors. Reach out and touch a bubble. When you take a walk outside, listen for sounds. Be very quiet and then exclaim or remark on what you heard.

Listen to music — great music, popular music, children's music, silly songs, and tunes you just make up. Sniff the roses and other fragrant flowers, too. Smell the aromas of food, baby soaps, shampoos, and lotions. Taste those things that smell good and are safe to taste. Join your baby on the floor and scoot or crawl around together, stopping to explore various things as you go.

Offer your baby the world. Go out often. Use everyday activities to explore the world, both close and far.

2. MENTOR

Mentor in basic skills, showing the whats and whens, the ins and outs of how things and people work.

Many parents ask us what we mean by "mentor." Is this the same as teaching? And what *are* the basic skills infants need to know? Mentoring is a form of teaching, one that is highly effective and takes place in the context of a caring, established, and long-term relationship. The word "mentor" is defined as a wise and trusted advisor or counselor. The word comes from the Greek epic, *The Odyssey,* in which Mentor was a close advisor to Odysseus and entrusted with the care and education of Odysseus' son, Telemachus.

Mentoring builds on the unique, responsive bonds between adults and children. A lot of the really important learning in life does not happen in a formal, structured format. It comes from daily experiences, small and large, that offer useful information and insights. A baby is eager to learn about everything — about people, places, things, feelings, and who "I" am and what I can do.

"Walk the walk" matters. Children learn what they live. They learn from what they see and hear their parents *do* — how parents make things work, how they solve problems, what behavior is acceptable or not, what types of cues and words win positive responses. Parents can and do mentor through their everyday actions and words.

Most real learning in the first eighteen months occurs in natural exchanges. Parents frequently aren't aware of how much or when they are "teaching." There are dozens of ways young infants learn about associations, consequences, symbols and abstractions, and how human beings attend to and respond to others. We reviewed many of these in the earlier chapters on cause and effect, intelligence and learning, and social and emotional development.

As we have cautioned earlier, there are very few absolutes infants must learn. The basics include learning the names for objects and people in their lives, general concepts about relationships between things (like above, below; inside, out; close, faraway; up, down) or qualities of objects (like big, little; loud, soft; wet, dry). What matters most is that your child is actively learning. Remember that mentoring extends to the social and emotional realms, too, like learning to greet and part (hello, bye-bye), to show consideration (please, thank you, excuse me), and to understand approval versus disapproval (yes, no). The varied ways that people can show love, affection, interest, delight, pride, and joy also are important to learn.

Do babies need to learn colors? Shapes? Letters of the alphabet? Tunes to songs? Basic number concepts? Probably not. Maybe even decidedly not.

But can they? Probably yes. Do they enjoy this? Try it and find out. Clearly, children can be introduced to such ideas, symbols, and words long before they need to use them. What you — your child's first and most important mentor — choose to pass on should be what comes naturally and what feels right and enjoyable. Beware: Do *not* think that teaching something such as colors or letter recognition very early will necessarily last or make your baby smarter or better prepared for school.

What will prepare your baby for later success, including doing well in school, is that he or she is learning and is acquiring a *love of learning*. In general, the *what* of learning does not seem too important, with one exception — language. Babies absolutely need to learn the basics of language: Speech perception; making diverse, interpretable sounds; saying words and sentences (in any order); plus other means of showing intentionality and communicating feelings, thoughts, questions, and needs.

Which language (or languages) your child learns does not matter. What matters is that she learn early and appropriately about ways to communicate successfully and efficiently. Language is closely tied to other forms of learning and also to social-emotional development.

Why is mentoring important? Mentoring provides the broadest basis for learning. Learning helps the brain get wired properly, just as the brain's development helps to improve learning. Babies build a lifelong foundation for learning when they have many positive experiences with different forms of learning from someone who loves them, someone they trust. Once learning is established as an easy and enjoyable part of everyday life, your child will continue to be an active learner.

The best kind of learning is associated with pleasure, both from neurochemical changes in the brain to the actual learning event. There may never again be a time when the joy of learning is so readily visible to you as in these first eighteen months.

Mentoring enhances the attachment between parent and child. This is the deep and lifelong relationship that goes beyond meeting basic survival needs. Your child will know that when you teach, you teach with love and with his own individuality and best interests at heart. Don't worry about lesson plans. But seize the many opportunities you will have to share what you know and how you think the world works. Be prepared. Soon he will challenge you and ask you about things you cannot answer. Then together you will continue the adventure of learning.

More ideas about things to do for mentoring. What you teach your child will change rapidly as the months go by. Here are some ideas to give you a feel for what's in store. Some pertain to the very youngest babies, others only to a talking or walking child. Mix and match. Rarely can you go wrong. And be sure to use all the ideas about responsive caretaking. Don't be too insistent; don't demand attention when your child is fussy or tired or bored. Don't interrupt the flow of her self-initiated behavior. Don't wait too long or not long enough. Her behavior will guide you so you will know what to do when and for how long.

Show your fifteen-month-old how cabinet doors open and close. Give your four-month-old a rattle, say "shake" as you move it and make sounds together. When you talk on the phone, let your eleven-month-old hear what is happening (do remember to tell your phone partner what you are doing!). Pretend to have a conversation with play phones with your sixteen-month-old by taking turns talking or just making sounds.

Help your toddler to work age-appropriate puzzles if these seem interesting. Allow time for trial-and-error learning, as well as helping with words and movements. Don't admonish when he makes mistakes, but provide useful instructions and ideas to guide his behavior to help him succeed next time. Do the same with toys that come apart and fit back together and ones with moving parts.

Sing lots of songs to your child. Accompany them with hand gestures or dramatic faces or body movements. Let your toddler try on your hats, and tell her what you do when you wear each hat — "This is mommy's running hat.

Mommy wears this when she goes jogging." "This is daddy's hat. He wears this hat when he plays (baseball, golf, tennis)." Teach about articles of clothing and everyday objects. Point out things and name them when diapering, dressing, feeding your child. Show some of the different things they can be used for.

Group things together. Lots of big things, or red things, or soft things, or smelly things. Help your child figure out when something is different and does not belong. Sometimes this can be very funny, like putting baby's clothes on you, or having something unexpected appear or reappear after something else was hidden.

Remember that babies' responses to activities such as these will vary, depending on their level of understanding and their alertness and interest level. Something that is interesting or silly at one age, or on one afternoon, may not be so at another age or time. Sometimes it may even be confusing or frustrating. For example, there are some toys with objects suspended inside that babies cannot reach. Giving this to an infant who is eager to hold and manipulate can lead to fussing or crying. Store it away for a later time.

Never allow extended periods of distress to occur when playing. But a few moments of upset, brief and intermittent, are simply part of growing up. This is the trial and error of learning for you and your child.

Toddlers love to help their parents in "adult" tasks. When you are cooking, let your child stir or pat or touch some of the ingredients. Yes, you can make real pat-a-cakes as well as pretend ones. Your child can stir with one spoon while you stir with another, or you can stir together.

Most babies go through periods when they love to throw things. Is something being learned here? Yes. First, your child gets you to pick up the objects, or to join in and throw them, too. Second, some things can and should be thrown. Get a ball — although you will be mostly rolling it in these first eighteen months rather than throwing it. Perhaps your child will learn to throw trash away and help you clean up (although the idea of cleaning up is a bit advanced for most eighteen-month-olds to understand).

Most simple household tasks lend themselves to learning for your child. So can most of your outings, whether routine tasks or social visits. Special occasions or trips to art museums, zoos, and gardens are great for learning, long before your child can take full advantage of all that these places have to offer.

Another classic, timeless source of learning is books. In the early months, the rhythm and flow of words teach fundamentals of language. You can point to pictures and to the objects found in your own home. You can put your child in the story and substitute words and ideas freely. Select books that delight you, and your child will be delighted and learn as well.

Through mentoring activities like these and many more, your baby learns the basics — the fundamental relationships, ideas, concepts, and activities of our world. This learning helps children to make sense of the world, and to be more capable in their own actions. Your mentoring is timely and priceless.

3. CELEBRATE

Celebrate developmental advances, for learning new skills, little and big, and for becoming a unique individual.

Celebrating achievements is great fun for parents and children alike. Some milestones are universally noticed, especially first steps and first words. Most parents can't help but show their pride and joy. They may jump up and down with glee, clap their hands, exclaim, smile, laugh, pat their baby on the back, and tell family and friends. Everyone likes to be noticed for something wonderful they have achieved. Babies are no exception.

"To get the full value of a joy, you must have somebody to divide it with."
—Mark Twain

Why celebration of your child's behavior is important. When someone "makes a big deal" over their behavior, babies learn that what they do matters and is noticed. Also, parental joy is contagious, and babies feel good when their parents show pride and pleasure in their developmental progress.

A parent's response to a child's achievement is directly linked to the child's growing awareness of self. This, in turn, leads to a sense of self-efficacy. There is also evidence that the pleasure of learning and reinforcement helps release chemicals in the brain that facilitate learning. So praising achievement can bring about more learning. Finally, parental celebration helps keep parents and babies tuned in to what they are doing, noticing change, and appreciating everyone's individuality.

Celebration can come from many people in addition to parents. Praise and cheers from relatives, friends, and other caregivers all reinforce a baby's growing understanding that a competent person is emerging. These people all clearly convey to a baby that learning is wonderful and valued. This, in addition to your baby's own delight with the consequences of learning, sets the stage for continued willingness to take on new challenges of development. Babies, like all of us, like having personal cheerleaders. When your children grow, they will remember you as someone who gave them the confidence to know that they could succeed at whatever they put their hearts and minds to doing.

More ways to celebrate, and what to celebrate. Fortunately, most parents need no instruction in this department. There are lots of individual and cultural differences in what people do to express joy and pride. All can be effective.

What parents need to remember is that they cannot stay "tuned out" or pre-occupied with other things for extended periods and forget to notice what their child is doing. Even little celebrations, signs of pleasure related to what your baby is doing, need to be shown daily. Trying a new food, smiling a big smile, giving you a nice stroke or touch, or waiting patiently — all are cause for celebration.

In the early months, timing is of the essence. Celebration needs to be almost immediate for your child to connect your outward signs of pleasure with what he has just done. Babies can't remember past a few seconds. Happily, babies practice new behaviors over and over. You will have many daily opportunities to keep responding.

Allow your own ways of expressing joy to shine through. Don't force your celebrations. Don't overdo anything in a way that is not you. If you are phony or exaggerated in how you respond, you will not want to keep it up for long.

Should you or others in the family experience extended periods of depression or the blues, be sure others are available to help with the positive side of life and to notice what your baby is doing. Your child is too young to comprehend why someone who used to be responsive is no longer so.

Cheer new achievements with smiles, sounds of delight, hand-clapping, kisses and hugs, a pat on the back, and lots of words — to your child and to others, too. Celebrating your infant's developmental progress does not mean making her the center of attention always, or noticing every little thing she does. As always, your good judgment and personal style are important in deciding how you and your family choose to express your pleasure and pride in her advances.

4. REHEARSE

Rehearse and extend new skills, showing your baby how to practice again and again, in the same and different ways, with new people and new things.

Babies, like everyone, improve their new skills with lots of practice. Rehearsal and practice underscore what's important. Learning continues as your child has more and more experience with a new skill, whether it be people-oriented or one that engages objects. Your help in expanding on a new behavior is an extension of mentoring. But beware, not every new skill will be ready for vigorous practice or application, at least not immediately after it appears. What is important is that your infant has a chance to try things, again and again, and to continue the journey of learning about how to adapt and refine each emerging skill.

Guided rehearsal and extension of new skills are extremely important for your child's development. Most new skills can be expanded and improved. This allows your baby to discover more fully what it means to be able to reach, to grasp, to manipulate objects; to smile and engage your attention through playfulness and reciprocal interactions; to scoot, crawl, walk, run; and to babble, in ways that increasingly approach real language.

Your own actions can serve as suggestions or ideas to guide your child's behavior. You can give helpful hints about what can be done next, about how to vary what has just been learned, and about how many different ways there are to do things. Learning can become even stronger with help from you.

Why helping to extend new skills matters. Skills benefit from practice and trial-and-error experimentation. This is how children learn to see when and where these skills can be used, and how they might be improved. Most achievements of infancy follow a natural path, from simpler milestones to more complex operations. This applies to social and emotional development as well as to language and cognitive achievements. In some ways, this daily essential is really just an extension of mentoring. It's more teaching with love and commitment.

Not every single skill needs rigorous practice and extension. Not every skill needs to be actively worked on right away. What matters is the cumulative building and encouraging of competency, being there when things do not work out, when frustration may appear, when confusion might set in. These mildly negative experiences are inevitable and natural. You cannot and need not prevent them. But be there to keep them in bounds so your child doesn't become extremely frustrated, disappointed, or confused.

Your goal should be to respond appropriately to your child's behavior. You can build on your infant's interests and accomplishments, rather than push a predetermined list of skills to be learned at some set age or stage.

How to use rehearsal to make the most of your baby's new achievements. Show, talk, encourage. Set up the world so some things can happen, perhaps a bit more easily than otherwise. Point things out. Be there to play games and engage in trial-and-error learning.

Neither give up too easily, nor push too much. Observe your child's behavior carefully. Look for cues, and respond with loving appropriateness. Do not worry that your baby will grow up too fast. See your infant's increasing maturity as exciting and praiseworthy. Children need their parents' attention and guidance for a long time, at least another two decades — probably more, if you are good parents.

Be prepared to do some things over and over again for the sheer joy of it and to help your child gain mastery and to appreciate new skills. Also, be prepared to see your child sometimes learn the same thing at different ages, but at a new level of understanding or skill. Good mentoring is expansive, patient, gentle, thoughtful, and competent. A child with more than one mentor is truly blessed.

5. PROTECT

Protect from inappropriate disapproval, teasing, neglect, or punishment.

This essential is as much about what *not* to do, as it is about actions to take. Parents must ensure that they and others do not respond inappropriately to a child's behavior in ways that could be permanently harmful or slow down the child's development.

Protecting your baby from inappropriate disapproval, teasing, or punishment is all-important. No child under one year of age is able to understand right from wrong, or dangerous versus safe, in the adult sense of these words. Be sure that your baby is not reprimanded inappropriately for simply being a baby.

Babies never need to be punished, treated harshly, teased, or made fun of in a rough or insensitive manner. (See more on guidance and limits in Essential 7.) What makes punishment, disapproval, and teasing "inappropriate"? The answer is: an excessively negative or punitive response for something that is normal, healthy, inevitable, or unintentional.

Parents sometimes get angry for things that, in their more rational moments, they knew could not be helped. Every parent has moments when it may appear that their baby must have done something just to make them mad, to control them, to make them worry, to damage or dirty something. If you find yourself in this situation, stop. Think about your child's age. What is your child's level of understanding about what has occurred? Could a six-month-old possibly know that electrical cords are dangerous, even if you've repeatedly said so? When does your child realize that spilling liquids or making a mess with food dirties a special outfit, either yours or your baby's? Many of the same behaviors that are constructive and appropriate in one situation, or with certain things or people, are decidedly not appropriate in other situations or with different objects and people. This process of socialization about the rules of acceptable behavior will take a while.

The best safeguard is to anticipate how your child's natural behavior and growing achievements might be a problem. For example, baby's books should include some with big cardboard pages, ideally ones that are laminated, so your child can directly touch and explore books. And magazines for play should be old ones that can be torn, because tearing is a skill and makes fun noises.

Parents must protect their children from harm. But yelling or punishing babies for reaching out to a hot pan on the stove is not the way to do this. A firm and consistent "no," with an explanation of "hot," is always okay, but very young infants may not yet understand.

More sophisticated rules of social conduct, such as not interrupting adults, are far beyond a young baby's ability. Early practice will help with later mature behavior. Self-control regarding pain and discomfort also is not possible or desirable in young infants. They need to communicate what their needs are in a timely way. When your child learns to talk and ask questions, encourage him. There will be plenty of time to teach subtleties about not asking too many questions. Older children have the understanding and self-control to learn not to interrupt adults, not to ask too many inquisitive or direct questions, and not to complain when they are uncomfortable. But these are not lessons for infancy. Try to know what your baby can and cannot understand. Unrealistic expectations can only lead to frustration for everyone.

Why do young children need to be protected from inappropriate punishment, disapproval, and teasing? Many actions that lead adults to say "no" are ones that can cause harm, either to the baby, to others, or to valued objects. But these forms of exploration don't call for punishment or harsh reprimands. Punishment absolutely cannot be effective for babies of this age. Worse, it can bring out negative emotions or cause withdrawal and disengagement, and the wrong lessons are learned.

Sometimes parents tease in ways that are meant to be playful or innocent, but are too rough or mature for an infant or toddler. Making fun of a child may lead to a type of self-consciousness and subsequent unwillingness to show new behavior or to try to do something new in the presence of adults.

Once in a while, parents may defend such behavior by saying they have to show older siblings that all the children are treated the same way. This is a terrible precedent to establish because children need to be treated individually. Techniques that work with older children don't work with infants. To adopt a rigid, "one-size-fits-all" approach would be as inappropriate as requiring an eight-week-old and a five-year-old to eat the same types and amounts of food, or get the same amount of sleep, or be spoken to in the exactly the same way.

Teasing sometimes has a way of running through the generations. In some families and cultures, some forms of teasing are thought to be constructive or instructive. We cannot imagine how this could be so for very young infants. When parents make fun of a child's imperfect actions or mistakes, the child too often gets the message, "You are not capable." This is especially problematic in the second year as the sense of self emerges.

Babies do not need to get "toughened up" for the later teasing they will likely experience. You will not produce an overly sensitive or self-conscious child by respecting your infant's right to develop at his own pace and in his own style. Part of maintaining the best of early attachment and parent–child bonding is to extend this protection through the later months and years when children acquire more independence and voluntary control.

We note, with grave concern and sadness, that abused children often show "lots of love" for their abusive parents. Wrongly, some people think this is affirmation for a harsh and cruel style of parenting. There are very clear reasons why children who are abused continue to seek their parents' love and approval. Indeed, such children often seem overly attached to their parents at later ages. There is a continuum of parenting from highly appropriate and effective to truly abusive and ineffective. Please be unsparingly honest in appraising your own behavior and the behavior of all the others who take care of your child. The emotional scars of enduring maltreatment are deep and often transcend generations.

How to be sure your child is not treated inappropriately. Do not scream at, hit, punish, or frighten a baby. Do not let others do this to your child. When your child pulls a tablecloth off a table or goes near the stairs, realize that these are things babies will naturally do in the course of exploring. Parents should remove the temptation, or the infant, rather than punish the child. When your child can understand, you can teach by using "no," and guiding her to a new activity or place.

Don't bite or hit your child to demonstrate why it's wrong to bite or hit. The child only becomes overwhelmed, and this reinforces the idea that people do bite or hit. Instead, talk to your child and gently show that those things hurt.

Do not ridicule a baby's first efforts at speech or other activities. Don't tease your baby mercilessly about anything. Babies won't be able to pronounce a word correctly until after much practice. They won't become independent in eating until after lots of messes (which sometimes are funny). A bit of tickling is all right, but never tickle until a baby cries.

Be attentive and loving to your child. You can't give a child too much love or attention, and you can't spoil a baby. Have plenty of playtime. Talk your baby through daily events. Have plenty of playthings on hand, and sit on the floor with your child as she plays with them. Laugh with her as often as possible. Even very young children can have an astonishing sense of humor. Doing all the other good essentials will keep you busy, enjoying your times with your child, and right on track with this essential.

6. COMMUNICATE

Communicate richly and responsively with sounds, songs, gestures, and words; bring your baby into the wonderful world of language and its many uses.

Rich and responsive communication is paramount for learning and social-emotional development. Language is the major way we communicate. Language is also central to high-order mental processing — our ability to label, categorize, sort through, and reflect on all aspects of our lives.

Language also contains a magic of its own, a multisensory experience to delight the ears, the tongue, the eyes, and bring out emotions and insights. Language is used in instruction, in love, in discipline, in exploration. The value of language to your child's growth and well-being is beyond measure.

Children need lots of exposure to language every day in ways that are directed toward and responsive to them. Language from a recording, a tape, or a television program is not sufficient or effective.

Person-to-person language is completely different. Hearing one's own name, the names of others, learning what names go with what things. Discovering words to describe qualities of objects, feelings of people, characteristics of relationships. Imitating words. Inventing words. Saying words more clearly. Saying things that mean something, that get a great response, that tell others what a baby wants, that let others know the baby matters. What parent doesn't naturally marvel at and delight in a child's initiation into the world of language?

Why the language environment has a lasting influence. A large space in the mature cortex of the brain is dedicated to speech and language processing. It is closely connected to many other aspects of thinking and reasoning as well. New research shows the complex ways in which brain-behavior connections are expressed and influenced by early language experiences.

There appears to be a sensitive period when the young child's brain is open to a range of new experiences, and then increasingly becomes specialized. Also, there are bursts of phenomenal language growth in children's spoken language, indicating that young children have an exceptional talent for acquiring and using speech.

Older children learn more by listening to others in conversation than they can when they are very young. Young children probably learn some things when they overhear others talking, such as the components and rules of speech turn-taking, cadences, phrasing, and intonation, and how volumes are adjusted to different settings. But they learn these things best when they directly listen to, speak to, and talk with others.

While infants learn a great deal about language in the first eighteen months of life, they will keep on learning for at least several more decades. For many of us, learning language is a lifetime endeavor, as well as a source of information and great enjoyment.

In the second and third year of life, you will see how much your child can learn about language (and other things) from being with other children. But parents will continue to be a child's primary dictionary, grammarian, reader, and listener even in the later preschool years. A good, strong language foundation in infancy — intimately connected with communication itself, long before children can produce clear sounds and words — begets better language development later.

For healthy mental, social, and emotional development, a child's early language environment, especially the responsive and rich language of their parents, is perhaps the most important and powerful influence. Children who are tuned into language and have many opportunities to learn about it in all of its forms are also most likely to succeed in school and in other academic pursuits.

Ways to enrich your child's language environment. Research on parents who are the best natural language mentors reveals that they have many similar skills. They typically:

- ❀ Listen closely to their children's speech.

- ❀ Look for other indications of intentionality and meaning.

- ❀ Respond to the messages their child communicates.

- ❀ Repeat and elaborate on what their child has said.

- ❀ Check out whether they have understood their child correctly.

- ❀ Help their child learn new ways, better ways, to say something.

- ❀ Label things, naturally and easily, in an ongoing stream of conversation that accompanies much of what they do. (This does not mean, however, that there should never be silent times.)

- ❀ Encourage their children verbally to help them figure out that there may be two or three different words that mean the same thing.

- ❀ Use other people's names, and use the child's name often and appropriately.

- ❀ Openly express pleasure and delight in their child's verbal advances and efforts.

- ❀ Do not ridicule or reprimand their child for language mistakes.

- ❀ Use "parentese" — a form of highly engaging speech that captures their child's attention — in the early months. Then gradually they shift to more mature, adultlike forms of speech as their child is ready.

- ❀ Permit playing around with sounds and words.

These parents also like to read, tell stories, chant nursery rhymes, sing songs, and simply play around with words. They also use lots of repetition. They will sometimes focus on helping their child master a few words or phrases. Then they expand and elaborate. They then wait patiently while their children try. They don't interrupt or complete their children's sentences, but let the children communicate on their own much of the time.

Anyone can learn and use these skills of linguistically talented parents. Don't feel self-conscious talking to your two week-old, or two-month-old, or fifteen-month-old about things that seem way too advanced. Just get in the habit of talking and sharing with words. Try talking to your child as though he can talk back. Describe what you're doing as you do it. Ask him questions, too. When he begins to babble and coo, babble and coo back. Use his name often. Repeat words and rhymes over and over.

Read simple word and phrase books to your baby; then advance to longer books as he grows older. You will be able to tell which books and topics hold his attention, and which do not. It is exciting to see a child learn to love reading and books. Soon your infant or toddler will be asking you — in many different ways — to please read those favorite books again and again. Ditto for telling great stories.

Let your child "talk" on the phone, even before the verbal skills for a real conversation are fully in place. It's a thrill for grandparents and others to hear your baby's cooing, and it gives your child a sense that he has something to say. This establishes ongoing connections with other people. And phones are not the only medium for this. Try electronic mail, or tape recorders, or videotapes, and even old-fashioned letter writing and card sending. All use language and provide ways to stay in touch.

7. GUIDE

Guide and limit behavior to keep your child safe and to teach what's acceptable, and what's not — the rules of being a cooperative, responsive, and caring person.

Guidance and limits are an essential part of encouraging your child's development. For many parents, it seems that just around eighteen months of age, and approaching the two-year-old birthday, there will be many more times when your child is "testing the limits." This really is just part and parcel of normal and healthy development for toddlers.

We are extremely reluctant to advise formal discipline and limit-setting in the first eighteen months. There has been a recent explosion of books on the market about disciplining your child and treating behavior problems. These are not for parents of babies. Some are a blatant response to the troubled youth and frightening headlines about children who are out of control, not connected to other people, not caring or empathetic. Understandably, parents want to be sure their child will not turn out like these children!

But setting up a regimen of strict discipline and limits cannot, and should not, occur in infancy.

Rather, there are "preliminaries" that can be put into place. These preliminaries will help to set the stage for the more appropriate demands you will be able to ask of your child later. These preliminaries include establishing healthy routines for certain times of day and certain activities. These routines will teach your child about the order in your lives. They will also teach about different ways of behaving, depending on when and where you are. These will not be memorized by your child. Instead, your child will begin to grasp that there are quiet times, or loud and playful times; that when someone is hurt, you show concern and help; that there are some things that are not allowed — the "no's" of life — and that there are reasons for them.

Another way to help set limits is to show your child by your example. Parents who live what they believe, and display the behavior they expect from their children, have the best results. Parents who verbally command their children to be a certain way, and not to do certain things, but who themselves violate these commands and expectations, have the most difficult time of all with their children "misbehaving."

Being consistent is important. Also, parents should pick a few things to teach that are most important about "good behavior." For example, beginning around eighteen months of age, manners are very easy to teach. Children like to copy and please adults. If you encourage your child, and if you say "please" and "thank you," she will pick these up effortlessly and with pleasure. If you try to force these behaviors, or don't use them yourself, the results will be disappointing.

How important is limit-setting in infancy? Even though we have included this as a daily essential, we are guarded in our certainty that there are many limits that a child actually needs to learn this early in life. Research findings deal mostly with parenting practices for older children. Some findings also come from retrospective reporting (memories) of parents about what they did during their children's younger years.

In general, a style of parenting described as "authoritative" wins out in the research to date. Authoritative parents have much certainty and knowledge, much consistency in their own behavior and expectations, and consistency in the consequences they provide for both good and bad behavior.

However, authoritative parents also show flexibility and individualization. They are neither laissez-faire and extremely permissive, nor are they absolute and rigid. They display a natural balance and good sense, which often go hand-in-hand with knowing when children can and cannot do things.

Even in infancy, some behavior patterns will get set in place. Starting off in the right direction will be a big help. Safety, of course, is paramount. For instance, you should insist that your child is properly secured in a car seat that is just right for your child's size. Don't give in when she fusses or cries by having someone hold her when the car is moving. This is in no one's best interest. Instead, be sure there are interesting things to look at or play with; that you provide interesting conversation and continue to respond to her (without compromising attention to the road and traffic); that there is music; and that her basic needs, such as food and diapering, have been met.

The same approach applies to gently and consistently teaching your child about not touching or exploring dangerous objects. Show why things are not good or safe to do. Such teaching is appropriate and workable as your toddler matures.

Punishments, time-outs, and withholding positive things aren't appropriate in the first year of life, other than minor withholding of signs of pleasure. Techniques that can be effective with a three-year-old will be confusing and seem random to a twelve-month-old. Save these techniques for the right time, when they can be important assets in your parenting tool kit.

You can express displeasure in ways that will be effective after your child is about one year of age. You can also express concern and worry, and you can indicate what is out of bounds. But remember to be highly selective and to have a good reason for your actions. There will be plenty of time to teach lots more about behavioral and social norms in the next several years when your child can understand and respond to your intentions. For now, establish some family rules and begin to talk about them, even though they won't really make sense or register yet.

"No" often seems to be a toddler's favorite word, usually close to two years of age. This is a fundamental developmental advance. It means your child is developing a sense of self and recognizing the different roles of people in your family.

When possible, try to deal with your child's "no!" playfully. Sometimes your toddler's "no" does not even really mean "no." Let her know you are listening and observing, and that of course your child can have a say in things. Gradually, you will see signs that she is learning to compromise, to wait, to take turns. These behaviors will add to her sense of well-being, confidence, and security. Also notice if you are saying "no" all the time, yourself.

Parents should talk with each other, and other regular caregivers, about values, techniques for positive behavior control, and beliefs about effective discipline. For your older child, consistency among all caregivers will be very helpful for your child to learn what is most important.

Most parents want their children to be considerate, well-mannered, engaging, and self-controlled. As we described earlier, these behaviors will be learned from the everyday interactions with others, from emotional expression and reading others' emotions, and from cause-and-effect relationships.

Focus on the positive. Fill many waking hours with interesting things, learning through play and everyday transactions, and being responsive to each other. Love and good behavior will follow, albeit with some ups and downs and challenges. Get prepared, but don't prematurely embark on a formal program to teach all the social rules too early. To do so is just as inappropriate and ineffective as pushing your six-month-old to recognize letters and words in the hope that you will have an advanced reader in the third grade.

Can I Really Do All of These Things Lots of Times, Every Day?

We hope we have not overwhelmed parents with the "Essentials" your baby needs. Our advice at the beginning of the book, and in this chapter, should not be lost. Have fun. Bring your own personality and preferences into being a great parent. Keep an open mind and try out lots of different things. But mostly use what you see works. Learn from other parents, as well as from books. And even if your own parents were not perfect and never read anything about baby development, they likely have many good suggestions. They, too, can read this and other books about the "new" findings. You may have great fun talking over these discoveries.

In the second section of this book, we provide many more ideas about how to put these essentials of good parenting into practical use, depending on your child's age. Each age section includes suggested activities that come from tested and proven infant programs. You will be able to add hundreds of other things to do with your child. Have fun, and pat yourself on the back, too, to celebrate all the good things you have learned! ✿

Section II

Your Baby's Development

Introduction

❋

TIMELY WAYS TO ENHANCE
YOUR CHILD'S DEVELOPMENT

This section covers some of the highlights of infant development in the first eighteen months of life to guide your activities as a loving, responsive, and mentoring parent. Look at these highlights as windows of opportunity to encourage, support, and celebrate your child.

Each chapter corresponds to an age period, but only approximately. Parents and grandparents, pediatricians, and psychologists all mark a child's overall development chronologically. This convention is so well-established that we dare not try to overturn it. But we caution:

Children's development is not strictly linked to the calendar. Development is orderly, but there are many differences in the timing and sequence of achievements.

Most parents have books to document their baby's progress. These books list the major milestones that parents universally notice and value. But the books leave room for parents to record the age when each occurred because babies do not reach milestones at the same ages. There is also space to write down stories about where and how your child "did" something new, wonderful, exciting, or amusing. Together, these memories are part of your family's lore — the special stories that delight parents and children for years to come. Above all, these books celebrate a child's individuality and specialness. They show children how much they are part of a family. Indeed, babies help to shape the course of family development just as much as parents shape babies.

You are about to enter into a period of your lives that is like none other. There are untold delights and challenges ahead. Enjoy. Rest assured that you have good knowledge and guidance for this wondrous journey.

For each age period, we have identified a central theme. None can capture every-thing important or interesting, and each extends far beyond the few months when it becomes readily apparent. We offer an overview of what's likely to happen in different areas of development. We also provide lots of ideas for things parents can do with and for their babies — ways to be sure your baby has the Seven Essentials every day, at every stage of development.

We are confident you'll discover many personal touches and try lots of other activities, too. There are many different ways to successfully enhance your child's development. None requires special training or a lot of money. Most require time and care. All can fit into your daily rhythms and family lifestyle. Be creative and enjoy!

Cherish and support your child's uniqueness. Challenge with patience. Teach with kindness and enthusiasm. Show your pride, and offer constructive guidelines and appropriate limits to promote positive development. Have lots of fun. Give your child the essentials and the tools for a wonderful life that is balanced and filled with love, joy, and contributions. ❀

CHAPTER 11

Getting Oriented and Building Trust

First Month

A NEWBORN BABY IS AN INCREDIBLE BEING. AS SMALL AND HELPLESS AS HE IS, RESEARCH SHOWS HE IS ABLE TO TAKE IN A SURPRISING AMOUNT OF INFORMATION ABOUT HIS NEW WORLD. BY THE END OF THE FIRST MONTH, HE WILL SHOW REMARKABLE BEHAVIORAL CHANGES IN MANY AREAS.

What's in Store

All facets of your baby's growth will surge during infancy. Development in the first four weeks may look small. Much of the time your baby will be asleep or feeding, being diapered or bathed, but important things are occurring. A lot is happening. This is a time of many wonderful beginnings in your baby's life and in yours.

This is the time to appreciate and play to your baby's senses to help her delight in her new world and to make order out of this strange new place that is her home. This is a time to experiment to learn what works best to comfort her and to capture her attention. This is a time to think about, read about, and practice being a parent. Talk with other parents, including grandparents and valued relatives. Find lots of time to rest. The little things in life, *except for your baby,* can all wait. Most of all, this is a time to celebrate the wonderful new being who has entered your world.

Your Baby's Style

Your baby arrived with a special set of behavioral qualities — his "temperament," — the precursors of later "personality." They reflect the likelihood that your baby will behave a certain way. Some qualities will seem to stay with your child for a long time; others will change or disappear.

Even in the first month, parents report considerable individual differences in activity levels, curiosity, irritability, consolability, sociability, positive emotions, sensitivity to touch, and adaptability to different situations and surroundings. Even before birth, infants show different amounts and patterns of activity (body and limb movements), as well as different responses to external sounds, movements, and changes in their mothers' behavior.

Some of your baby's attributes may make your job as a parent more difficult. Parents of easygoing babies may seem to have a lighter load than those who care for babies who are more sensitive, or more demanding. But in each trait lies the seed of a quality that can be nurtured and developed into a positive attribute — another asset for a happy, healthy child. The important thing is to be flexible and enjoy learning about your baby's traits and temperament. If you do, you will find it easier to respond to his needs in ways that are most effective, and to shape each trait into an asset that will serve him throughout his life.

A great deal of research has focused on the relative importance of these early temperamental differences in influencing the way children develop. Although findings consistently and strongly suggest that some individual tendencies are visible early and remain fairly constant over the early years, there is ample evidence that parental responsiveness and stimulation are of paramount importance in shaping the person an infant becomes.

The individuality of each child and the many ways you can respond to that individuality will be continuing themes in this section. By focusing on your child's own way of acting and responding, you are tuning in to her cues, her way of communicating, getting to know her. This happens as she is seeing, hearing, smelling, tasting, and touching — new sensations, most of them pleasurable. Most especially, she is tuning in to you, your face, your voice, your predictable and responsive holding, caregiving, rocking, stroking, and "just hanging out together."

Not every minute needs to be spent doing special or extra things. The minutes, hours, and days will float by. Talk to your baby. Sing to him. Listen and look. Smell him. Massage him. Try different ways of holding him, feeding him, burping him. Follow the excellent and expert advice in the most up-to-date, revised baby manuals. Our favorites are prepared by leading pediatric associations or multiple authors who contribute different areas of expertise when it comes to the "baby basics."

At this early stage, you are getting to know each other. In this first month, there will be much time for surprise, delight, and experimentation. Use this wonderful time to look, listen, learn, and enjoy.

Elements of Growth

PHYSICAL GROWTH IN NEWBORNS

A newborn's average length is about twenty-one inches long, and average weight is approximately seven and one-half pounds. A quarter of this size and weight is taken up by the head — a disproportionate setup.

Babies reflect differences in parents' sizes, ethnicity, and prenatal nutrition. Babies also vary according to their gestational age, their more precise biological age. If your baby was premature, your pediatrician can help you adjust his "age" by counting it to be closer to when he was supposed to be born. Often this involves subtracting the number of weeks born early (such as three weeks early, six weeks early) from the chronological age (the time since his birth date). This is like giving your baby a new birthday — the one he would have had if born full-term. Such re-aging can be very helpful when you look for developmental achievements.

Once this timing adjustment is made, the so-called delays in development for many premature babies turn out not to be delays at all. Likewise, some babies are really older when born. Their development may appear more mature if their ages are not adjusted.

The ungainly movement you see includes lots of reflexive or automatic movement, plus the lack of good voluntary control over body parts. What may be less apparent is the rapid maturation of your baby's physical senses, the primary avenues by which he will discover and learn until his motor skills develop to give him additional means to explore.

Movement and Coordination: The imbalance caused by babies' relatively large heads affects much of their total body movements. For example, your baby will soon strive to hold her head upright. Despite her valiant attempts, always support her head when she is moving or is held in vulnerable positions.

Many of your baby's reflexes are deceptive. Newborns show "stepping" and "walking" movements if held at just the right angle and moved slightly forward through space. Of course, a newborn can't really walk. Years ago, scientists experimented to see if lots of practice with this walking reflex would accelerate or improve later voluntary walking. Babies who practiced did walk a bit earlier, but not better. And by a year and beyond, there were no differences at all in the babies who did and did not have extra practice.

Other fun reflexes: Place your finger in your baby's palm and see how he grasps it; brush your fingers over the back of his hand and notice how he loosens this grasp; see how he blinks in response to a gentle blow or bright light; and the most important and useful reflex we know of, gently stroke around his cheek and mouth and press gently upward on the roof of his mouth to get him to root and suck.

Babies' instincts, coupled with close attention from caregivers, help ensure survival. These reflexes cease over time and are replaced with purposeful, controlled actions. But during the first year, your well-baby checkups will include checks for these reflexes and their diminution.

Dr. T. Berry Brazelton, the trusted Harvard University pediatrician, helped to create a special test for babies in the first month of life, the Brazelton Neonatal Assessment Scale. (The word "neonate" refers to a baby in the first twenty-eight days of life.) This is a fun experience for parents to watch, since they can see what a large and responsive repertoire of behavior their very young infant already has. But no formal testing is really needed for all babies.

Baby tests were developed for use in research, such as in studies of the development of children who may have been exposed to prenatal conditions of unknown harm or benefit (remember, it was not that long ago that every obstetrical book in the world said that drinking alcohol was perfectly safe and could not harm a baby before birth). Other studies measured how very small, subtle differences in the first month affect the way parents take care of their babies, or what types of later skills and interests babies develop.

The Senses: As we discussed, babies are a lot more receptive and aware right from birth than we used to believe. All of their senses are active, even though some are in the early stages of development.

Sight: Your newborn's vision is fuzzy, and color is not of much importance. But his sight is good enough to focus on objects that are eight to twelve inches away — just about the distance to your face when you feed and hold him. From the first week, your baby will enjoy looking intently at people, especially your eyes and your mouth. Remarkably, many babies will imitate facial or hand gestures. Try sticking your tongue out clearly and repeatedly. See what your baby does. What about a big pout? Or a wide-open mouth?

This imitation seems quite sophisticated, because your baby is able to translate a visual image in some way that leads to matching or copying. There still is some debate about how conscious your baby is in this imitation, or whether this is another instinctive way babies connect through their own actions to the people around them.

During this first month, visual preferences appear. Your baby will soon be able to distinguish familiar images from new ones. (Holding your baby upright directly stimulates and enhances visual functioning.) Soon your baby will enjoy looking at patterns rather than solid expanses of color, and will appreciate the interest from angular designs and stripes, as well as his earliest favorite — circles.

Smell: A newborn's sense of smell is well-developed. Fortunately, very few babies will smell the unpleasant odors they do not like. What will enthrall your baby totally is your own unique fragrance. The oldest, most primitive part of the brain controls smell sensations. But this in no way diminishes the lifelong importance and joys, not to mention the good warnings, that can come from smell.

Hearing: A newborn's hearing is also well-developed, even though sounds are somewhat muted. They hear better those sounds that are somewhat higher in pitch, including "parentese." Without training, almost all parents speak to their babies in a voice that is distinctive. They speak close to their baby's face and ears, softly and clearly, in a higher pitch, using coos and other sounds many parents never even knew they had in them. This truly captures and holds your baby's attention. If you feel self-conscious using "parentese," spend time alone with your baby to get used to it. You will soon find that you naturally go in and out of this "parentese." Laugh at yourself and see how well it works.

Babies know their mothers' voices just after birth. Soon they recognize their fathers' and other special people's voices as well. Babies do not always turn toward the sound, but their body and limb movements may change to show their attention. See how your baby tells you she is listening.

Touch: A baby's sense of touch is not only well-developed at birth, it is the basis for a number of instinctive physical reactions. Physical stimulation of babies' bodies is an inevitable and integral part of caretaking. The importance of physical contact for establishing early bonds and promoting development is well-documented. These findings have led to radical changes in how hospitals handle babies and how parents are encouraged to touch and massage their infants. This is especially true for babies with special health needs, such as very premature babies or babies with infections.

It wasn't that long ago that new mothers were hospitalized for two weeks, and their babies were mostly cared for separately by nurses. That most parents and babies survived this unnatural separation underscores the adaptability of babies and parents alike. No longer are babies kept away from parental contact. Parents now learn careful ways to handle, stroke, stimulate, or rock their babies, all adjusted for each baby's own developmental stage and preferences.

But all things considered, earlier and more natural physical contact is to everyone's benefit, biologically and psychologically.

Taste: Newborns have a well-developed sense of taste and can distinguish mild flavor differences within a few days of birth. They will also show preferences, especially for sweet tastes. Yes, mother's milk does have a wonderful sweet taste and fragrance. Formulas try to match breast milk, but none has totally succeeded.

BREAST OR BOTTLE?

A number of recent, highly publicized studies have suggested that babies who are nursed for extended periods of time have more optimal brain growth and show improved development in many areas, including higher intelligence. In some ways, these findings seem to defy common sense, because everyone knows highly accomplished, successful adults who were not breast-fed. At the same time, few people doubt that nursing is "nature's way." The question then becomes: How compelling is the evidence about the benefits of nursing? There is no doubt that nursing is the preferred way to feed young infants, affording many benefits and few or no risks – although there are hassles, personal preferences, and difficulties that some families may encounter.

At the same time, the research concerning the value of nursing for brain development and intelligence is far from conclusive. Research has not resolved the extent to which the positive outcomes for breast-fed infants are due to the quality and amount of mother–infant interactions and touch, to the nutritional composition of mother's milk, or a combination of both.

It is clear, however, that bottle-fed babies can be healthy, happy, and accomplished when they receive both good nutrition and good stimulation. Increasingly, parents are combining breast- and bottle-feeding to allow fathers and other special people (grandparents, older brothers and sisters, dear friends) to share in feeding.

COGNITIVE AND LANGUAGE DEVELOPMENT

Your baby is already a cognate being capable of an elementary type of learning. Learning is an integral part of cognition and intelligence. Experiments with newborns and babies in the first month have produced exciting revelations about the brain's capacity to make connections and to make order of experiences in these earliest weeks of life. (Rest assured, these experiments were well-controlled, brief, and quite pleasant for the babies.)

Babies are primed for information that is simple, highly regular or predictable, and directly connected to their own actions. What you do and what happens are already teaching your baby about the world. But there is no need to rush into anything this first month. Plenty is happening for your child, if you are simply there and noticing — showing what most of us think of as love and responsible parenting. Remember, there is no such thing as overindulgence or spoiling your baby at this stage. Ignore anything you hear or read to the contrary.

Your baby's learning is mostly about who does what. He is learning to anticipate different behavior from different people. By the end of this month or next, he will clearly show you how great his people awareness is. At later stages, a more playful parent will elicit more active movements, such as thrusting of legs and arms, than will the quieter parent. This behavior means "I know who you are. I am ready to play with you!"

At this time, however, a baby's memory is very short when learning something brand new. Show a toy, remove it from sight for a while, show it again, and your baby will think it is "new." More importantly, if your voice, your rocking, your response occurs quickly when your baby needs you, your baby learns to expect help. If you routinely delay, your baby won't identify you as strongly as a source of relief. However, not every gurgle or coo, whimper or "aah" must immediately and always get a great big response from you and others. This would be impossibly exhausting. Somewhere in between, and mostly toward your natural tendencies, is the right way.

In these first four weeks, babies should rarely be alone for long periods, except when they are sleeping soundly. Most parents keep their baby in the same room with them or nearby for many good reasons.

Surprisingly, components of language development start even before birth. Scientific studies have shown that babies prefer stories that were repeatedly read aloud by their mothers before they were born. Their memory capability allows them to retain the rhythm and cadence of the repeated verses or passages, and they visibly show a preference for these patterns. This underscores how early the imprint of language is on their young, very receptive minds.

Do we advise parents to read lots before a baby is born, and to keep this up after birth? Our advice here, as elsewhere in this book, is: If this sounds fun or interesting, try it. It can't hurt. But this is not essential, nor has it been linked to extra language ability, reading skills, or IQ points. Parents who enjoy this also tend to read more later to their children. They, themselves, also read, and they also like talking and listening to their babies. The talking and listening are what matters — not a book per se at this age.

Talking to your baby, especially face-to-face, is invaluable right from birth. As stated earlier, it may seem awkward at first to carry on a one-sided conversation. Just remember how great the benefits are. An easy topic is whatever you are doing: "Now I'm washing your hand and your arm," "Let's put on your T-shirt," and so on. Your baby will love it.

STATES OF ALERTNESS

All babies have several states of alertness. As your baby grows, these states will become more distinct. The overall level of alertness in newborns is low. But in a few weeks, you will find your baby increasingly alert during part of her waking hours. Experts classify these states somewhat differently, but they generally agree that the following should be included:

- **Deep sleep:** motionless sleep with no response to moderate or sustained outside activity

- **Regular or quiet sleep:** sleep with slight movement and variations in respiration patterns

- **Light or disturbed sleep:** sleep with some movement, eyelid-fluttering, and vocalization, such as sighs

- **Drowsy:** awake with a glassy look in open or partly open eyes, some movement and vocalization

- **Quiet, alert wakeful:** wide awake with eyes wide open, but infant is not attentive to any particular person or object

- **Active and alert wakeful:** playtime!

- **Fussy:** irritable and/or crying

EMOTIONAL AND SOCIAL GROWTH

Right from birth, babies show distress when their physical needs require attention. Just as early, however, they show interest, which is a positive emotion. Smiles are there, but we cannot say exactly why or when. True social smiles appear by four to six weeks, sometimes a little earlier.

Attachment to parents and other caregivers builds throughout the first year. The foundation for this essential emotional and social aspect of development begins right from birth. Happily, as we explained above, the parenting activities that nurture a baby's soul and spirit also build her body and mind. These are some of the most rewarding recent findings. When you hold your baby in your lap and read her a story, the physical contact builds her brain, and the words boost her language development. But she is likely to stare, not at the book, but at your face. She is most interested in you. Your story reading builds her trust in you and her bond with you because, in this instance, you are a source of pleasure to her.

Look for signs of social and emotional responsiveness. This is the foundation for the many social and emotional exchanges that will continue to be part of the back-and-forth, give-and-take, synchronous ways that the generations support each other. This is the period of falling in love. Interestingly, scientists never study love directly. Instead they try to measure it in different ways through observation, interviews, and even the physiological reactions of babies and parents.

The heart of emotional and social development in the first month is trust: the beginnings of your baby's reliance on the way you respond to your infant. These early weeks and months are an important period when children begin to learn to trust others. Babies are especially receptive at this stage to learning to rely on those who respond to their needs.

In light of this information, delaying food to meet a schedule rather than your baby's hunger just doesn't make sense. Ignoring a baby's discomfort only produces stress. Stress, in turn, produces hormone swings that, over time on a repeated basis, actually impair cognitive and motor development. Moreover, delay undermines the trust that your baby needs and that you want to establish. So we recommend attending to your baby's needs as much as you can, as soon as you can. This is the best way to show your love for your baby at this important stage.

There will be times when your baby just cries, no matter what you do, and this will be heart-rending. It is for every parent. But don't give up trying new things to calm him. Experimentation can yield wonderful results. This is the only way to learn what your baby's different cries mean and what works for him. During your first weeks, you will be learning your baby's behavioral style and temperament. Responding as best you can should minimize the upsets, even though you won't be able to eliminate them entirely.

CALMING YOUR BABY

In our experience, far too many babies are categorized as fussy when they really aren't. The result is unnecessary anxiety and stress for parents and babies alike. Some babies are sensitive. For example, some have exceptionally sensitive skin and may be irritated by clothing or touch. Others are highly sensitive to sound, light, movement, or the way they are held. Whatever the cause, most such sensitivities can be managed to a good degree, if only parents will experiment enough to find the cause and discover the best remedies.

Too many parents are incorrectly advised early on that there's nothing they can do. So they give up trying, and everyone suffers. Alternatively, some parents persist with something that clearly isn't working, such as rocking or bouncing, perhaps even harder. If what you do doesn't work, stop. Take a break. Try something else. Keep experimenting.

TOUCH
Clothing
- Experiment with different weights and fabrics.
- Try loose-fitting versus snug clothes.
- Test clothing with or without elastic bands at wrists and ankles.
- Try different detergent brands, or extra rinsing to eliminate residue.
- Remove tags.

Holding
- Use different positions (cradled, upright).
- Try different types or amounts of stroking or massage.
- Some babies respond well to being held for long periods in a carrier or sling.

Movement
- Avoid sudden movements. Slow down. Or, try gentle rocking movements.

Sleeping
- Let your baby sleep unfettered in the crib or surrounded by crib blocks.
- Use alternatives to cribs, such as the car seat.

SMELL

Clothing

◈ Use fragrance-free laundry products for baby and caregiver clothing.

Hygiene

◈ Use fragrance-free products for baby. Adults can also use fragrance-free toiletries and eliminate perfumes and colognes.

Household

◈ Minimize odors of cleaning and other household products. Replace vacuum bags.

SOUND

Voices

◈ Vary the volume, pitch, and speed of talking.

Background

◈ Vary the volume on TV, radio, CD's.

◈ Play different types of music at different volumes.

◈ Vary the volume of beepers, telephones, answering machines, doorbells.

◈ Minimize the impact of vacuum cleaners and other noisy appliances by closing doors or putting the baby temporarily in another room away from the noise source.

SIGHT

Indoors

◈ Vary the wattage of light bulbs.

◈ Avoid sudden changes in light intensity. (Dimmer switches are easy to install on lamps.)

Outdoors

◈ Shield your baby from bright sun.

FOOD/TASTE

Quantity

◈ Be sure your baby is getting enough food.

Formula

◈ Try different formulas for bottle-fed babies.

Burping

◈ Be sure to burp your baby well, since gas can upset your baby's stomach. You might try burping several times during a feeding.

TEMPERATURE

Babies often prefer warmer surroundings than adults. If you can control the temperature of his room, you might try setting the thermostat a few degrees higher than you would choose for yourself. You might also add an extra layer of clothing for your baby or cover him with an extra blanket. But be sure not to make your baby overheated.

We want to add some special words for parents who must spend some time away from their very young babies. This may occur when you or your baby has an emergency medical condition, or when something outside your control happens, which you must attend to without your baby. We know of no evidence that such separation causes irreparable harm if others provide care during the short period of separation. If you can avoid or minimize the time apart, do so. If not, we are optimistic that overall, good foundations can still be laid for your child's life.

Trust is the theme of this chapter because it is the cornerstone on which so much will be built in the coming months. The benefits of the good habits you build now in your response and attentiveness to your baby will last a lifetime.

BACK TO SLEEP

New research on Sudden Infant Death Syndrome (SIDS) has come up with dramatic findings: Babies who sleep on their backs or sides have substantially lower risk of SIDS than babies who sleep on their stomachs. This is another case where new research has upended a long-held belief. But the benefits for babies are without question on this issue. All babies should always be placed on their backs or sides for sleeping.

Activities

Your baby will be alert only a small portion of the time he is awake. But the care and attention he receives during this time are important to his development. You can help him get the most benefit from his alert periods by holding his interest with talk, music, play, touch, and being tuned in to his cues. You may hold a brightly colored object for him to look at. You can read to him, sing songs, massage his body, and describe to him what you are doing.

Feeding, bathing, and changing are wonderful opportunities to engage his attention and to establish regular routines that he can look forward to. Be sensitive to his interest level. When he has had enough, he'll let you know. As we have said, too much stimulation is as bad as too little. Babies need downtime, too. They also need you to "listen" to their behavior, rather than bombard them with "good stimulation."

The most important component of all of these activities is you. Your attention, words, and touch are the paramount aspect of play and stimulation for this period because you are building the trust that your baby will need in the months ahead.

At this point, toys are for everyone's benefit but the baby's. Friends and relatives love to give toys. Parents love them, too. Other than occasionally looking at an object, however, infants do not have much interest in toys the first four weeks. But the supply you are collecting will be well-used in the coming months.

By the end of the first month, your baby may enjoy looking at a mobile with appropriate bold colors or black-and-white geometric designs, circles, and faces. You can easily make your own. Just be sure it is securely attached and out of your baby's reach. Position the mobile where your baby will see it. Babies normally turn their heads to one side or the other, rather than looking straight up. So you should place it to that side, rather than overhead. You may also rotate sides to encourage your baby to look in both directions. Your baby may also look to find the sources of gentle rattles or bells.

A nonbreakable mirror attached securely to the side of the crib is another item that will attract your baby's attention as the month progresses. As with the mobile, the mirror should be positioned so that your baby can see his face. This generally requires tilting the top of the mirror slightly toward him. The mirror can also be alternated between sides of the crib.

SEVEN ESSENTIALS
Activity Examples for First Month

Encourage Exploration

- Become aware of your baby's reflexive actions, including sucking, walking/stepping.
- Concentrate on learning about your baby, especially to read his cues.
- Swaddle for security and warmth.

Mentor in Basic Skills

- Soothe and comfort as needed.
- Observe how your infant responds to sounds.
- Provide soft clothes and blankets and sweet smells.
- Look into your baby's eyes and marvel at her being.

Celebrate Developmental Advances

- Share with others your hopes and dreams for your child.
- Celebrate your own developmental advance for having welcomed a child into your life.

Rehearse and Extend New Skills

- Pay attention to what kind of schedule your baby likes. (Playtime will increase as your baby grows older.)

Protect (and Comfort)

- Support your baby's head when you carry her.
- Have a secure, safe, and quiet place for your baby to sleep.
- Always use car seats.
- Never leave your baby on a changing table alone – never, not even for a second.
- Help brothers and sisters understand their protective role.

Communicate

- Spend as much time with your new baby as you can and accept the help of others who are in your social network. They will feel special in your life if they meet your baby early and can help you and your family.

Guide and Limit

- Take some time for yourself and the rest of your family.

CHAPTER 12

Discovering the World

Two to
Three Months

THIS IS A WONDERFUL TIME IN YOUR BABY'S LIFE — THE BEGINNING OF REAL AWARENESS OF HER ENVIRONMENT. SHE SPENT HER FIRST MONTH ADJUSTING TO LIFE. NOW SHE IS BECOMING ORIENTED AND DIRECTING MORE OF HER ATTENTION TO THE PEOPLE AND THINGS THAT MAKE UP HER WORLD. AS HER MIND, SENSES, AND PHYSICAL SKILLS GROW, SHE IS INCREASINGLY ABLE TO DISCOVER THAT WORLD.

What's in Store

You will see the great physical gains your baby makes as she learns to sit in a propped position, to hold her head up when placed on her stomach, to lift her legs and hold them up, to grasp and feel objects, and to focus on ever-more-distant objects. She will bring her hands together in front of her and clasp them, a precursor for active play with objects. Her formerly clenched fists will have loosened, allowing her to discover her hands and fingers, which she will study intently. These new skills are powerful aids to her orientation and discovery.

As her vision develops, she is fast becoming aware of, and fascinated by, her surroundings and the people who care for her. She will stare at you intently.

Much of her development — especially her emotional, social, cognitive, and language skills — will be less evident or even hidden. Nonetheless, this development is occurring, and your active participation is essential for it to proceed as well as possible.

This is also a rewarding time for you. All the wakeful nights, erratic schedules, constant feeding and changing of the first month are paying off in many ways. Your baby is settling into a more regular routine, developing daytime and nighttime patterns of behavior. She may be sleeping for longer stretches at night. Her alertness increases in both length and quality. And best of all, she is beginning to smile.

Your Baby's Style

Your baby is a unique combination of the preferences and predilections he was born with, plus what he learns and absorbs in daily living. However that combination is achieved, your baby has been from the start, and will always be, one of a kind.

You have already learned much about your baby's rhythms, moods, needs, and likes. In this period, you will see how these shape the way he plays and learns.

Styles of discovery are as varied as every other aspect of babies' lives. Infants differ greatly in their interests and attention spans. Some babies are intensely interested in their surroundings, and can stare at objects for long periods. Others may intently explore objects they can reach and hold. Still others are energetic and athletic, batting, dropping, and throwing everything in their reach. All of these styles are developmentally effective. Each infant is simply discovering his new world in his own way and at his own pace.

As your baby grows, stimulation is increasingly valuable to his continued growth. By playing with him during his lengthening periods of alertness, you can enhance his development on all fronts. The important thing to do is follow your baby's cues. Provide stimulation as long as it holds his attention. When he averts his eyes, loses interest, or becomes fussy, move on to something else. Change to a new activity or let him enjoy some quiet time. (Babies, too, need "personal time.") The challenge for you is to learn what works best for your baby. What works, however, is a moving target, one that will continually shift as he grows.

Your baby will begin to show preferences for a number of things, including favorite sleeping positions, the direction he likes to turn his head while he's lying on his back, and toys or objects he likes to see or hold.

He may show a new or continued sleeping preference. For example, he might like being next to a surface, usually the corner or top of the crib. This has a soothing effect for some babies, perhaps re-creating the closeness of the womb. Most experts suggest letting him do what he likes. The exception is that babies should always sleep on their backs or sides — never on their stomachs — in order to reduce the chances of Sudden Infant Death Syndrome (SIDS).

He may begin to show a preference for turning his head to one side, rather than the other. Over time, this can cause a slight flattening of the head. This condition is not serious and will go away as he begins to sit up and move around for increasingly longer periods. However, you may be able to get your baby to alternate sides by drawing his attention to toys or objects on his non-preferred side. You can also place him at the other end of his crib so that he needs to look the other way to see his room. You can also tip his mattress very slightly toward the nonpreferred side to encourage his gaze in that direction.

Elements of Growth

PHYSICAL GROWTH

Physical coordination and sensory development take big leaps forward in these two months. Both allow babies to make great strides in discovering their environment. They also give you many new ways to enjoy and play with your child.

Movement and Coordination: Physical strength and coordination build rapidly from this stage on. The variety of things your baby enjoys will grow dramatically in this period. Her body control is increasingly voluntary, not just reflexive. She will be intrigued by her hands and feet, aware that they are extensions of her. Her coordination and control progress swiftly. The reflex actions she had at birth will begin to fade. Her once-jerky movements will be replaced with more purposeful, smooth, and efficient actions as she learns to grasp, hold, and explore objects within her reach.

You'll see a lot more arm movements, leg thrusts, and head lifts. Limited, gentle exercise can be a wonderful way to play with your baby, one that will help build both muscle tone and attachment to you.

While such exercise is not necessary to your baby's physical development, freedom to move is. Babies who spend large amounts of time in strollers, high chairs, or infant seats lose valuable opportunities to strengthen their muscles and to develop their coordination. Whenever possible, your baby should be free to move and practice new skills. Since your baby isn't mobile yet, he won't need that much space. A floor mat will do fine.

During this period your baby may learn a number of physical skills, such as using her arms to prop her chest and head up, and supporting some of her weight on her legs when you hold her up. You can encourage all of these movements by turning these skills into games. As she gains new movement skills, be sure to adapt your safety standards to keep pace.

The Senses:

Sight: Your baby's vision improves dramatically during this period in four key areas: color, focus, convergence, and tracking. Color-blind at birth, your baby can now see bold colors. Brightly colored toys, books, and objects will attract his attention now and provide you with a growing array of ways to play with him.

His focus improves greatly. At the beginning of the second month his best range for focus will be eight to fifteen inches. By three months, he will be able to focus on objects several feet away and will turn to smile at you halfway across the room.

During this period, he will also develop the ability to turn both eyes inward (convergence) so that he can track an object that moves toward him. Before this, he would have seen a double image of such an object. Combining focusing and convergence, he will start to perceive objects of different sizes and at different distances, whether they are still or moving.

At about the same time, he will be able to track moving objects smoothly. You can encourage this skill by holding an object about one foot from him and moving it slowly from side to side.

Smell: Babies expand their reactions to various smells in this period, indicating that they differentiate more than before between types and intensities of odors.

Hearing: Your baby's hearing becomes almost fully developed during this period. Hearing paired with his growing cognitive skills enables him to distinguish the sources of sounds and follow them. But just as he prefers your face to other sights, he will prefer your voice over other sounds. When he hears your voice or footsteps, he will turn to watch you and follow you as you move about.

Touch: Touch is an important learning tool for your baby. His growing coordination during this period enables him to start taking advantage of this sense. Now that he can grasp and hold objects, he can explore the way they feel against his hand or cheek. He will increasingly use his hands to explore surfaces and objects. You can encourage him by giving him toys and objects with different surfaces and textures.

Your baby is increasingly able to control his hand and arm movements so that he can bring his hand to his mouth and suck on his fingers or fist. This is a normal and important complement to feeding, and it will be a helpful self-comforting routine as time goes on. He can also bring to his mouth anything he picks up. His mouth will quickly become just as important as his hands in discovering the "feel" of his growing world.

Pacifiers can be helpful, providing they are not overused. The goal is to support your baby's interests and learning, not to suppress them. Pacifiers should not be used to keep a baby quiet and inactive.

Taste: Taste becomes a growing part of exploration as babies begin to mouth everything they touch or pick up. While infants can clearly discriminate between one taste and another, their desire to discover is so strong that even the most objectionable taste won't always discourage them. This preference for discovery will continue for many months. This is why household cleaning products and other dangerous substances must be kept out of your baby's reach. Even the most dreadful taste won't stop a baby from ingesting everything from solvents and detergents to medicines and cosmetics.

COGNITIVE AND LANGUAGE DEVELOPMENT

Your baby's growing awareness of his world is the driving force in this period. His intense focus on you and everything within his range of vision, hearing, and touch build his awareness and collection of memorized images. Each of these images, in turn, creates new neural pathways in the brain, the foundation for the next layer of memory and learning.

As the weeks progress, he will show a growing ability to deal with more than one thing at a time, an important sign of both physical and mental growth. For example, he may be able to stare fixedly at an object and suck on a pacifier at the same time. He can look at and listen intently to an object that makes sounds.

During this period, your baby's language skills also move to the next level. In his first month, his "vocabulary" was limited to crying. Soon he begins to add a variety of other sounds that correspond to different moods and behaviors. He will also increasingly make noises in response to sounds he hears, a big step in interaction.

You can encourage his growing vocabulary of sounds by repeating the noises he makes back to him. Your responses encourage his communication with you and his further experimentation with sound. As you continue to talk, read, and sing to him, repetition helps him learn the sounds of the words he will soon speak.

For this reason, we don't encourage the use of "baby talk." The most effective way to promote language skills is to speak slowly and clearly in short, simple sentences.

How babies discover: The words, sounds, and images that fill your baby's hours fuel the staggering rate of growth in the brain that is a hallmark of the first three years. Just as adult memory can be reinforced by repetition or fade from lack of use, so a baby's brain connections are forged early by what she sees, hears, and does over and over again. Repetition is the key to your baby's learning and central to her development.

New research has shed light on how fast babies' memory skills develop. These findings are in sharp contrast to the beliefs of just a few decades ago, when babies were viewed as having minimal cognitive capacity until well into the first year. We now know that the number of repetitions required to create a memory pattern declines briskly right from birth as memory retention grows stronger.

Therefore, while your baby's memory is limited, repeated reacquaintance with specific sights, sounds, smells, and touches build up her repertory of familiar experiences. Repetition builds memory by forging connections — synapses — between the brain cells. She will use this same repeat-to-remember process all of her life, as she masters her tennis backhand, crams for her Spanish midterms, or learns the names of co-workers at a new job. The infant brain is primed for this explosive growth. That's why the attention and care a baby receives has such a strong impact.

The process is cumulative. As a baby's stored memories grow, they provide an ever-larger foundation for new learning as she moves on to new sights, sounds, reactions, and activities.

By the end of this period, you will begin to see increasing signs of this extraordinary brain development from the routines that you have established. In particular, you will see two signs of her growing short-term memory capability. First, she will get bored with a particular activity or toy after she has learned it. She will then want to move on to something else. Second, you will see signs of her growing recognition of familiar objects and people. For example, if you have promptly responded to her cries in the past, she may quiet just at the sound of your voice or footsteps now.

EMOTIONAL AND SOCIAL GROWTH

Your baby's growing awareness of you, and his attachment to you, are the centerpieces of this period's emotional and social growth. As his alertness and memory develop, so will his interaction with all those who regularly attend to him. You will start to see different patterns of response to each of the central figures in his life. He will become increasingly expressive about what he finds pleasing and displeasing. This is both fun to see and helpful in learning his likes and dislikes.

Trust in you continues to build every time you help your baby. This trust is as important as ever in building the confidence he will need in the coming months to explore and learn as fully as possible. At this stage, your baby is beginning to learn patterns of behavior. Your treatment of him and response to him are the most important of those patterns.

Repetition of your prompt response to his needs not only builds trust, it also begins to provide predictability in his life. Predictability is a new aspect of the trust you want to continue to build. Predictability creates security for your baby, just as it does for you. His confidence that his needs will be met frees him to use his growing abilities to develop and learn. He won't waste energy needlessly on stress and anxiety.

As time goes on, his cries will begin to abate just at the sound of your steps or voice. Even though the need that prompted his cry has not been met yet, he either knows that help is on the way or he is able to divert his attention from his upset to the person who is approaching. Both of these explanations — anticipation of relief and control over where he focuses his attention — are evidence of new levels of learning and awareness. These important learning steps are key to your baby's emotional development, central to his growing relationship with you, and a wonderful acknowledgment of your parenting.

As your baby's cognitive skills grow, your responsiveness starts to have another benefit: He begins to gain a sense — even at this early stage — that his needs are important and that his behavior can have an effect on others. This is a critical achievement in his development, one that will mature over many months and deeply affect his self-image. It will help shape his understanding of his ability to control some aspects of his environment. It is essential for him to see himself as an agent for change which, in turn, is a vital component of self-image for productive adults.

As smiling grows more purposeful, it also becomes more frequent. Babies smile at human faces, sometimes beginning as early as two weeks after birth. But by the third month, most babies have learned to turn on the charm, smiling at anyone and everyone who comes near them.

As your baby begins to distinguish people from one another, he is more likely to reserve his smiles for the most important people in his life. The more these people smile and coo at him, the more he will smile back. However, we know from numerous studies that children whose smiles are not returned will gradually quit smiling. This is yet another example of how valuable your attention is to your baby. He responds to the way others treat him. His socialization starts very early. Even this early in your baby's life, you can have an enormous impact upon his personality by reinforcing desirable behavior.

What Works/What Counts

ROUTINE BEHAVIOR

This is a good time to develop routines that can help your baby continue to build his trust in you and feel secure in his world. Babies love consistency. It is a needed balance to all the new sensations of their expanding world. Routines are a wonderful way to provide both consistency and predictability.

Routines can help calm your baby during the crying bouts normal for this age. Routines can also help you cope with unsettled nights, which are another by-product of the rapid advance in your baby's discovery. All babies go through varying cycles of sleep, including deep and light sleep as well as a semiconscious state. Your baby may well use her semiconscious time to rouse herself to practice whatever new actions she has recently learned. This is no problem for her, but it can keep the rest of the household awake.

Bedtime and naptime routines may involve bathing or reading stories. Some aspects of play can be predictable, as well. Your baby learns that when you move to the rocking chair, she is about to be fed; or that when you put her on the floor mat, you are going to play with her. Such predictability is another type of consistency, one that is comforting to your baby and one that can establish patterns that will make feeding and sleeping easier in the months to come.

This is not a call for rigidity. Change is a part of life. Babies need to learn to respond to variations from routine and expectation. By routines, we are speaking of general patterns. Periodic alterations are not only unavoidable, they are healthy.

In general, however, your baby will never outgrow this new and growing desire for consistency, routine, and predictability. Even as a mature adult, she will not want surprise or uncertainty in areas of life that are important to her — just as you don't. Most babies fuss less, and enjoy life better, the more predictable their daily living routines are.

Activities/Toys

Now that your baby is alert and active, play becomes a more important — not to mention more rewarding — component of every day. You can develop some play routines that you and your baby look forward to. In addition to regular playtime, bathing, feeding, changing, and bedtime are excellent times for toys or songs or books.

Continue to follow your baby's cues. His natural curiosity and enthusiasm will lead him to discoveries that are interesting and enjoyable at every stage. When you follow your baby's lead, he will learn more and develop more quickly. He will also learn that his own interests have merit. By your applause at his accomplishments, he learns early that success is rewarded. And playtime will be fun for you both.

When he loses interest or gets fussy, move to another activity or let him rest. Just like adults, babies need both active and quiet time.

You do not need expensive or "educational" toys to play with your child. Friends and family will no doubt buy all kinds of gifts. But your baby will invariably enjoy basic objects, just as babies have done for countless generations. Balls, blocks, rattles, and containers win out over the elaborate constructions nearly every time. Socks, rags of different fabrics, measuring cups, and the like offer great fun and learning at no cost. Below are a few ideas. More suggestions will be found in the Seven Essentials chart on the following page. As before, these are just "starter" suggestions. Make up your own play ideas. Be inventive.

- Encourage object tracking by moving small objects slowly toward or across in front of your baby. This is a good attention-getter because, at this age, your baby will invariably follow the object. After three months, however, his attention to a moving object will diminish as he becomes less reactive and more proactive in choosing where to focus his attention.

- Mirrors will continue to interest your baby at this stage. Periodically check to be sure the mirror is still positioned correctly to be easily viewed from your baby's newest favorite position, and make sure it is nonbreakable.

- Hold your baby with his feet on your thighs or another surface and allow his legs to support some of his body weight. Gently bounce him while you recite rhymes or sing.

- Use sturdy crib or floor gyms. However, discard them when your baby shows signs of being able to pull up to a sitting position. These toys are not sturdy enough to withstand the weight of this action.

- Mobiles will continue to attract your baby's attention. Change the objects to give your baby variety and to keep up with his improving vision. You can also attach a ribbon from your baby's ankle or wrist to the mobile. He will be delighted with the mobile's reaction to his movements. However, do not leave your baby unattended this way. *Remove the ribbon before you leave.*

- Take your baby out with you when you shop, go to your church or synagogue, or "take" walks. The sounds and sights of many environments are great aids to growth and learning. Involving your baby in your own daily activities gives him variety, as well as wonderful new ways to learn and enjoy your company.

SEVEN ESSENTIALS
Activity Examples for Two to Three Months

CONTINUE ACTIVITIES FROM BEFORE, PLUS

Encourage Exploration

- Help your baby to track small jingle toys by moving them slowly, seven to ten inches from his face.
- Hold her in an upright position and look at posters, pictures, etc., on walls.
- Call his name from different positions.
- Hang mobiles over her crib.

Mentor in Basic Skills

- Place small grasping objects in his hand.
- Comfort her by holding her close and quieting her.
- Smile and talk to him while maintaining eye contact.

Celebrate Developmental Advances

- Smile and comment as she tries to hold up her head.
- Pay attention to his movements while bathing and diapering, and make silly noises or sing to him.

Rehearse and Extend New Skills

- Keenly notice her reactions and temperament and adjust your actions to achieve comfort and joy.

Protect (and Comfort)

- Make sure all toys and rattles are safe.
- Give your home a thorough health and safety inspection and make whatever changes are necessary. (See, for example, *Caring for Your Baby and Child: Birth to Age 5*, from the American Academy of Pediatrics, 1998.)

Communicate

- Read your favorite books out loud while holding him.
- Draw her attention to your face just before feeding by talking to her and smiling.
- Coo and talk to your baby in a face-to-face game in which you take turns.

Guide and Limit

- Keep building your baby's trust by your prompt response to her needs.

CHAPTER 13

Becoming a Social Being

Four to
Six Months

YOUR BABY'S WORLD EXPANDS DRAMATICALLY IN THIS PERIOD. IN THE LAST STAGE, HER ENVIRONMENT EXTENDED ONLY A FEW FEET FROM HER EYES AND INCLUDED ONLY THE PEOPLE AND OBJECTS IN THAT LIMITED RANGE. BUT NOW HER RAPIDLY IMPROVING EYESIGHT ALLOWS HER TO SEE AND TAKE IN A WHOLE ROOM. SHE WILL CONTINUE TO BECOME MORE FOCUSED AND PURPOSEFULLY ATTENTIVE WHEN SHE IS AWAKE.

What's in Store

Along with her increased focus and attention, her growing motor skills give your baby greater ability to explore objects. She can now hold and play with small toys, and she will study them in great detail. She probably will also play with the hands and faces of her parents.

At about four to five months, your baby will take a big leap forward in her socialization. She will smile frequently and begin to laugh and giggle. This is the period in which parents become passionately captivated by their baby because she is such a delight to be around. She is utterly thrilled with life, perhaps more so than she will be at any other time. Everything is a game for her — each new sound, action, and sight. And she is beginning to develop a sense of humor. This is definitely a period for you to enjoy.

Through all these activities, your baby is learning that her actions cause certain reactions from objects, such as the way they sound when banged together and the way they move when batted or dropped. She is also learning that her behavior causes predictable responses in people, especially her parents and other primary caregivers.

As we discussed in detail in Chapter 4, this is the evolution of her understanding of cause and effect — a major step that affects every aspect of her development, especially socialization. It begins as she learns that her repetitive actions cause the same reactions in toys and objects — generating the same noises from rattles, squeeze toys, and the like. She also learns that certain behaviors — cries, smiles, coos — produce predictable responses from people.

What allows this to happen is her increasingly sophisticated cognitive skills. As her short-term memory builds, she can observe the effects of her actions, from the reaction of an object she squeezes to the response from you when she cries. She is learning that she can be an active agent in her world, not just the passive receptor she was just a few weeks earlier.

The collective result of these changes makes this an exciting time for parents. You can see the many facets of your baby's development come together to produce an increasingly active, curious, and intelligent child.

- ❁ She will repeatedly drop objects on the floor, knowing that you will pick them up.
- ❁ When you come into the room, she may vocalize to get you to come and play with her.
- ❁ She will perform repeated actions on her favorite toys to get them to move or sound in the same way.

All of these behaviors, and many more, show elementary memory and planning, along with her growing physical skills and her emerging understanding of object permanence — that an object continues to exist after it disappears from view. The combination of all these skills allows your baby to see herself increasingly as an independent agent in her world, capable of wanting something, remembering how she got that something in the past, and repeating the actions that worked before, so that she will get what she wants again.

As her memory grows, she recalls patterns of actions by people in the games she has played. She will soon learn to initiate those games. Parents who covered and uncovered their faces in peekaboo will soon find their baby covering her face to start another round.

A major aspect of your baby's new cause-and-effect awareness involves her relationships with others. She is becoming a more social being. As part of her growing awareness, she learns that other people react differently to her. She learns to anticipate behavior from those she sees every day. However, she may become warier around strangers and those she does not see regularly because she won't know how they will behave toward her. This stranger anxiety is normal, and will probably increase over the next several months.

Throughout this period, your response to your baby's enthusiasm and to her cries of discomfort continue to work to build her attachment to you. If you keep attending to her cries, she will continue to associate your presence with comfort and care.

In this period of increasing playfulness and activity, your attention is also integral to her enjoyment. If you regularly play with her and show your delight in her pleasure and at her accomplishments, she associates you with joy. Moreover, your positive reactions encourage the joyful disposition she shows at her successes.

Your Baby's Style

As their socialization progresses, most babies become increasingly interested in people. They enjoy the interaction, and love to use their newly acquired physical control, smiles, laughter, and vocalizing skills. However, some babies are quieter and more intent on observing their surroundings. The appearance of another person may distract them from whatever they are doing, and they may become very quiet. This is perfectly normal. Neither pattern by itself, whether active or quiet, says anything about intelligence or future behavior. Once again, the best advice is to acknowledge and enjoy your baby's unique character and respond to him accordingly. In so doing, you give him the strongest foundation to develop all of his natural talents and abilities.

Reactions to unfamiliar people also vary widely among infants. They may be wary around those they don't know well as early as five months, as late as nine months, or never at all. Again, none of these is better as far as your baby's well-being is concerned. Less anxiety on your baby's part does, however, make life easier for you.

Another emerging aspect of socialization deals with favorite objects. Children also behave very differently in this regard, but many begin to show an attachment for a particular toy or blanket during this period. Such objects provide security when parents are not around. This transference of security is important to a child's growing sense of independence.

This object attachment is not a rejection of the parent. Instead, it is a reaffirmation of the bond the baby has established with that parent. Children who are most trusting of their parents' love can most easily make the transference of security to an object.

Finally, with growing muscle strength and coordination, babies begin to move in new ways. From here on there are wide variations in the timing and order of the various movements infants learn. No individual pattern is linked to any aptitude or level of intelligence, and all are normal and healthy. These variations underscore children's ingenuity. Many of your child's early attempts at movement will be downright comical. We encourage you to enjoy them, and not to worry about them.

Elements of Growth

PHYSICAL GROWTH, MOVEMENT, AND COORDINATION

You will see a big leap forward in your child's physical activity during this period. He will learn to sit up unsupported and will master the skill of reaching for objects and transferring them from one hand to the other. These two activities will greatly expand his world, because now he can explore it on his own. In particular, both of these skills help him understand cause and effect.

The simple action of reaching for an object is so basic that we take it for granted and tend to overlook the achievements needed to make it possible. But it serves as a good example of how your baby's many skills are being integrated to allow him to learn at an ever-faster rate.

To reach for an object, your baby has to see the object, direct his hand to it, and grasp it — a complex integration of vision, purpose, eye-hand coordination, and small muscle control. These skills, individually and collectively, are a major achievement that opens the door to a new level of exploration.

These motor skills are complemented by growing eye-ear coordination. Your baby will generally turn to detect the source of even small noises. He will almost certainly look in your direction whenever he hears your voice.

Your baby's growing agility also gives him new vistas for exploration. Beginning in the fourth month, he may be able to turn at least halfway over, freeing him to see more of the room he is in. He may enjoy being held in a standing position, even though he can only support part of his weight. By the sixth month he may be able to roll himself into a near-sitting position. He sits up straighter, a result of the growing strength of his back and abdominal muscles. He is also developing some preliminary locomotion skills as he twists and turns his way around the floor. He may start to creep, using outstretched arms and legs to push his body, belly to the floor, to some new destination. He may also raise himself up on hands and knees and lurch forward. It is common for these early perambulations to be backward. Don't worry; he'll figure out forward soon enough.

From the beginning of this period, your baby is active enough to require closer attention. He can flip off a changing table, squirm to the edge of a sofa and fall, or wrestle himself out of a carrier if he isn't strapped in. It is essential that you keep a close eye and firm hand on him whenever he is above ground level. If you must leave for a moment, put him on the floor.

By the sixth month, your baby's first teeth — the lower central incisors — are likely to appear. Teething tends to make babies irritable. They usually want to bite on anything and everything, increasing their already strong tendency to put everything into their mouths.

The Senses: By this stage in your baby's life, virtually all of his senses are close to those of an adult. The most important change involves vision, which was the least developed sense at birth.

Your baby can now see a full range of colors and light/dark contrasts. He can focus on objects throughout a room. He can perceive depth and distance. He can track objects moving from side to side, toward or away from him.

His new vision is a big factor in the rapid expansion of his curiosity. Now he can see everything in the room, not just the items within a few feet. He has a whole new world to explore. His curiosity and desire to get to everything in sight will be big factors in his compulsion to start moving. Since he can't reach all the objects he can see, he now begins to want to get to them.

COGNITIVE AND LANGUAGE DEVELOPMENT

By the beginning of this period, your baby is starting to make sounds with the saliva in his mouth. He will soon begin to imitate sounds he hears — an essential element of learning language. Then his learning of language really kicks into high gear. This coincides with his burgeoning interest in communicating — by vocalizing, movement, and expression — with anyone who will pay attention. He will be in love with his own voice, cheerfully babbling away, uttering long strings of repetitive syllables, regardless of whether anyone is approving or even listening.

He learns to make sounds by watching the mouths and faces of those who talk to him. Therefore, the first letters he sounds out are those he sees most readily because they are made with the lips — p, b, and m. Mama, baba, and dada are typical first words. The next group of consonants are t, d, and n — those formed with the gums and teeth.

Your baby may show signs that he is beginning to understand the meaning of a few words. Repetition and reinforcement are the basis for learning language. So if his father shows up or smiles whenever the baby says "dada," he will commit this to memory that much sooner. Your responses to your baby's utterances are central to helping him develop language skills, beginning with sounds, then words, and, ultimately, grammar and syntax. Naming objects, describing tasks, and rhyming phrases are all excellent ways to promote such learning.

His cognizance of the physical world continues to grow more sophisticated. Pointing, reaching, and grabbing for objects are the primary signs of this new growth. If he drops an object, he will look over to see where it went. He can recognize an object even if he sees only a part of it. He may even remove obstacles to an object he wants. But he is still some months away from a full understanding of object permanence.

One of the most delightful developments of this stage is your baby's budding sense of humor. He will begin to giggle and laugh at the unexpected. If you make funny faces, put on a clown nose, intentionally use a wrong word in a familiar song, make strange sounds or do anything that departs from what he is used to seeing and hearing, he will be delighted.

The onset of this kind of humor signals an important cognitive achievement. It means your baby has learned to understand order and to distinguish things that change, such as the clothes you wear, from things that stay the same, such as your face. This achievement involves increasingly sophisticated memory and sorting. Your baby will find humor in anything that marks a change from what he is accustomed to seeing. This pattern of humor will last all his life, albeit in increasingly subtle forms. The delight adults find in everything from puns to pratfalls has its origins in what your baby is now learning.

EMOTIONAL AND SOCIAL GROWTH

By the beginning of this period, your baby may start to cry to get you to come and play with her. Having remembered how you behaved in the past — responding to her cries — she will begin to see if she can cause you to behave that way again. Such a cry is not a call for food or comfort. It is a call for your company.

This behavior may begin in the fourth month but typically doesn't become regular and purposeful until the end of the sixth month or even later.

It takes your child to a new dimension of socialization, one where your response is extremely important in helping her to develop into a happy, independent child who is a delight to have around. But its onset indicates that you have succeeded in building your baby's trust. She believes you will come when she calls you. This is a wonderful achievement for both of you.

Clearly, your responses are central to the "worldview" she is developing, as well as to her sense of independence and worth. These are invaluable foundations for her later development. While it doesn't show yet, her growing sense that she matters and that her needs will be met are vital ingredients to the confidence and eagerness with which she will explore and learn as her cognitive and motor skills grow.

The play and attentiveness your baby gets from you at this stage is central to building her confidence and reinforcing her enthusiasm for discovery. It may sound strange to be talking about self-confidence in a baby this young, but we now know that mental development is rapid and advanced at this stage. However, because your baby can't talk, much of this development remains hidden, and the results don't show up for several months.

Rest assured that your baby is absorbing your love and your reactions like a sponge. Care, attention, and enthusiasm make deep and lasting impressions at this stage, as do neglect, impatience, and apathy.

Every story you read to your baby, every game you play with her, every expression of delight at her accomplishments are "money in the bank" for her future as a happy toddler, an inquisitive student, and, believe it or not, a well-adjusted teenager. The love and support you give your baby now will be repaid many times over.

Virtually every child development specialist agrees that the socialization your baby learns in the next eighteen months will have a profound effect on the attitudes and behavior she will exhibit for years to come, and on her personality.

This is the period when a number of aspects of your baby's growth emerge and converge:

❀ **She will become highly imitative of your actions, moods, and behaviors.**

❀ **Your actions will make especially deep impressions on her.**

❀ **She will increasingly seek your approval.**

All of these factors work together to make it possible for you to shape your child's emerging personality in positive ways. Your baby's desire for your approval is a powerful ally for you to use in channeling her behavior into happy, confident, secure patterns.

During this highly impressionable time, what you teach your baby and what she learns every day from watching you will shape her disposition. If you are happy and playful with her, you help her to be cheerful, cooperative, and a pleasure to have around.

Daily Routine

In this period, your baby's daily routines, such as sleeping and eating, become integral to his growth in new ways. Sleeping patterns may be affected by his daily activity to a greater degree than before. And eating will become a new avenue for learning.

SLEEPING

The intervals of your baby's daily routine continue to lengthen. He is awake and alert for increasing amounts of time. Three to four naps daily is the norm. However, his increased energy and activity are likely causing him to wake up during the night, often more than once. He's excited — you're not.

Routines: This is the time to develop routines for putting him back down. The simpler the routine, the better.

Tiring: Playtime and feeding before bedtime may tire your baby out enough so he sleeps with fewer interruptions. However, some babies get excited with play, which can make it harder for them to get to sleep. You need to adjust to your baby's style.

Security toy: Make sure his favorite security toy or blanket is available in his crib.

TEETHING

Drooling begins often by the fourth month — a precursor of the arrival of his bottom teeth, which usually come in around the sixth month. The arrival of teeth may pose occasional challenges to nursing mothers when their infants bite. This is invariably accidental, but still unwelcome. Move your baby gently away or give him something else to chew.

DIET AND FEEDING HABITS

Solid foods (meaning semi-liquid strained foods, whether homemade or store-bought) should not be introduced before four months at the earliest and preferably not until the sixth month. Earlier, a baby's digestive system isn't up to handling complex foods. Partial digestion, indigestion, and food allergies are among the more common unfortunate reactions when solid foods are introduced too early.

Once solid foods are part of your baby's diet, feeding tends to get messier, but for good reason. Food and mealtime become important to his learning. Meals become increasingly social, with your baby's interest centered on the person feeding him. He is also increasingly squirmy, and it takes little to distract him.

Then, too, the food itself offers a whole new world of objects to explore and discover. Eating is also great for practicing newfound dexterity. Playing with food is a fabulous new game, one that can teach your baby a great deal. But be prepared for the mess. He will smear food on his face, in his hair, on his clothes, and on you. He may blow food out of his mouth. He may toss food on the floor. Spilling will become the norm.

Newspapers on the floor under the high chair and a hefty supply of washable bibs are good damage-control devices. A washable smock (for the baby and/or you) can be a good back-up for especially creative and energetic youngsters when you are dressed and can't change before you go out.

Self-feeding is an important step for your baby, both physically and emotionally. Since mealtime is a social time for the family, his "grown up" participation is another element of his growing independence and confidence. When he starts reaching for the spoon when you feed him, give him a spoon to play with. Show him how to use it (it will take some practice before he gets much food into his mouth). Give him pieces of solid food — fruit, vegetable, or bread — to hold and play with while you feed him.

By the end of this period, many babies are delighted to be using a cup, even if their attempts at drinking are less than successful. Encourage slow, sip-at-a-time learning. For most of his liquid intake, your baby will drink either from the breast or a bottle.

Patience should be your guiding principle during this learn-to-eat stage. Feed your baby when he is hungry and pace the meal to his interests. Allow at least some game-playing. Attempts to control him are likely to frustrate him and make him more obstinate about eating in the coming months. Table manners can best be taught in later months, when your baby's control and understanding are both up to the task.

VISITS, TRAVEL, EVENINGS OUT, BABYSITTERS

This is a good time to visit friends and relatives for a variety of reasons. Your baby is especially sociable and largely good-tempered at this stage. She is still lightweight and easy to transport. The motion of cars, trains, and planes puts most babies to sleep. Her lack of mobility keeps her under physical control.

Nonetheless, babies are creatures of habit and routine. Breaking these routines may require some adjustment, both to the place you visit and when you return home. Your baby may fuss and abandon the sleeping and feeding routines that she had acquired prior to the trip. If you are visiting groups of relatives, there is bound to be a good deal of excitement at her arrival. But if you can keep things relatively calm and maintain as many of your baby's bed, bath, feeding, and play routines as possible, the adjustments will be easier.

Some babies show little or no separation anxiety. Others do, and this behavior may grow more pronounced as the months go on. It may also wax and wane several times over the coming months.

Going out for an evening and leaving your baby with a sitter will not have caused problems before this stage and can usually still be finessed. But because your baby is becoming more sensitive to strangers, including a regular sitter, even weekly outings may begin to cause some problems because your baby won't remember this person. Things may go more smoothly if you introduce the sitter to your baby each time by allowing your baby to see you and the sitter together for a short period. Many babies will have no problem with this, especially if the sitter comes often and your baby gets to know him or her. However, others will kick up a fuss.

Activities/Toys

At this stage, your baby will most enjoy the activities and toys that encourage her understanding of cause and effect, that allow her to explore new objects, and that help her to gain new physical skills.

- Give your baby toys to hold, feel, mouth, bang, and throw, such as balls, rattles, spoons, plastic or metal cups, blocks, plastic keys. Make sure none is less than one and one-half inches in diameter to prevent swallowing or choking.

- Encourage play with toys that show cause and effect, such as busy boxes, pop-up toys, squeeze or push-pull noisemakers, music boxes.

- Continue to use mirrors (nonbreakable) attached to the crib, angled to be easily seen from your baby's favorite resting position.

- Play old and new games, such as peekaboo, I'm coming to get you, pat-a-cake, tickling games, counting fingers and toes, touching and naming parts of the face and head.

- Encourage your baby's sense of humor. Do things that your baby will recognize as unusual — making funny faces and unusual noises; inserting strange or silly words into favorite songs and rhymes.

- Help your baby to stand; bounce her on your knee or lap in time to rhymes or songs.

NOT RECOMMENDED

We counsel parents against the use of walkers. Our guide in this matter is the American Academy of Pediatrics, which has taken a position against the use of walkers because they can be dangerous. As many as 25,000 accidents a year are caused by walkers. The most serious involve falls down stairways.

The only advantage to a walker is that babies generally love them. Given the disadvantages of this item, it's better never to use one in the first place. Your baby won't miss what he never had.

SEVEN ESSENTIALS
Activity Examples for Four to Six Months

CONTINUE ACTIVITIES FROM BEFORE, PLUS

Encourage Exploration

* Gently pull your baby to a sitting position while on your lap and support her in the position for several seconds.
* Prop him with pillows so he can see his hands more easily.
* Let your baby see herself in a mirror as she makes face and body movements.
* Show pictures of household objects and talk about them.

Mentor in Basic Skills

* Help him to reach for, grasp, and hold small objects of various shapes and textures.
* Play beautiful music and find simple tunes that she likes.
* Aid in first efforts to crawl.
* Hide small toys under a cloth or pillow and help your baby find them.

Celebrate Developmental Advances

* Pick up your baby and smile and hug when he does something cute like cooing or making his mobile move by jiggling his crib.

Rehearse and Extend New Skills

* Hold and drop objects that she can track visually and adjust your actions to achieve comfort and joy.
* Play repetitive peekaboo games.
* Introduce variations on turn-taking games to maintain longer spans of attention.

Protect (and Comfort)

* Smile and talk as you comfort mild distress.
* Use a rocking chair to comfort your child. Find a rhythm that you both enjoy by trying variations.

Communicate

* Coo and babble back and forth as if you were having a conversation — vary rhythm, intonation, pitch, speed.
* Read books together and point to pictures and describe them.
* Imitate your baby's gestures and sounds.
* Look at pictures and laugh and giggle together.

Guide and Limit

* Enjoy your baby. Do things that make your baby as happy as possible as often as possible.

CHAPTER 14

Thinking and Experimenting

Seven to
Ten Months

THIS PERIOD BRINGS TWO WONDERFUL DEVELOPMENTS IN A BABY'S LIFE — MOBILITY AND A NEW LEVEL OF SOCIAL SKILLS. BOTH WILL DRAMATICALLY ALTER FAMILY LIFE AND THE ROUTINES OF CAREGIVING. THEY ARE ALSO DELIGHTFUL TO WATCH AND BE PROUD OF.

What's in Store

Mobility marks a sea change in your baby's development and in your life. He can now get to things that for months he could only stare at. He has additional means to satisfy his burgeoning curiosity — a critical element in both his mental and physical development. He has an expanding world in which to test his growing understanding of cause and effect. He is also becoming adept at learning which of his actions stimulate which responses from you. Growth in all three areas — mobility, curiosity, and cause and effect — make parenting more challenging and demanding, but also even more fascinating than in the preceding three months.

This is a time when your child's energy is highly visible. Parents marvel at the boundless energy of their newly mobile babies who are bent on exploring most anything in reach. They may also be worn out as they try to keep up and watch over their new explorer.

Social interaction also grows at this age as babies become increasingly aware of, and responsive to, adults. They may show greater differentiation and stronger preferences as well. They may fuss and refuse to go readily into the arms of a stranger. They also clearly want you and your attention.

At this stage, babies begin to imitate more, copying what others do. You will see this in hand-clapping, putting things in and taking them out of another object (like a box or a shoe), and turning handles or pressing keys to make toys do something special. Such imitation will continue for many months, and even years. Vocal and verbal imitation provides for lots of fun games, as do social gestures and silly movements.

Your Baby's Style

Your baby's uniqueness will become more evident in more facets of her skills and interests during this period. There are many ways to learn the physical skills of this period, and the ways she meets the social and emotional challenges are just as varied. No longer content to observe the goings-on, she will increasingly want to be included in what's happening.

As babies grow older, variations in temperament, preference, and style become more pronounced. Different activity levels are especially noticeable. Some babies are very quiet and cerebral. Others rocket around like cartoon action figures. What they focus on at any given point can vary just as widely as their energy levels.

While we try to give as broad a description as possible of each phase and development, no book can do justice to the infinite variety of children. We cannot emphasize too strongly the importance of allowing your child to be herself, the unique individual that she is.

Competitive parenting isn't new. It is natural for parents to be proud of everything their baby does ahead of "average." Unfortunately, it is also increasingly common for them to worry if something doesn't happen "on time." This is especially true of the locomotive achievements common to this period.

However, unless there is a serious developmental problem, such averages may do more harm than good. The less you are concerned with them, the better. Rest assured, your baby will learn to crawl, stand, walk, and run unless there is a serious medical problem. You don't need to do anything special in order for her to learn these skills. But do enjoy the antics and marvel at the inventiveness and determination your baby will show to master them.

On the other hand, healthy social and emotional development cannot and will not happen by itself. It requires your direct intervention. A great deal of the foundation for this development is occurring at this stage. Your attention to it will be rewarded many times over.

Elements of Growth

PHYSICAL GROWTH, MOVEMENT, AND COORDINATION

Mobility may be the most dramatic physical change of this period, but it is far from the only one. Big advances occur in overall body strength and coordination as well. These gains allow your baby to use mobility with increasing efficiency. For example, he can bring himself to a sitting position and remain there for longer periods. This allows him to play intently and to concentrate on a new discovery without interruption. With his hands and arms no longer needed for support, they are free for play and learning. His coordination and control improve, allowing him to bend and stoop as he learns to stand.

As he enters his seventh month, he is probably mastering creeping and may well start to crawl. The top-down path of body development governs the way most babies learn to crawl. Their hands and arms work the problem a good while before their legs cooperate in the effort. As a result, your baby may initially pull or push himself along the ground using only his arms. He might use one arm and one leg. He could also scoot across the floor in a sitting position. The possibilities are endless.

As the legs finally gear up to help, they may do so in a lopsided or lurching fashion. It takes time for leg action to become smooth and controlled. In the meantime, the variations your baby may try can be amazingly inventive, not to mention entertaining for you to watch. Through all this, be sure to appreciate your baby's determination and drive. He is likely to plop on his face repeatedly as he masters crawling. Falling down is a regular part of walking. He may be tense until he masters his latest skill. But nothing is going to stop him from learning to move!

The timing and order of the stages of locomotion vary widely. Some babies skip creeping or crawling and move right to standing and learning to walk.

Others learn to stand between creeping and crawling. Some start climbing as early as eight months. If this happens, be sure to set up stair guards immediately.

Babies learn things in spurts. It is not uncommon for babies to focus for some period on working with their hands, rather than their legs. Then they may reverse their attention and concentrate on the next locomotion option.

Babies learn how to stand, only to have to figure out how to sit down again. Eventually your baby will learn to stick his bottom out and just plop down. You can help teach him this. But until he masters sitting on his own, he is very likely to fall, usually backward. Therefore, it is a good idea to cushion areas where he might fall and get hurt.

After your baby can crawl and stand, there is a period of consolidation in which he perfects these skills before moving on to walking.

Whatever your baby does on the locomotion front, it will all work in the end. He will walk just fine. The point is to marvel at his discovery process. Don't push him to do something before he is ready. You can encourage him. For example, you can periodically place a favorite toy just out of reach. But don't overdo this. Let him learn on his own, but keep an eye on him and be ready to rescue him from frustration.

Fine motor skills improve greatly during this period, too. Your baby's thumb now fully opposes his fingers, increasing his dexterity and control. It's a rare moment that a baby in this stage is without a toy in one or both hands. He is gaining enough control to be able to do such things as stack blocks. He knows in advance whether he needs one or two hands to lift an object, and how big his grasp will have to be to pick it up.

Your baby will have joy written all over his face when he first manages to creep and crawl, and as he figures out different, more efficient ways to move about. The physical skills are essential, but just as important are his growing sense of accomplishment and his understanding that persistence pays off, both in his achievements and in your praise.

Your baby's new mobility will entail a flurry of activity — countless phone calls to friends and relatives, numerous photos, a whole new set of games you can play with him, and a mad scramble to baby-proof your home. In the midst of all this frenzy, it is easy to overlook the emotional impact of what your baby has achieved. For weeks he struggled to attain a goal, never giving up, and he finally achieved what he set out to do.

This is how the programming for early development creates patterns of success, and expectations that perseverance will be rewarded. These are patterns you want to continue to encourage. When this vital support is lacking, the signs are unmistakable. Dr. T. Berry Brazelton has found that infants as young as nine months old show clearly by their behavior whether they expect to succeed or fail at a new task and whether they expect praise for their accomplishments. The attention you have lavished on your baby since birth has been instrumental in reinforcing his growing sense of accomplishment. Your continued encouragement and praise are vital to his confidence and to showing him that determination is rewarded.

Safety first: As your baby starts to move, safety becomes a paramount concern. This is the time to recheck every precaution you have put into place.

While basic safety precautions should be taken throughout your home, there should be some areas that are both safe and damage-proof, places where your baby can explore without danger to herself or the contents of the room.

The goal is to provide some safe spaces where she is free to do what she wants and where you won't have to stop her at every turn to protect her or the furnishings. Her own bedroom or playroom and the family room or den can be good choices. She should have the freedom to explore and learn where her enthusiasm and curiosity don't have to be quashed at every turn, and you should be free from worry.

Distraction is your best bet for guiding your baby to safety. If she does something that could cause harm, gently remove her (or the dangerous object) and turn her interest to something else. Give her a different toy or game, or take her to a different room. Her short-term memory is improving, but it isn't good enough yet for her to remember what she wasn't supposed to touch or do once she has been distracted. This is why distraction works well at this age. However, as her memory improves, you will need bigger distractions for this approach to remain effective.

Listed below are some commonly recommended safety practices for this period. For a comprehensive list for various ages up to five we recommend the discussion by the American Academy of Pediatrics in their book, *Caring for Your Baby and Child: Birth to Age 5.*

- Put plastic covers on all unused electrical outlets.

- Move electrical cords out of your baby's reach and path.

- Install safety locks on doors, cabinets, and drawers.

- Cushion sharp corners of furniture against falls.

- Keep floors clear of small items such as buttons, pen tops, paper clips, batteries, toys with small parts, and objects less than one and one-half inches in size.

- Keep cords of window blinds and telephones out of reach.

- Never leave your child near a bucket of water, even if there's only half an inch of water in it.

- Store valuable books and objects out of baby's reach.

- Block off stairs with gates.

- Beware of foods a baby can choke on, such as grapes, nuts, and hot dogs.

COGNITIVE AND LANGUAGE DEVELOPMENT

Mental development continues at a fast pace during this stage. Your baby is quickly building his store of associations and memories, which are increasingly complex. He is learning to anticipate actions, such as the evening arrival of a parent home from work. He is also learning to put small actions together to enable him to achieve something he wants. For example, he will move pillows to create a platform he can climb on to reach something. His understanding of the physical world grows as he learns more about quantity and spatial relationships.

There are many different styles of learning. Some babies work peacefully on multiple possible solutions to achieve a desired end. Others are driven to exhaust one possibility before moving on to another. Whatever your baby's style, it is important that you encourage and mentor, but not be overly helpful. Your baby needs to learn how to learn.

Infants whose exploration has been patiently tolerated and encouraged are likely to be more inquisitive and better able to entertain themselves for longer periods as they try out new activities with abandon. Infants whose parents follow consistent routines are likely to adapt more quickly to the changes of growing up.

On the other hand, infants with overprotective and anxious parents may have more limited curiosity and may seek parental assistance at every turn. If you have been too quick to assist, your baby may already be acting helpless, expecting you to do things you know he is capable of doing on his own. If so, be a bit less attentive. He will fuss at first. But at this age, he will quickly adapt and start picking up his toys, asking for things by name, and learning the skills he needs.

Constructive, positive learning and behavior patterns are good signs that you are "reading" your child correctly and responding and encouraging him appropriately. If, on the other hand, you're not pleased with some of his behaviors, you might reassess the situation: What could be the cause? What adjustments might improve things? What could you do to encourage your baby to solve his own problems, to entertain himself?

There are no quick or easy answers. That's why parenting is such a challenge. Each baby's evolving personality is a product of many factors including the temperament and tendencies he was born with, his daily experiences, and the people around him. Constructively channeling a child's temperament and interests is a one-of-a-kind job for each child. We can give you common practices, typical patterns, and usual results. But none of these will apply precisely to your baby. You will need to adapt each strategy.

Repetition continues to be key to learning. However, you will notice that fewer repetitions are needed before your baby has absorbed a new idea, skill, or concept and wants to move on to something else. He will get bored much more quickly, and will require more sophisticated stimulation to hold his attention.

From the beginning of this period, you will see signs that your baby is beginning to learn the meanings of a few words. From this point on, comprehension will surge ahead. However, it will probably be some time before he starts actually saying words, since speech can lag behind understanding by weeks or even months. However, his babbling is growing to multisyllable vocalizations. This is usually the last step before your baby begins to say real words.

EMOTIONAL AND SOCIAL GROWTH

This is an enormously important period of emotional and social growth for your baby. This growth springs from two primary sources — delight in her physical achievements and her rapidly growing awareness of what she can control or cause to happen. The impact of her growing understanding of cause and effect is so dramatic at this stage that it shapes or affects virtually everything she will think or do.

A major component of your baby's development has been to discover an ever-growing array of things she can cause to happen. From her physical achievements and experiments with language to the way she plays with toys, she is learning that she can initiate the activities and cause responses she likes. She has also learned that her cries bring your presence, attention, and pleasure or relief from discomfort.

Her physical growth may be slower than in previous months. But the rate at which she is putting concepts together and understanding how the physical world works is dramatic, indeed. Add to this her new mobility, and you can see how and why she starts to exert some independence. You can also see how your efforts to continue to build her trust will be more complicated, but just as essential.

You will see the rewards of all your care and affection to date in the confidence with which she moves into her rapidly expanding world. You will also find new ways to encourage your baby, to show your love, and to provide a safe and secure base for this new phase of her growth.

Your baby's attachment to you continues to grow throughout this period. As his cognitive and physical skills increase, he needs more stimulation to keep him engaged. Consider the following:

Routines: Your baby will enjoy routines. You should continue the nighttime, mealtime, naptime, and other routines you have already established. But you can add new ones appropriate to his expanding skills. For example, as he begins to crawl, you can set up floor-play routines, times for the doorway jumper (complete with music), etc.

New challenges: Provide a variety of toys and materials that engage his interest. If his attention is occupied, he won't need to call for you to relieve his boredom when you are otherwise occupied. Change the assortment of toys to hold his interest and to eliminate items he no longer plays with.

Encourage independence: Help him use his emerging independence to solve his own problems. The routines you use to quiet him should be ones he can emulate on his own and without your assistance. This is especially true when it comes to sleeping and self-comfort.

It may help to periodically stand back and look at your child's overall development. Identify what's changed recently, what's working, what needs a different tack, and where some extra encouragement could help. As you see the strides to independence your baby is making, you will find it easier to understand her actions and her mood swings. You will also see why some parenting techniques are likely to be more effective than others in managing the changes.

If your baby has not shown signs of stranger or separation anxiety before, you may see signs during this period, perhaps even when you leave her presence for just a few moments. While this anxiety can be frustrating, remember that babies who exhibit separation anxiety have loving relationships with the adults they don't want to leave. Separation anxiety is a good sign that your baby has grown to trust you.

There is disagreement in research circles as to the cause of this anxiety. Most theories point to your baby's growing attachment to you, a need for greater security in the face of all the new challenges and opportunities she faces, or a growing dislike for change in important aspects of her life. It may also be that her newfound mobility comes with the scary realization that she can be separated from you — hence the clingy behavior. Patient acceptance of her anxiety will actually speed an end to this behavior and accelerate her independence.

It may also not be as bad as your baby makes it seem. You may face heart-rending cries as you leave your baby with a sitter, only to have the sitter report that the baby quickly recovered after you left and had a fine time that evening.

The solution to both separation and stranger anxiety is gradual introduction. Let her see you together with the babysitter before you depart. Let her see you talk to grandparents and friends before they attempt to approach her. The visual "bridge" of seeing you with a new person is, in most cases, enough to eliminate or at least greatly reduce stress for your baby.

If your baby is still distressed when you leave, it is important that you be honest and straightforward. Trickery is no solution to separation anxiety or any other behavior you would just as soon avoid. When she protests your leaving, promise you will come back. When you return, remind her that you kept your promise. She may not be happy about your next departure, but over time she will come to trust that you do return as you said you would.

Your baby may also become anxious with activities or sounds that have previously not bothered her at all. The sound of the garbage disposal or vacuum, or bathing or being put in her high chair may set her off. Something may remind her of a previous experience that frightened her, such as a big dog that barked loudly. Gentle reassurance that all is well will get her through the upsets.

Daily Routine

SLEEPING

Babies vary widely in their sleeping habits, but most sleep less during the second half of the first year. Thirteen hours per day is average, but the range can be from nine to eighteen hours.

As he becomes more wakeful at night, the sleep routines you have set up should continue to assure that he and you get the sleep you need. However, you may need to alter your approach and remind him of his self-comforting routines, or make up new ones. Keep his favorite toy in his crib. Teach him to sit back down after he has pulled himself up to a standing position in the crib.

If your baby has trouble falling asleep, don't pick him up. Just talk to him, pat him, and leave. If sleeplessness becomes a major problem, you may have to let him cry it out. But this should be a last resort and done rarely.

It is not uncommon for babies at this age to bang their heads repeatedly against the crib or to hug their legs under their stomachs and jounce rhythmically. These behaviors often occur when the baby has been put down for sleeping. No one has discovered for sure why babies do this. A common theory is that these practices relieve built-up tension. Both practices will cease in time, sooner if you just ride it out and don't try to get your baby to stop. Making the bedtime or naptime routine extra-soothing may help ease any tension.

The head-bangers won't injure themselves if you use well-padded crib bumpers. You can protect the crib and the wall from the jouncing by installing temporary padding over the exposed areas.

DIET AND FEEDING HABITS

Mealtimes continue to be messy. Smearing food into his mouth with the palm of his hand is the usual approach for the seventh month. But patience and latitude with the mess will speed his learning and increase the amount of food he eats. Just cut the pieces into small bites, and give him a few at a time.

His ability with a cup is limited, but will improve with practice. You can minimize spills by putting only small amounts of liquid in the cup. You can also let him practice with a cup in the bath tub, where his spills won't matter.

As play with food increases, many mothers become concerned that their baby is not eating enough. Babies invariably eat enough unless they are ill, but fearful mothers may attempt to assure adequate intake.

One common approach is to pressure or trick a baby into eating. This usually fails. At best it can be counterproductive, leading to clenched jaws and absolute refusal. At worst, it can lead to lifelong patterns of eating disorders.

Another common approach is to give the baby only what he wants, no matter how unnutritious his desires. This, too, backfires. It is fine to respect reasonable preferences. But good nutrition should be your guide.

Activities/Toys

Toys and activities most appropriate to this period are those that will encourage your baby to practice her mobility and explore her environment. A few suggestions:

- Create inviting spaces for your baby to crawl to, in, and around.
- Have her crawl to you as you sit in one place or move around the room.
- Place objects on the floor, such as pillows or soft blocks, that she can crawl to, over, and around.
- Put different textured materials on the floor for her to crawl on.
- Help your baby to learn to stand by supporting her, bouncing her gently to rhymes or songs, and showing her how to sit back down.
- Toys and games that present challenges for your baby to master are excellent for helping her to explore how things work in her world. These types of toys and games also build her self-image and her sense of autonomy.
- Provide a good assortment of classic toys that allow ample opportunity for imaginative play, accomplishment, and problem-solving. Good toys include balls, blocks, nesting toys, big beads, busy boxes, rattles, big puzzles, and toys that can be pulled apart and put back together.
- Put a collection of small objects (make sure they are at least one and one-half inches in diameter, to avoid a choking hazard) into a container for your baby to empty and then refill.
- Allocate a cupboard or drawer for him to empty and refill.
- Give him an assortment of pairs of objects to match, such as gloves, mittens, and socks.
- Give him old magazines to look at and tear.
- Continue to provide mirrors (nonbreakable) for your baby to watch himself in as he develops his motor skills.

SEVEN ESSENTIALS
Activity Examples for Seven to Ten Months

CONTINUE ACTIVITIES FROM BEFORE, PLUS

Encourage Exploration

- Change mobiles to vary visual stimulation.
- Point to objects near and far and describe them.
- Let your child see you hide objects and help her find them. Make a big deal when she finds them.

Mentor in Basic Skills

- Play finger or hand games in which your movements are contingent on something that your baby does, like smile, talk, or move.
- Dance around the room with your baby in rhythm to music.
- Give your child objects to drop, which you pick up and give back.

Celebrate Developmental Advances

- Let him find objects hidden in your hand and act surprised and delighted when he does so. Introduce variations on this game and in your responses.
- Show pride in your infant's crawling.

Rehearse and Extend New Skills

- Elaborate on simple contingency games like peekaboo.
- Play the same games in different parts of the house or with slight variation in the same place. Attend to your baby's reactions and cues.

Protect (and Comfort)

- Prepare your house for a crawling infant. Look at each room from the perspective of a crawling infant and baby-proof the premises.

Communicate

- Kiss and hug your child in front of a mirror and observe his reaction.
- Describe your child's actions out loud: "You are drinking from a *cup*," "Now we are going to *swing*," "We are getting *dressed*."
- Label body parts – here is your *hand, foot, nose, leg*, etc.
- Match pictures to objects.

Guide and Limit

- Introduce some finger food and help him feed himself.
- Support her attempts to walk.

CHAPTER 15

Independence

Eleven to
Fourteen Months

WALKING AND TALKING! THIS IS A TIME OF MAJOR ACHIEVE-
MENTS FOR YOUR BABY. EVERY FACET OF HER GROWTH
SURGES DURING THIS PERIOD, PROPELLED BY A GROWING MASTERY OF
MOVEMENT AND RAPID SOCIALIZATION. SHE CAN PHYSICALLY GET TO A
MUCH WIDER WORLD. MOREOVER, SHE COMPREHENDS THAT DOMAIN,
ESPECIALLY THE PEOPLE IN IT, TO A FAR GREATER DEGREE THAN SHE DID
JUST A FEW SHORT MONTHS AGO.

What's in Store

Look for your child to become more self-aware, to understand more fully the
separateness of other people, and to exhibit a wider range of emotions.
Imitation will figure prominently in her learning as she carefully matches or
copies increasingly complex sequences of movements. She may show signs of
affection for dolls or stuffed animals. This is a wonderful acknowledgment of
your parenting because she is copying your loving behavior.

How you respond to her initiatives is increasingly important to her,
and you will be guiding her behavior more visibly than before. This is a good
time for her to begin to understand what is expected of her. You can also support her emerging independence that comes as she begins to walk and talk.

At the outset of this period, your baby is probably taking steps while
holding onto you or furniture. She may move on all fours and show a lot of
variety in how she moves about. By eleven months, some babies have already
taken their first steps. Others may wait for two to three months before they
begin to walk. How much help they want or need with locomotion will likely
change. Some babies become perpetual motion machines at this stage, intoler-
ant of restraint. Others are less eager to cruise around.

Language is the other phenomenal achievement of this period. Each baby does it "my way." A few babies will have said a word or two already, but most will have their first real words appear soon after their first birthday. These will be simple, and you will become an expert translator over the coming months as her vocabulary quickly grows.

With all these new skills, your baby will increasingly want to do things on her own. As this independent spirit and determination grow over the next years, so will your baby's need for your reassurance that keeps her protected and connected. This back-and-forth between wanting to be "on my own" and wanting help from you can be confusing for parents, especially when the timing seems off. Just when parents want their children to do something on their own, they may want their parents to take over, and vice versa. Don't rush the process. Just go with the flow.

These new achievements all build on the developments you have seen to date. As the first birthday nears, you will undoubtedly look back with delight and amazement at how remarkably accomplished and capable your baby has become in just twelve months.

Your Baby's Style

Your child's early temperamental style will show itself in some new ways in this period. Some children are more active, while others are quieter. Some are adventuresome and fearless, while others are more cautious. Some are shy, and others are gregarious.

No matter what style your baby started with in this period, you may be in for some surprises. Some infants try out new styles (which is not limited to any age period). You may also see changes in how much sleep your child needs; how often and how long he naps; how willing he is to try new foods; and how much he likes different tastes, smells, and textures. These changes will then influence how you act.

Surprisingly, behavioral qualities in one area do not necessarily extend to others. For example, a child may be absolutely fearless in physical movement, but unwilling to eat any new food.

Parents always notice and appreciate characteristics such as sweetness, charm, inquisitiveness, persistence, cooperativeness, and social responsiveness. Provide as many opportunities as you can for the best sides of your child's personality to shine.

As babies begin to do and learn more things simultaneously, the order and variety of ways they learn grows, too. As we have said before, parents often focus on physical achievements because new motor skills dramatically change household life. Then, too, comparison with other children is virtually unavoidable on such big items as talking and walking. We hope, however, that the information on all facets of your child's development will help you to appreciate all your baby's wonderful achievements throughout this period.

Elements of Growth

PHYSICAL GROWTH, MOVEMENT, AND COORDINATION

As the end of the first year approaches, physical growth will begin to slow down. Babies will gain about five or six pounds during all of the second year, compared to the average of sixteen pounds they gained in the first year. But there will be big changes in your baby's body type. The typical chubby, rounded shape of his first year will become leaner and more muscular from practicing new motor skills. However, appetite often decreases in this period because your baby's slower weight gain doesn't require the calorie input of the first year's growth spurt.

This period may start out relatively quietly as your baby gathers strength for the big leap to walking. Quieter babies, on the other hand, may show a real burst of energy and activity. However, variations in the timing and progressions of locomotion vary tremendously. Your baby may start this period by mastering cruising. However, many babies skip this step altogether, content to crawl until they are ready to walk.

While most babies in this country learn to walk between twelve and fourteen months of age, the range of "normal" is very broad, partly because active crawling is such a viable alternative. Unfortunately, our competitive culture can lead parents to unnecessary worry or pointless pride if their baby's learning timetable varies from the average. Our advice is to relax.

Learning and perfecting physical skills require both physical practice and mental development. Pressuring your baby to master any new skill will likely cause more frustration than success. While you can certainly encourage your baby's first steps, don't overdo it. It is much better to let each child develop at nature's own pace. Remember that experimentation is integral to learning anything.

Moreover, extensive research shows *no important correlation between the age at which a baby walks and the level of any skill later in life*. Babies who walk later than average usually are just honing other skills — fine motor, language, cognitive — and they will get around to walking when they have mastered their current learning project, whatever it is.

Your baby will also become increasingly adept at understanding space and depth. By now spatial coordination is improved to the point that he knows how far away objects are. Finding hidden objects behind your back or under a cup is now just "babies'" play.

As your child's arms and hands strengthen, his dexterity improves, giving him greater skill with everything from toys to spoons to large crayons or pens. During this period he will gain a great deal of skill in manipulating multiple objects, able to do more than one thing at a time. Most children begin to prefer one hand (and foot) over the other around this time. However, it is too early to tell reliably whether a child will be right- or left-handed later on. You may see your baby use one hand to hold objects, and the other for more active manipulation. But he may switch.

COGNITIVE AND LANGUAGE DEVELOPMENT

As this period progresses, your baby will spend more time with physical objects and play. She will study objects intently for long periods of time. She will explore objects by touching and mouthing and perhaps by banging, dropping, and throwing. Whenever possible, she will figure out how to do something with objects, and then proudly show you what she has learned. Simple puzzles may begin to hold your child's attention. Try them and see.

Imitation is an important learning tool. It is also a clear sign of your baby's growing cognitive skills. Imitation signals both observation and memory capabilities. Babies are keenly observant, and they will copy as much of your behavior as possible, good and bad. Throughout this period, imitation will become increasingly sophisticated and complex, moving from simple actions, such as wiping a table with a cloth, to complex patterns, such as hiding a familiar object and waiting for you to look for it.

Imitation is also vital to learning language. By the first birthday, most babies understand a large and fast-growing number of words, even though they may say very little. They can point to many objects by name, including body parts, toys, and household items. They also understand phrases.

The lag in speech is physiological. The neck, jaw, larynx, vocal chords, and all the muscles of the mouth, throat, chest, and abdomen need to develop before clear speech is possible. Also, new teeth initially get in the way of word production. Finally, the brain needs to develop to coordinate interaction among all these body parts before a child can make a desired sound or sequence of sounds.

In this period, many babies are beginning to say words. However, some babies don't start talking until later. Babies reared in bilingual homes often don't start speaking until around their second birthday, at which time they will talk in both languages. During the previous quiet months they have been absorbing both tongues, learning to distinguish one from the other and learning the vocabulary and pronunciation of each.

Although babies who are precocious in their early language development tend to be quite capable in terms of their cognitive skills, there are many very bright children who are not the earliest or best talkers. A year from now, almost all children will be talking lots, and they will have traveled quite a few different developmental pathways in their month-by-month progress in terms of their vocabulary size, their use of syntax, the number of words they chain together, and their comprehension of what others say.

There are many good ways to support and promote your baby's language development. Continue to speak in ways that are easy to understand. Use simple sentences, and be clear and distinct in what you say. But be sure to include the rich and diverse components of language. Continue to read books, and talk together about the names of things and their qualities, the actions between objects or people, what happens when someone does something (or does not). Ask your child to tell you what is happening, or to point things out to you. Recite rhymes. The words themselves provide pleasure, and they teach new skills and provide practice with pronunciation and the lilt of language. This is a great time to act out poems and stories. Avoid excessive baby talk. Don't worry if your baby uses baby talk.

EMOTIONAL AND SOCIAL GROWTH

Social contact continues to be important in this period. But some babies may seem less interested, in part because they can do so many more things on their own. Most babies are remarkably friendly at this time, and openly show their love and affection for their helpful caregivers. Their behavior often says "thank you" long before they can pronounce the words or know exactly when these words should be said.

Emotional development shows a big leap at this stage. Your infant will seem much more tuned in to the feelings of others, and will show a range of emotions reflecting greater intellectual understanding of the world and what is happening. As babies acquire a more sophisticated awareness of cause-and-effect relationships, there are more things that contribute to feelings of joy, interest, disappointment, surprise, excitement, sadness, frustration, and confusion.

Throughout this period, your baby will become increasingly aware of the self, that he is a distinct being capable of operating independently in the world. In the next stage, from fifteen to eighteen months, a more mature version of selfhood emerges.

Around eleven months, two important developments occur. First, your infant will be able to understand "no" or "no-no" and simple prohibitions. Second, he will begin to test some of the limits you set. When you are watching, he may reach for an object or approach an area that is off-limits. This is a way of learning and checking out his understanding.

As we stressed earlier in this chapter, it is important that parents and other caregivers continue to set good examples and show appreciation for your child's good behavior. You should also be patiently guiding behavior to assure safety. The more skillfully and faster a baby moves, the more can be explored, discovered, learned. And the more your child might encounter trouble. Safety continues to be a paramount concern.

Along with your baby's growing social awareness comes a widening array of behaviors that indicate self-initiative. Many of these will be delightful, such as imitation, role playing, and asking for assistance. As your child begins to be more assertive, you will discover you have both more and less "free time." On the one hand, he will find more ways to entertain himself. However, this calls for increased monitoring on your part.

You need to keep tabs on your child and be available. Try to find ways to do so that allow you to do things you enjoy at the same time. However, there will be times when your child really wants your undivided attention for longer periods of time than before, sometimes for activities that you find tiring or boring. Your child is gaining in his ability to keep his attention focused on one activity for longer periods of time. This is a vital skill for learning difficult tasks that take time to learn and practice.

This is the age when many books discuss the onset of temper tantrums. We are not aware of any systematic studies on temper tantrums in infants, surprising as that may seem. Undoubtedly many children have them. But not all do. The best advice we know, based on studies about promoting positive behavior, is to try to minimize the circumstances that elicit extreme or out-of-control behavior. If such behavior occurs frequently, analyze the conditions that precede it and test out ways to shorten or end the tantrum. In any event, a calm response on your part is best.

What Limits Should You Set?

The line between constructive and unnecessary limits is hard to define, especially for first-time parents. We recommend that you set the minimum number of limits needed to ensure safety and a reasonably smooth-running household. This is easy for us to suggest. But what does it mean in practice?

You really have to trust your own judgment and to observe your baby closely. She is still absorbing an enormous amount of information every day. So you want to set needed limits, but avoid unnecessary ones. Limits at every turn will be counterproductive. You also have to balance your baby's legitimate need to explore with the requirements of others in the household. This is a matter of trial and error. It is a learning experience for every parent.

Safety is paramount. There can be no compromise on limits that ensure a child's safety. Safety limits are mostly common sense.

As this period progresses, most babies become increasingly adventurous when it comes to heights. Your baby may have started to climb as early as eight months, and will most certainly be doing so during this period. Babies start by climbing heights of about eight or nine inches, the height of a typical stair step. So stair guards are essential as soon as you find your baby learning this skill.

Babies learn to climb up before they figure out how to get back down. You will doubtless hear cries when your baby wants to get back down, but can't manage this feat on her own.

In the next stage of climbing, babies master greater heights. When it comes to more height (or depth), babies don't completely trust their vision as to how far away something is. But they get bolder by the day on the climbing challenges they will tackle. Safety dictates that you recheck the rooms your baby uses to make sure climbing opportunities don't pose any danger. You should periodically update the baby-proofing of your home as your baby's mobility and reach take her to previously unattainable areas and objects.

Behavioral limits, on the other hand, are more subjective. Babies' behavior patterns at this stage are fascinating. Much of their learning is based on repetition, which is central to building memory and mental skills.

At this age your child will enjoy more complex activities and will repeat them over and over. They will repeat words and actions over and over. They are delighted to have you read the same story again and again. They will endlessly bang the same toy, open and close the same kitchen cabinet door, turn the stereo volume control, play the same tune on one of their toys — all to the point of distraction for many adults.

Setting limits on such behavior poses two problems. First, much behavior that may be annoying to adults is valuable to a child's learning. You don't want to stifle this growth. Second, attempts at limiting such behavior are difficult to maintain on a consistent basis because you will invariably be more patient on some days than others. Your baby, however, won't understand why you permit something one day, but not the next.

When you are near the point of exasperation, remind yourself how important this behavior is to your child's learning. This is the most valuable and practical advice we can give. Just visualize your child's brain growing as she replays that same nursery rhyme on a music box for the hundredth time, because that is just what's happening.

Another common problem for first-time parents is their baby's reactions when limits are enforced. The hurt look and cries of an infant whose plans are thwarted invariably make new parents feel guilty. As you become more experienced, you will appreciate that some negative response is a normal part of growing up for every child. In time, you'll gain confidence in the way you are managing this important process because you will see the good results your efforts are producing.

Maintaining limits: The trust you have built with your baby in the preceding year will be invaluable in maintaining limits. Moreover, consistency in maintaining limits will continue to build that trust.

Choose simple rules, ones your child can readily understand. Simple rules are not only easy to follow, they teach your child that there are such things as rules. If limits are too complicated, your child may not understand them. Moreover, he may miss the point that limits exist.

At each stage, understand and respect what your child can and cannot understand. His language skills are building. He can understand reasons for some limits, such as "hot" or "hurt." But it will be a while before he grasps concepts such as the monetary value or ownership of objects.

To be effective, limits must be consistently applied. Ideally all caregivers would adhere to the same limits, and apply them as regularly as possible. If you apply some limits consistently but others only sporadically, your baby will just be confused.

You should not have to repeat a verbal warning more than once to get compliance. If your baby persists, you need to intervene to stop the unacceptable activity. Do so firmly but gently. Babies at this age want your approval, and they want to please you. Calm and mild disapproval will reinforce the idea that limits, and your child's adherence to them, are required.

Babies are unbelievably determined and single-minded when it comes to exploration. This is an essential element of their drive to learn. Even though they know an area or object is off-limits, they may break the rules repeatedly because something has caught their attention and they want to touch, hold, smell, and learn about it. However, your baby may also be testing the limits you have set. When babies test limits, they want and need those limits to be maintained.

Just saying "no" and drawing your baby away from an "off-limits" object or activity may not break her concentration and determination. You will have more success if you redirect her attention to something else — a different toy or activity. Humor can help with the transition.

As the complexity of your child's activity grows, so will the scope and volume of his play. He used to be happy taking one box out of another. Now he wants to take everything out of an entire cupboard or even pull the whole drawer out of the chest. If this causes problems for you, try to find constructive ways to channel these activities in ways that don't limit their learning potential. Give your baby a special cupboard or drawer that's his to empty and refill. Babies love to dump things out. If he's dumping all his toys on the floor, make a game of putting them back, such as singing as you do it, or chanting a rhyme.

ENCOURAGING INDEPENDENCE

Besides setting and maintaining limits, you also want to encourage your baby's independence during this period. To do this you want to encourage imitation and exploration. Unfortunately, efficiency is often a casualty in this process. Daily routines will require extra time as your baby learns to do more on her own and wants to join in almost everything you and your family do.

She will openly ask for your help during this period. Your responses are important in shaping her willingness to turn to you for aid and information in the future. So you want to be responsive. But you should also allow time and opportunities for her to discover things independently.

You should continue to be available for your infant's requests, but you don't need to drop everything all the time. If your child is repeatedly left to handle problems that are beyond her capability, she can become discouraged. On the other hand, if you intrude too much or try to fix everything for her, you may inhibit her development, and she may become passive.

You can encourage independence with your praise. Your baby is especially eager at this stage to win your approval. Show your enthusiasm and offer praise when your child succeeds. For the most part, ignore mistakes and errors. Notice how much your approval means to your child.

Daily Routine

Lots of babies seem kind of messy at this stage, whether playing, feeding, bathing, or exploring. However, your patience with the mess will be a great help to learning.

Bedtime routines should be fairly settled for most families by now. Sleep continues to be important for your baby to be at his best when he is awake. As he learns to walk, be sure his sleeping environment is safe, should he wake up and want to cruise around.

Eating for some babies may seem more sporadic. Parents are often alarmed as food intake drops even as their baby becomes increasingly active physically. Such alarm is unfounded. At this stage, a baby's physical development is geared much more to greater control and much less to gain in size. Watch what your child eats over a three- to five-day period, and things will look a lot better. Try to avoid making mealtimes too rigid in terms of what you expect your infant to consume.

By about one year, babies are mostly able to get food into their mouths, but you'll be there to ensure food is the right size and a safe temperature.

Activities/Toys

The range of games, toys, and activities that will interest your baby mushrooms during this stage. He is developing many new skills that are fun to practice and perfect. Activities that give him a sense of self-initiative and accomplishment will be high on the list of favorites. As he builds independent skills, your praise and applause will work wonders. Some favorite activities include the following:

- Word books and naming games to build vocabulary
- Puzzles, stacking rings, and building blocks to teach spatial relationships, sorting, and ordering
- Boxes and containers to empty and refill with objects
- Simple discovery games that encourage learning
- Chasing and hiding games
- Balls and games with balls
- Push-and-pull toys, especially those that make noise
- Toys that encourage make-believe, such as dolls, puppets, play telephones, and child-sized household items, such as brooms, mops, and kitchen sets
- Beginning at about twelve months, your baby may be able to hold a crayon and scribble. Demonstrate very simple things to do – a line, a big dot – so your child can try it. Markers with scents or that sparkle or glow in the dark can be fun, too. But just creating lines is plenty fascinating for babies.

SEVEN ESSENTIALS
Activity Examples for Eleven to Fourteen Months

CONTINUE ACTIVITIES FROM BEFORE, PLUS

Encourage Exploration

- Help "introduce" your baby to other adults and children in a friendly manner. Be a model and let your child see that you enjoy exploring yourself.
- Help him to push boxes and toys.
- Play together with water, ice, sand, soap, blocks, or mirrors, and talk about the sensations.

Mentor in Basic Skills

- Use familiar objects (two alike and one unlike) and play same/different games.
- Scribble with crayons and big sheets of paper.
- Introduce simple yes-or-no questions, yours/mine distinctions, push/pull, and other "opposites" concepts.

Celebrate Developmental Advances

- Show pride and joy in your child's accomplishments and let her hear you comment about her behavior positively to other adults.
- Clap.
- Sing or dance a special way.

Rehearse and Extend New Skills

- Make towers of two or three blocks and knock them down.
- Let him name objects and pictures of objects. Give lots of practice and variety.

Protect (and Comfort)

- Toddler-proof your house. See *Caring for Your Baby and Young Child: Birth to Age 5* from the American Academy of Pediatrics.
- Examine your child's total environment, not just your home.

Communicate

- Ask her to point to nearby objects.
- Play "position" word games: up–down, in–out, over–under.
- Ask him to point to, or name parts of, pictures.

Guide and Limit

- Help two young children to play in the same space, to notice one another, to touch, etc. (They may or may not actually play together.) Provide plenty of toys and monitor their behavior and comment on what each is doing.
- Praise good behavior.

CHAPTER 16

Self-Competence

*Fifteen to
Eighteen Months*

FIFTEEN MONTHS MARKS THE BEGINNING OF TODDLERHOOD, A STAGE THAT WILL LAST UNTIL MIDWAY THROUGH YOUR CHILD'S THIRD YEAR. THE WORD REFERS TO YOUR BABY'S MOBILITY — HE IS NOW TODDLING ALL OVER THE PLACE.

What's in Store

Even more important and interesting than your child's mobility is the person who is emerging from all the growth and newly learned skills and behaviors. His concept of self takes a big leap forward during this exciting stage. He begins to understand himself more fully as a separate being. He becomes more sophisticated in his awareness of how other people respond to him and how he can cause predictable responses from different people.

He will work vigorously to consolidate all of his learning and his newly acquired physical skills. Naturally, he wants to test all of these abilities, just as he has practiced everything else he has learned. You will see whole new patterns of behavior emerge as a result.

Autonomy: He will want to do more things by himself, and he will try to exert more control over events, things, and people.

Negativism: One way children this age sometimes try to express their independence is defiance. They can refuse to do what parents ask. They typically test limits. "No!" may become an important word, especially at mealtime if pushed to eat when they don't want to.

Imitation: He will increasingly copy and mimic adult behavior and actions, a wonderful way for him to learn and delightful for you to see.

Affection: He will initiate affectionate behavior — smiles, hugs, kisses.

These social developments are only one aspect of the dynamic growth of this period. Your child will also show big strides in language, intelligence, inquisitiveness, and socialization. Using all of these skills, he will increasingly want to take the lead and do things on his own. He is becoming more self-reliant and self-sufficient, a big step forward.

Language: Your child's language skills surge ahead, and his understanding of words will accelerate dramatically. By the end of this period, he will be learning many new words every day. He is also likely to start speaking words and phrases. Even if his speaking begins later (not at all uncommon, especially for children in multilingual homes), he is understanding more and more of your conversation. Once he begins to communicate, he has a new tool to use to challenge your authority. But you also have a new means to maintain it.

Intelligence: Your child will begin to make more complex associations between objects, actions, and behavior. He will also start to show preliminary problem-solving abilities, a big leap forward from his earlier trial-and-error approach to challenges.

Inquisitiveness: Your child's attention to objects will focus less on what they look and feel like and increasingly on what they do, what they can be made to do, how they work, and how they can be manipulated.

Socialization: Your child is getting ever more adept at understanding what kind of behavior on his part produces which reactions by others. He is also enjoying the attention he receives. He continues to want your approval. This gives you golden opportunities to encourage the behaviors and traits that will stand him in good stead all of his life — a sunny disposition, cooperativeness, affection, respect, curiosity, and a will to succeed. This is a great time to start teaching manners — "please," "thank you," and the early stage of waiting one's turn.

For the most part, this period is truly enjoyable for parents, especially those who have consistently provided the love and guidance their child needed in the preceding months. Children fortunate enough to have had this kind of care will spend more of their time in this period on enjoyable and productive pursuits.

Your baby's rapid gains and integration of achievements are wonderfully entertaining. His every success will prompt a big grin and a delighted "See!" for you to applaud. His personality is taking shape and becoming more evident every day. All this adds up to a major new phase of self-awareness and competence.

Your Baby's Style

At this age, your child is reaching a whole new level of personhood. Her understanding of the world and her active participation in all aspects of family life reach new levels of sophistication and complexity. This is a time to celebrate everyone's achievements, including yours as a parent.

Language soars in this period. Your child will add prepositions and words about location: in, on, under, high, low. She may begin to put two words together, possibly even three. All your hours of turn-taking games, such as pat-a-cake and peekaboo now have big payoffs. These games laid the foundation for the back-and-forth of genuine conversation. Even more important, they set the stage for a new level of your child's social sophistication using language as the medium.

This period also marks the onset of abstraction. Your child is beginning to be able to think conceptually, to transcend the here and now in her own thoughts. She will still be concerned with objects and people. But she can now think about them in new and increasingly sophisticated ways. She is coming to see that they have attributes beyond their own physical properties. She will study how objects are different from each other and how they are alike.

Finally, the most important milestone: By the end of this period, your child will have developed a sense of self. For the first time she will understand herself as a separate, independent person.

This is a period of wonderful growth for your baby with many new ways for you to enjoy each and every unfolding talent and ability she displays.

Elements of Growth

PHYSICAL GROWTH, MOVEMENT, AND COORDINATION

As walking is mastered, your baby's newest project will be climbing. This is an exciting new challenge for her, but one that needs careful supervision to assure safety, both indoors and out. Her desire to imitate may lead her to scary new territory, such as the top of a slide, from which she will want to be rescued. Fearless youngsters may attempt feats beyond their skills. If they become hurt or frightened, they may shy away from repeat encounters for months. The challenge for parents during this phase is to allow their baby's skills to develop safely.

Toddlers of this age are extremely sensitive and receptive to fine detail. You can encourage your child's sensory capabilities by pointing out details and asking her to point details out to you in items that involve virtually all of the senses, especially sight and sound.

COGNITIVE AND LANGUAGE DEVELOPMENT

You will see big gains in your child's memory in this period. Not only can she remember increasing sequences of actions and events, but she is also developing the ability to mix and match those memory bits into more complex actions. For example, exploration of objects, combined with imitation, moves learning to a more purposeful level. Where a baby previously was content to bang items, she will now increasingly imitate her parents in using them. She will use a brush to brush her hair, use a spoon to stir the imaginary contents of a bowl, and so forth. Moreover, she no longer has to rely on haphazard trial and error, since she is beginning to think through, in advance, what she must do to achieve her goal.

Your child will add many more words to her spoken vocabulary throughout this period, and her learning rate will grow rapidly. She may show that she understands an increasing number of words, even if she says little or nothing.

It is not uncommon for children, including highly intelligent ones, to delay speaking until well into their second year. If your child speaks less than the norm, you should not be concerned as long as you have ruled out any physiological cause for the delay. Even a slight hearing impairment can slow the development of language. So, too, can prenatal stress on brain development caused by drug or alcohol abuse.

However, it is more common for children of this age to begin to use words to describe or ask for things, and to state what they want. You can encourage your child's vocabulary by naming objects, playing word games, using short sentences, and reading.

It takes longer, however, before children begin to combine words into sentences. Children can learn many words before they start constructing sentences. They may memorize and say short phrases. However, they will not initially be able to recombine the words of that phrase into different phrases. They have learned the phrase as essentially just a longer word.

EMOTIONAL AND SOCIAL GROWTH

The care your baby receives from all caregivers is especially important during this phase and through his second birthday. This period is as important as any in shaping everything from his enthusiasm to good behavior. Socially acceptable behavior and self-control require patience and teaching on your part. Children will not learn these essential skills on their own.

It is easier to teach good behavior and self-control now than at any other time in a child's life. This is the prime time to firm up the social contract you have with him. There are two factors that make this period so ideal for getting your child off on the right foot: imitation and desire for approval.

Imitation: Your baby is as attentive to you now as he will ever be. Imitation is a driving force in his learning. He will copy your moves, mimic your expressions, and follow your actions. Therefore, he is especially impressionable and susceptible to learning and copying what you do. Telling him what to do isn't enough. He needs to see you following your own advice and instructions.

He will pick up everything, from saying "please" and "thank you" to waiting his turn, from smiling when people are nice or helpful to showing affection. If the general disposition in your home is warm and sunny, it will be reflected in your child's attitudes and behaviors as well.

Desire for Approval: He is also increasingly aware of, and enjoying, all the attention he can attract. He is becoming more discriminating between the different responses he can cause. Therefore, your responses should encourage the traits that will be most enjoyable for everyone and most useful to your child as he grows up.

- **Positive reinforcement:** By your smiles, hugs, and approval when your child learns something new and behaves the way you want, you send powerful signals to keep him doing more of the same. This kind of positive teaching is every bit as important as consistently maintaining limits when your child misbehaves.

- **Physical behavior:** Babies will experiment at great length to see what kind of reaction they can get. They will poke, prod, tickle, hit, hug, and kiss people. Fathers tend to be more accepting of hits and pokes, which they may see as humorous. However, because babies of this age are so impressionable, we believe parents should use the opportunity to encourage the best behavior.

- **Performance:** Most children enjoy performing for others at this stage because it's fun, and they like the applause. Within reason, this is a wonderful way to build your child's self-worth and outgoing style.

Independence: Using her new abilities to move, communicate, and explore, your child will increasingly want to exert her independence and to do things herself. Whenever possible, let her do as many things as her skills allow. Her ambition will often exceed her dexterity, and her efforts will often be slow. But your encouragement will provide a great boost to her confidence, and with practice, her efforts will speed up.

Her independence can cause problems when she insists on doing something she is unable to do. A variation on this involves choices. Toddlers love to have choices, but they can have great difficulty actually making choices. Independent activity and choices are important to a child's growing sense of self and accomplishment. But they shouldn't be allowed to thwart limits, important routines, or the needs of others.

There will doubtless be difficulties with some situations. Keeping the event as uncharged as possible is more likely to lead to an easier resolution than if parents allow a prolonged conflict to go on, or if they make a big fuss.

Sometimes it's good to let a child have his way. Children need to win occasionally. However, on important matters, especially where safety is concerned, firm resolution is needed. Otherwise children quickly sense that their negativity can be used in a manipulative way.

If you have already established boundaries and found ways to consistently maintain them, coping with negativism will be a logical progression from what you have already put in place. A few ideas:

- When your baby yells "No!" you can turn this into a silly game. Start saying "Yes!" and then switch to saying "No!" so your baby begins to say "Yes!"

- If your baby struggles when you're trying to get him dressed, take a few minutes to play. Or drape the item of clothing over your head. When he's in a better mood, continue dressing him.

- If you're planning to take your child somewhere, tell her at least ten minutes in advance: "We're going to go to the grocery store in ten minutes." Then tell her when five minutes are up, then three, then two. When it's time to go, she'll be more ready to drop what she's doing and come along.

Negativism: A key element of an infant's growing sense of self is a nascent understanding of individuality and power. Negativism is one way children test these attributes. Beginning around the thirteenth or fourteenth month, your child may begin to try the three variations of negativism: not wanting to do what you want, doing what you don't want, and being very choosy about some things.

All babies go through this stage to one degree or another. But if you are consistent in maintaining the limits you have set, in praising your child's achievements, and reinforcing her desirable behaviors, she will emerge from her negativism in about six months, secure in her understanding that you mean what you say and of her place in the household. This is the first, best, and easiest shot you will have to achieve these important ends. If you succeed, everyone wins. It is well worth the strain on your patience to do so.

Behavior Modification: Behavior reinforcement techniques will be needed throughout this period. Now that your baby's language skills are developing, as is her willfulness, you will need to do more than just change her focus to get her to behave. If she is defiant or acts objectionably, you must be ready with an effective response that all caregivers agree on and use consistently. At the same time, when she obeys, you need new ways to praise and encourage her.

At this stage, reasoning doesn't work well with children. Their socialization isn't mature enough for them to behave rationally. Their behavior is still impulsive. Simple explanations can be useful: "No, hot," "No, sharp." But involved descriptions of adverse consequences to come just won't register. It will take lots of experience before a child understands that he can benefit from not acting on impulse.

Strategies and Tactics: As stated earlier, we recommend that parents avoid spanking, hitting, and other forms of corporal punishment, for two reasons. First, such punishment teaches that violence is an acceptable way to settle differences. Second, because there are other approaches that are nonviolent and are far more effective.

Short-term separation from you can be an effective deterrent. Children want you in their sight and presence nearly all the time. When your child misbehaves, set up a doorway gate to the room you are in and put him on the other side of it. There is no physical force or fear involved, but he will be very unhappy, even with ten or fifteen seconds of this modest separation. If needed, increase the length of the separation.

Temper Tantrums: Your child may explode occasionally into temper tantrums. Your response should be calm and firm. You can either ignore the episode or move your child to a different location. If the tantrum is caused by frustration, your child will stop on his own when he is finished. If the tantrum is designed to get his way, your child will learn that this tactic won't work. The same calm firmness should be used to confront anger and aggression.

Praise and Reward: The flip side of punishment is reward. You want to encourage good behavior at every turn. Your smiles, hugs, kisses, and cheers whenever your child is especially kind or affectionate or helpful are just as important to shaping his behavior as is maintaining limits. Socialization skills, such as consideration of others, must be taught. These are essential building blocks in the foundation of your child's development. If that foundation is strong at this point, your child will be able to devote her energies to growth and learning, not to backtracking and correction. For parents anxious to give their children every advantage, few are greater than this.

Daily Routine

Bedtime: Established routines for bathing, bedtime, and meals will be helpful in minimizing negativity that is typical of this period. It may be useful to modify these routines within reason to accommodate your child's desires. This allows him an important element of choice, but still keeps the regularity of the routine working to your benefit.

If these routines have not been established before, they will be harder to set up now. However, it will be worth the effort to do so. Otherwise, daily activities can become regular battlegrounds.

Meals: Food-obsessed as Americans are, most parents worry about their children's eating habits all during this second year. As we have said in earlier chapters, eating will become a problem only if the parents fret and fuss. Children who are allowed to eat at their own pace and choose what they want from a wholesome selection will do just fine. When parents get anxious and try to cajole or force children to eat, however, the result is heightened tension, greater obstinacy, and even long-term poor eating habits or disorders.

This is a good time, however, to begin to introduce new foods. The variety you offer can help interest your toddler in eating a healthy meal. Introduce new foods slowly. By being careful about how and when your child tries new foods, you can develop his sense of adventure about food. You can make games to make food discovery fun and interesting ("What does this taste like?"

"What food is this?") But the guiding principle should be to avoid making a big to-do about eating.

Imitation: During this period your toddler will use imitation to copy a number of actions that help him become more self-sufficient. For example, he will learn to undress and dress himself — in that order. Don't be alarmed if he suddenly shows up in the living room with no clothes on. He will also become more adept at eating and washing.

Activities/Toys

Toys and activities for this period should encourage your toddler's quest for independence. They should allow him to imitate grown-up activities, to figure things out on his own, or to solve or complete some action. You should also provide play and access to equipment that allows him to practice his walking, climbing, and balancing skills. Pillows, climbing blocks, balls, indoor gyms, and playground equipment geared to toddler size are important for physical development. Perennial favorites and good toys include the following:

- All activities should be designed so that your child is consistently a winner. Children at this age are easily discouraged by loss. They are too immature to play competitive games in which there are winners and losers (unless, of course, they always win).

- Toys should be sturdy enough to withstand normal rough handling. There is no point in buying toys that will break.

- Toddler gym sets for inside the home and outdoors are widely available.

- Blowing is a new skill for this period. Blow bubbles, blow out candles, blow bubbles through a straw into a beverage.

- Expect your baby to become increasingly attracted to things you use — "grown-up" items, such as your keys, handbag, pens, comb, and brush, etc.

- Play games that include getting, hiding, retrieving objects.

- Play make-believe games and use fantasy toys, including soft dolls and puppets. These should not have attached eyes or ornamentation that could be torn off.

- Encourage your child to participate in reading, singing, rhymes, clapping hands, etc.

- Provide safe riding toys.

- Play with music and rhythm toys, including instruments and music boxes. Music tapes are also favorites at this period. There is a wide variety beyond "children's" tapes. Your baby may be fascinated with anything from folk to rock to country and classical. Your baby may like the original version, or music that has been adapted for young children. Remember that children learn by imitation. Be prepared to listen to whatever selection you provide over and over.

- Provide peg boards and toy work benches.

- Encourage scribbling and drawing.

SEVEN ESSENTIALS
Activity Examples for Fifteen to Eighteen Months

CONTINUE ACTIVITIES FROM BEFORE, PLUS

Encourage Exploration

- Push your child in safe swings, ride down slides together, ride on wheeled toys.
- Play with dough, clay, and other textures; smell different odors, play in the yard or park.
- Let him see you hide objects and then ask him to find them.

Mentor in Basic Skills

- Play a game of naming familiar people.
- Encourage her to use a spoon.
- Introduce words for feelings.

Celebrate Developmental Advances

- Praise him for beginning to help with routine care: removing socks, brushing hair, washing hands.
- Comment on and smile when she pushes, pulls, or throws toys appropriately.
- Pick him up and say, "Wonderful! You did it!"

Rehearse and Extend New Skills

- Read to your child frequently. Find out which books she likes and repeat them often.
- When you read, follow your child's interest and use the book as a prop for social interaction rather than as something to be read cover-to-cover in each sitting.

Protect (and Comfort)

- Emphasize health and safety routines.
- Provide prompt comfort for the bumps and falls that invariably occur.
- Pay attention to your child's playmates, particularly in childcare arrangements.

Communicate

- Respond to implied simple word utterances. For example, ask, "Do you want the ball?" in response to her "ball."
- Show how words and gestures go together: up – down; come here – no.
- Introduce concepts like table, chair, bird, and give different examples.

Guide and Limit

- Demonstrate and encourage affection and courtesy – "please" and "thank you," hugs, smiles.
- Show new ways to be helpful – picking up toys and clothing.

Looking Ahead

❧

AS THIS BOOK ENDS, YOU HAVE A HIGHLY COMPETENT, CURIOUS, AND ACTIVELY ENGAGED eighteen-month-old child, a remarkable developmental achievement when you think back to the first week of life. Your acquired wisdom and skill as a parent have undoubtedly progressed just as phenomenally.

We want to underscore the practical usefulness of the Seven Essentials and their scientific foundations to your child's continuing development well into the next several years. As far as we know, there are no entirely new ways in which children learn in these coming years. Rather, there continues to be a mix of both steady progression and intermittent leaps in developmental achievements.

Your increasingly capable family member will need new kinds of limits at this time, and will be ready for greater mental and social challenges. Provide these with love, enjoyment, and patience as a stable context for your relationship. Remember that as serious a responsibility as parenting is, it is also a source of great pleasure. If you ignore the fun side of the parenting equation, we think you will miss a great deal, as will your child.

Social and emotional development depend on many factors, including genuine happiness, interest, and natural give-and-take. You may be more likely to get bogged down, constrained, irritable, or worried if you are not enjoying parenthood. When things seem rushed, out of hand, disorganized, or overwhelming, take time to review, plan, and talk with those you love and trust about how to make things better.

Make sure you are getting enough rest, nutrition, love, exercise, and "whatever." The world's best parents whom we know are those who remain open, actively engaged in learning about both parenting and the world at large and who have discovered ways to feel fulfilled. You will be an inspiration to your children if you are this kind of parent!

Please continue to practice the Seven Essentials. By now, they should have become a way of life — a pattern of interacting almost without thinking. By eighteen months, there will be a much wider array of toys, games, equipment, computers, music, and social opportunities for your child. Take advantage of them. But don't forget that real learning and social-emotional development can occur without spending lots of money or doing anything that feels like "pushing" or "forcing" your child.

Your child's individuality, now quite apparent to you and others, will continue to flourish when the good elements are strengthened and given an opportunity to be expressed. Celebrate your child's differences from and similarities to you. Find ways to continue to explore, mentor, celebrate, practice, talk, protect, and set appropriate limits. Keep on finding ways to record your child's specialness, from photo albums or video documentaries to simple storytelling and displaying works of "genius" on your walls. You are helping to create memories, as well as strong skills, in another human being, and you are building an outstanding foundation for your child's entire life. ✿

With Best Wishes for a
Fulfilling Family Life!
Sharon & Craig

Professional References
and Acknowledgments

❦

BOOKS

Several key references parents may find valuable for more detailed information about infant research, early experience, and brain development include:

> Hetherington, E. M., & Parke, R. D. (1993). *Child Psychology: A Contemporary Viewpoint* (4th Ed.). New York: McGraw-Hill.

> Lewis, M. (Ed.). (1983). *Origins of Intelligence: Infancy and Early Childhood* (2nd Ed.). New York: Plenum Press.

> National Governors' Association. (1997). *The First Three Years: A Governor's Guide to Early Childhood.* Washington, D.C.

> Osofsky, J. D. (Ed.). (1987). *Handbook of Infant Development* (2nd Ed.). New York: Wiley.

> Shore, R. (1997). *Rethinking the Brain: New Insights Into Early Development.* New York: Families and Work Institute.

> Sternberg, R. J. (Ed.). (1994). *The Encyclopedia of Intelligence.* New York: Macmillan Publishing Company.

In addition, two very up-to-date, highly accurate general studies of the practical side of parenting are:

> *Caring for Your Baby and Child, Birth to Age 5,* The American Academy of Pediatrics, S.P. Shelov (Ed.). (1998). New York: Bantam Books.

> *What to Expect the First Year,* A. Eisenberg, H. Murkoff, S. Hathaway. (1998). Workman.

PROFESSIONAL REFERENCES

We owe deep gratitude to many colleagues the world over. First, we list those with whom we have collaborated on research and writing. Next, we list those whose research contributions have had a strong influence on our own research and have served to advance the field of infant research. We have undoubtedly, but inadvertently, failed to name some important contributors and colleagues. For this, our sincere apologies.

OUR RESEARCH COLLABORATORS AND COAUTHORS:

J. Adams, L. Baker-Ward, K. E. Barnard, M. Barrera, C. R. Bauer, P. Beckman-Bell, F. C. Bennett, A. A. Benasich, J. Bernbaum, C. Blair, B. Boat, W. T. Boyce, R. H. Bradley, B. Breitmayer, C. M. Brezausek, J. Brooks-Gunn, J. Brownlee, D. Bryant, M. Burchinal, E. C. Butterfield, B. M. Caldwell, F. A. Campbell, K. Campbell, P. H. Casey, G. Casto, S. Ceci, S. E. Cluett, A. M. Collier, C. Coons, R. J. Cooper, J. Crooms, P. S. Dale, C. Dent, B. Dorval, J. Dunn, D. C. Farran, R. R. Fewell, C. Figueroa-Moseley, N. W. Finkelstein, R. H. Fletcher, K. Gallacher, J. J. Gallagher, D. M. Gardner, B. D. Goldman, A. Gottfried, J. Gowen, A. Gray, M. Graham, R. T. Gross, V. Gunderson, M. A. Hammond, M. Hartley, R. Haskins, P. Hauser-Cram, F. W. Henderson, K. P. Hoffman, J. Hofheimer, M. C. Holmberg, A. Honig, H. J. Horacek, E. C. Howard, J. Jaccard, D. L. Johnson, H. Juliusson, C. Kasari, K. A. Kavali, L. S. Keller,

B. Keltner, D. Kindlon, M. A. Koch, H. C. Kraemer, R. Lanzi, L. M. LaVange, I. Lazar, M. Lee, C. O. Leonard, B. Lester, I. Lewis, K. M. Lutzius, C. Lyons, D. MacPhee, S. E. Malmquist, J. Markowitz, S. Martin, C. M. McCarton, M. C. McCormick, G. McGinness, J. D. McKinney, D. L. McMillian, S. Morse, H. Moser, K. E. Muller, B. A. Mulvihill, R. Orr, C. A. Parr, M. M. Phillips, D. Pierson, A. S. Ragozin, D. Redden, M. Reid, J. E. Roberts, R. Roberts, N. M. Robinson, S. L. Rock, J. Rorex, G. P. Sackett, C. Santoyo, M. A. Sanyal, E. S. Schaefer, D. T. Scott, K. G. Scott, C. Sells, R. Shapiro, E. J. Short, E. Siegel, L. S. Siegel, M. L. Skinner, D. T. Slaughter-Defoe, B. Smith, J. Sparling, D. Spiker, D. S. Stedman, A. P. Streissguth, T. M. Suarez, J. Sullivan, M. Swanson, T. Tivnan, R. Turner, J. E. Tyson, A. Wakeley, T. Walden, D. Walker, W. N. Washington, B. H. Wasik, J. S. Watson, R. A. Weinberg, K. O. Yeates, M. W. Yogman, P. S. Zeskind.

MAJOR CONTRIBUTORS TO OUR THINKING AND TO THE FIELD OF INFANT DEVELOPMENT:

L. B. Adamson, M. D. Ainsworth, A. Anastasi, D. R. Anderson, R. Aslin, R. Bakeman, S. Ball, P. B. Baltes, A. Bandura, K. E. Barnard, E. Bates, D. Baumrind, N. Bayley, L. Beckwith, H. L. Bee, R. Bell, J. Belsky, K. M. Berg, W. K. Berg, A. Binet, H. G. Birch, J. Block, J. H. Block, L. Bloom, R. Boothe, M. H. Bornstein, T. J. Bouchard, T. G. R. Bower, J. Bowlby, Y. Brackbill, R. H. Bradley, T. B. Brazelton, I. Bretherton, U. Bronfenbrenner, W. Bronson, J. Brooks-Gunn, J. V. Brown, J. Bruner, B. M. Caldwell, J. Campos, S. J. Ceci, S. Chess, C. Chomsky, D. Cicchetti, K. A. Clarke-Stewart, C. P. Cowan, P. A. Cowan, S. Crockenberg, P. S. Dale, R. Darlington, C. Darwin, A. DeCasper, V. Dennenberg, W. Dennis, V. Dobson, K. A. Dodge, B. Egeland, P. D. Eimas, P. Ekman, R. N. Emde, C. Feiring, A. Fernald, T. Field, T. M. Field, K. W. Fischer, N. A. Fox, C. T. Garcia-Coll, H. Gardner, N. Garmezy, J. M. Gottman, W. T. Greenough, S. Greenspan, M. Gunnar, W. K. Hahn, M. M. Haith, H. F. Harlow, W. W. Hartup, D. O. Hebb, E. M. Hetherington, R. A. Hinde, N. Hobbs, L. W. Hoffman, M. P. Honzik, F. D. Horowitz, J. M. Hunt, A. C. Huston, J. Huttenlocher, P. R. Huttenlocher, B. Inhelder, C. E. Izard, J. Kagan, M. H. Klaus, C. B. Kopp, A. F. Korner, P. Kuhl, M. E. Lamb, L. M. Laosa, I. Lazar, L. A. Leavitt, E. Lenneberg, J. V. Lerner, R. M. Lerner, B. Lester, M. Lewis, L. P. Lipsitt, E. E. Maccoby, D. Magnusson, M. Main, H. Markman, H. McAdoo, R. B. McCall, A. N. Meltzoff, D. L. Molfese, M. K. Moore, K. Nelson, E. L. Newport, M. A. Novak, J. D. Osofsky, H. Papousek, R. D. Parke, A. H. Parmelee, D. Phillips, J. Piaget, H. F. R. Prechtl, M. Radke-Yarrow, H. L. Rheingold, H. Ricciuti, D. Riesman, T. R. Risely, L. A. Rosenblum, G. C. Ruppenthal, G. P. Sackett, P. Salapatek, A. J. Sameroff, S. Scarr, M. D. Sigman, B. F. Skinner, R. G. Slaby, L. A. Sroufe, R. Sternberg, A. P. Streissguth, S. J. Suomi, D. Y. Teller, E. B. Thoman, A. Thomas, E. Tronick, T. D. Wachs, T. A. Walden, E. Waters, J. Watson, R. A. Weinberg, A. Yonas, C. Zahn-Waxler.

About the Authors

❀

CRAIG T. RAMEY, PHD is Director of the Civitan International Research Center at the University of Alabama at Birmingham and Professor of Psychology, Pediatrics, Neurobiology, and Maternal and Child Health. Major areas of professional commitment include: *intellectual and social competence development in children*; *early educational interventions to optimize child development and school success*; *at risk children, families, and communities*; *infant development and learning; children, families, and the media*.

Dr. Ramey serves as a consultant to local, state, and federal, and international groups, agencies and governments, including the National Head Start Evaluation Design Group (U.S. Dept. of Health and Human Services), the Commission on Prevention of Mental Retardation (Centers for Disease Control), and the U.S. Department of Education. He is the editor of two books and has developed two comprehensive early childhood curricula (from birth through age five) that are in widespread use throughout the world. He has also written more than 200 scientific and professional articles.

SHARON L. RAMEY, PHD is Director of the Civitan International Research Center at the University of Alabama at Birmingham and Professor of Psychiatry, Neurobiology, Psychology, Pediatrics, Maternal and Child Health, and Nursing. Major areas of professional commitment include: *treatment of mental retardation and developmental disabilities; enhancing the intellectual and social competence of infants and young children; effects of prenatal exposure to maternal stress and alcohol, nicotine, and cocaine; changes in the American family way of life, including children's perspectives on their parents and families; the use of scientific findings in the formulation of public policy; the transition to school and what makes children successful in school.*

Dr. Ramey serves as consultant to numerous government agencies, academic institutions, international organizations and professional associations, including the National Institute of Child Health and Human Development, the American Psychological Association, the Society for Research in Child Development, and the Congressional National Summit on Cultural Diversity. She is the author of more than 120 scientific and

professional articles, on the editorial board for many leading scientific journals, and is an elected officer and fellow in many national and international organizations.

The Rameys have four children and live in Birmingham, Alabama.

Also from Goddard Press:

❀

Me, Myself and I
How Children Build Their Sense of Self
18-36 Months
Kyle D. Pruett, M.D.

A definitive, up-to-the-minute book on the phenomenal growth of competence, personality and self-image in early childhood — and how parents can guide the process and shape the outcome for life. Filled with practical, proven strategies to help parents set each child on a lifelong path to confidence, joy and accomplishment.

Author Kyle Pruett is one of America's leading child development specialists and a clinical professor of child psychiatry at Yale University's Child Study Center.

Coming in May, 1999

❀

Going To School
How to Help Your Child Succeed
A Complete Handbook for Parents of Children Ages 3-8
Sharon L. Ramey, Ph.D. ❀ Craig T. Ramey, Ph.D.

An essential guide for parents on the all-important transition to kindergarten and the early elementary grades. Based on studies of thousands of children across the country, the Rameys show when and how to prepare children for the move to "big school" and how to support their early and continuing success academically, with teachers and their peers.

Coming in July, 1999